T0265864

SUZUKI

SUZUKI

The Man and His Dream
to Teach the Children of the World

ERI HOTTA

THE BELKNAP PRESS *of*
HARVARD UNIVERSITY PRESS
CAMBRIDGE, MASSACHUSETTS
LONDON, ENGLAND
2022

LIBRARY OF CONGRESS CATALOGING-IN-PUBLICATION DATA

Names: Hotta, Eri, 1971– author.
Title: Suzuki : the man and his dream to teach the children of the world/
Eri Hotta.
Description: Cambridge, Massachusetts : The Belknap Press of Harvard
University Press, 2022. | Includes bibliographical references and index.
Identifiers: LCCN 2022009252 | ISBN 9780674238237 (cloth)
Subjects: LCSH: Suzuki, Shin'ichi, 1898–1998. | Violin teachers—Japan. |
Violin—Instruction and study—Japan—Juvenile—History—20th century. |
Violin—Instruction and study—Juvenile—History—20th century. |
Humanism in music.
Classification: LCC ML423.S96 H67 2022 |
DDC 787.2092—dc23/eng/20220314
LC record available at https://lccn.loc.gov/2022009252

For Ian

Contents

INTRODUCTION

BORN IN 1898, Shinichi Suzuki lived through almost the entirety of the twentieth century. When he died, in 1998, the violinist, teacher, and humanist was best known as the founder of the hugely popular approach to early music education commonly known as the Suzuki Method.

According to the Talent Education Research Institute, an organization Suzuki founded in 1948, about 400,000 children around the globe are today learning to play music the Suzuki way. Particularly in the United States, where it was introduced in the late 1950s, the method has become synonymous with the musical education of preschoolers and school-aged children. Suzuki's influence has been so pervasive for so long that, today, the great majority of people who were very young when they picked up a violin—or cello, viola, piano, or flute—have likely come across his instructional approach in one form or another. Among top musicians who proclaim their Suzuki beginnings are violinists Kyoko Takezawa, Arabella Steinbacher, and Ray Chen. Many others, including Leila Josefowicz, Stefan Jackiw, Joshua Bell, and Hilary Hahn, had less thorough involvement with the Suzuki Method but were exposed to aspects of it in their early years. In 2020, Hahn became the third American violinist to record the repertoire accompanying the international edition of Suzuki's method books, following David Nadien and William Preucil.

Yet Suzuki's program was not intended to create professional musicians. His true goal, one that he maintained throughout his long career, was one of social transformation. He believed that the ills of his community stemmed from adults' failure to help children fully realize their potential and thereby become enlightened individuals. And by children, he meant all children—whether their potential was great or small, whether it lay in music, mathematics, poetry, or athletics. "This method is not education of the violin," he told a *New York Times* reporter in 1977. "It is education by the violin." To Suzuki, the achievement of a certain level of mastery on the violin was only an example—albeit a powerful one—of what any and all children could accomplish with proper guidance from an early age.[1]

Notwithstanding his success in motivating families across the globe to put kiddy-sized violins in the hands of their children, Suzuki's grand vision to redefine education remains little known. The primary reason for this neglect is that the Suzuki Method appears to work as a way of music instruction, and it is this, not the refashioning of society, that parents are looking for. Questioning the deeper meaning of education, and the state of existing educational systems, is not a task that most parents, guardians, and even instructors are prepared to take on when children sign up for music lessons.

For me, a historian and a mother who at one point projected her faith in the Suzuki Method onto her daughter, that is far from satisfying. Suzuki's ninety-nine-year life, and the ideas he developed, encompass too much to overlook. His work took him from his birthplace in Nagoya— where Japan's turn-of-the-century innovators and entrepreneurs, including his father, thrived—to the culturally resplendent interwar Berlin of the 1920s, where he studied. Eventually he found himself in Tokyo on the eve of the Pacific War, where he started teaching young children. Next came the scenic alpine city of Matsumoto in Nagano Prefecture, where he opened a music school after the war. Then came celebrity, as Suzuki toured the world from the mid-1960s onward, well into his nineties. His journey through these historical landscapes raises questions both specific and broad about the evolution of his educational philosophy and about what music and learning are supposed to mean in our own and our children's lives. What led Suzuki, who had no children of his own, to develop his approach? What propelled him to promote it with such passion? And in turn, why did his approach appeal so strongly to parents and educators both at home and outside his native Japan? To what extent was his larger educational philosophy, beyond the teaching and learning of music, accepted—or not?

Suzuki's life was a quintessentially twentieth-century phenomenon, embedded within many of its historical turning points. They include the two world wars, the Cold War, and the cultural and economic globalization that continue to shape our world. The twentieth century was, as historian Eric Hobsbawm put it, an "age of extremes," a time when opposing ideas and dogmas competed on a global scale to fundamentally change how people thought and lived. Exponents of influential ideologies—from socialism to internationalism, capitalism, and their countless variants—pressed their visions of a good society. Befitting the zeitgeist, Suzuki pressed his own. He was first and foremost a revolutionary, striving to create a world where all children could thrive because this world would be more just and humane than the one he knew. He believed that better lives for all could be achieved by changing the way we bring up our children and therefore insisted that his was not merely an educational movement but also a social movement.[2]

Central to Suzuki's revolution was his conviction that talent is not an innate property, exclusive to those born with it. Rather, Suzuki contended that all children could claim talent, and he aimed to prove it. Moreover, he believed that not just his philosophy but also his pedagogical approach could be applied to all kinds of learning, so that every child's talent could be nurtured—so that "all the children around the world shine like little stars."[3]

Suzuki advanced his project with unwavering confidence, which may explain the guru-like aura he exudes in the eyes of some of his method's followers. The pseudo-religious reverence of Suzuki's most dedicated acolytes has, I suspect, shaped much of the existing literature on his life. My aim for this book is not to put the man in a pantheon but to show him and his legacies in expansive perspective. Suzuki's life will also, I hope, serve as a lens through which we can see a panorama of cultural, artistic, and political shifts that marked his century. Perhaps, too, Suzuki's story will help us, living in the twenty-first century, better understand ourselves.

If Shinichi Suzuki was a revolutionary fighter, bent on changing the world—and not just the field of music—through his educational approach, what, exactly, did he try to change? First and foremost, he sought to change the way talent is understood. This was the obsession that inspired, energized, and organized his work, which he called talent education (*saino kyoiku*). It was only in the 1970s that the Suzuki Method brand name—a reverse importation to Japan from the United States—overtook the original label.

But what is this elusive quality called talent, anyway? And what makes a child talented? When we come across a child showing what we sense to be above-average abilities—be they in some academic subject, sports, music, visual art, or any other challenging pursuit—we are prone to say, without a moment's hesitation, "Oh, she is so talented!" To be sure, we debate whether the child in question was genetically predisposed, by nature, to win the talent lottery or is better prepared, by nurture, to develop and showcase her abilities. (The answer, I suppose, often lies somewhere in between.) Besides that, talent is something we think of as quantitative, measurable. The term is derived from the Greek *talanton,* signifying a particular weight of money or gold to be compared against other objects on a balance scale. Talent is something that one has more or less of; we take for granted that talents are unequally distributed.

Suzuki did not accept this common idea of talent, musical or otherwise. Irrespective of their myriad backgrounds and individual differences, all children, he thought, should be measured against their own potential—which he identified as "natural" or "raw" abilities—and not against anyone else's. He never denied that children demonstrated different levels of abilities, or that certain children learned easily where others struggled. Still, he was adamant that we all come into this world equipped with a tremendous capacity to learn, and that we can all become talented in our own ways. According to this view, talent is not a static, inborn quality, like, say, eye color. Rather, talent is a muscle that can be developed and strengthened regardless of genetics.[4]

In support of his position, Suzuki pointed to the universal capacity for language acquisition. As children, nearly all of us learn to speak our native languages fluently, ably commanding their intricate grammars, irregularities, and accents by the time we are four or five years old. For Suzuki, this was evidence that all children can be taught. He also believed that the lesson of mother-tongue acquisition could be applied to general education. Should children have difficulty learning, the fault lay not with the children but with the adults who did not take care to teach them. There were no dropouts in this world, he explained, only "dropped-outs" who had been compromised by adults. When adults guide their infant children toward language fluency, they bring to the task not just knowledge but also a spirit of love, patience, and self-reflection. If that same spirit were brought to all education, Suzuki thought, then every child would know the delight of learning throughout their formative years and beyond. They would not all achieve the same level of skill in any given endeavor, but they all would face and surmount obstacles en route to their own improvement, which is itself the key benefit of education.[5]

What better way to prove his point than to show that, with suitable instruction, any child could learn how to play the violin, an especially challenging musical instrument for beginners? A properly tuned piano allows anyone to produce the right pitches merely by tapping the keyboard; a beginner won't play all the correct notes with proper timing, but each note she plays will sound at the right frequency. The same is not true of the violin and other bowed string instruments: it is up to each string player to produce the correct pitches using precise left hand placement. And as for the right hand, that comes with another set of daunting challenges, starting with how to hold the bow. (Classical training demands that all violinists bow with their right hand and depress the strings with their left, regardless of handedness.)

The parallel Suzuki drew between general education and mother-tongue acquisition was novel. His philosophy also embraced notions of progressive, cumulative learning. Today, this is conventional wisdom, but early childhood music education looked very different in Suzuki's youth. Still, if others have caught on to some of Suzuki's pedagogy, it remains exceptional in practice. The Suzuki Method is characterized by a pervasive sense of inclusiveness and inventiveness, which bring elements of fun to otherwise-tedious drilling of musical skills. For instance, the method requires group lessons in addition to private instruction, with the goal of impressing on youngsters the joy of making music with their peers. The Suzuki repertoire reinforces this sense of joy. The early repertoire is full of catchy melodies appealing to preschoolers. Tellingly, the first of Suzuki's ten instructional books for violin starts with his arrangement of the universally familiar "Twinkle Twinkle Little Star," which has become something of a sacred hymn for his movement. The final two volumes feature demanding but equally hummable Mozart concertos.

The ten books guide the budding violinist step by step through the challenges that grow her abilities. These range from holding the instrument and the bow properly to producing a beautiful, even tone; to smoothly shifting left-hand positions over the fingerboard while accurately controlling bow movement with the right arm, and so on. Completing one Suzuki book and moving on to the next provides a great incentive for a young musician. This does not mean, however, that the challenges one has overcome in the previous books go away. In fact, the student is expected to be ever more mindful of past challenges and to continue reviewing old pieces. "Twinkle" is no exception. In group lessons, advanced students play it along with toddlers holding their tiny, 1/16-sized violins. This determinedly communal approach makes classical music seem less intimidating, more engaging, and accessible to anyone willing to do the work, no matter her background or inborn ability.

It is worth reminding ourselves that this Japanese man promoted his pedagogical approach and his larger philosophy through the vehicle of Western classical music. By that I mean not the music of the Classical period, from roughly 1750 to 1825, but the more capacious sense of classical music, itself difficult to define but perhaps easy to recognize—music that historically has been played in conservatories, in orchestra halls, and in salon concerts; music rooted in medieval ecclesiastical traditions; music that has historically enjoyed an elite status and has involved a canon including hundreds of years of notated works. Suzuki was inspired, in no small part, by his direct exposure to such music while he experienced the rich performance culture and high idealism of interwar Berlin, one of the capitals of European arts.

Today classical music can no longer be regarded as an exclusively European, Western, or even White cultural property, as the classical music world seeks ways to include various musical traditions and musicians from an array of backgrounds. Furthermore, the abundance of exceptional Asian classical musicians and instructors in our own time can make us forget that, until not so long ago, people seriously wondered out loud, in professional criticism and in casual dinner party conversation, whether Asian musicians were fit to play Western classical music. The now-clichéd line of argument, which I have often heard firsthand, was that Asians could at most achieve technical mastery, thanks to their single-minded diligence and tenacity. But these performers could not communicate the authentic spirit of the music; having been raised in a different cultural and historical context, they were assumed to be unable to feel that spirit themselves. As an Asian man, Suzuki had to circumvent such prejudices by appealing to the idea of universal humanism, itself arguably a product of the Western Enlightenment tradition.

It does not seem to me that Suzuki was able to put to rest the myopic debate about authentic performance. Those too-familiar arguments about perfectionism, diligence, tenacity, and the like are still marshaled to explain the prominence of Asian classical musicians today. And Asian performers, by the way, are not the only ones who have been positioned as outsiders whose conspicuous, confounding presence in orchestra halls demands explanation. Before Asians arrived on the scene, there was a feeling that the classical music world had been overcrowded by Jews. Referring to the abundance of Jewish performers in the principal positions of orchestras and as leading soloists, a television interviewer asked Nathan Milstein, one of the finest violinists of the twentieth century, "Why do Jewish musicians—why do they make good executive musicians?" With a straight face, albeit the corner of his mouth curled up mischievously, Milstein replied, "I know very many Jewish musicians that are not really good!" To Milstein, musical aptitude had nothing to do with "a race"; it was most likely the "social background that made some Jews take to the violin or piano." This observation wholly concurs with Suzuki's view that environment, not genetics, is the crucial factor underlying ability, an argument with ramifications far beyond the world of classical music.[6]

In any event, we tend to take for granted that classical music no longer occupies the central cultural space it once did in most societies, making the idea of a social movement rooted in its training seem anachronistic. Compounding that sense of classical music's waning relevance is the nagging suspicion that it never was as universally embraced as our selective memory has it. That suspicion is at least partially justified. Anxiety over classical music's seemingly small appeal is of long standing, hence, for example, the consolidation of music appreciation curricula in American schools in the early twentieth century. Such programs responded to public illiteracy surrounding Western concert music, in spite of the massive increase in the accessibility of classical scores during the nineteenth century and the simultaneous growth in the number and size of concert halls. Yet neither music appreciation nor the constant presence of classical music on early radio, in recordings, and on film could sway the wider population. The American-born violinist Yehudi Menuhin discovered as much while playing for soldiers during World War II. Twenty-five years old at the time of the Japanese attack on Pearl Harbor, the former child prodigy gave hundreds of recitals for Allied troops. More than three decades later, he recalled that playing for soldiers gave him new perspective on his cloistered art. Until then, "I had never played in cafes, cabarets," he wrote. "Nor had I been obliged to woo my listeners to listen. Now I had to please men who had never attended a concert, who were not bred to its conventions, whose patience could not be relied upon, far less their informed appreciation."[7]

It is in part because we exaggerate the popularity of classical music in our imagined past that we can also tell ourselves that classical music now is in decline. At least in the United States, this aura of decay is undeniable. How often do we hear about public schools cutting their music programs, while apparently fewer and fewer people attend classical music concerts? This is classical music's grand narrative today, notwithstanding the music's robust presence in new media and its clear and ongoing influence on other genres whose popularity either is unquestioned or simply not a source of angst. Today we are able to enjoy the cumulative and ever-expanding legacies of recorded and filmed performances uploaded to YouTube and other online platforms to the delight of enthusiasts and casual fans alike. And classical music continues to adapt, absorb, innovate, and cross over musical styles, exciting the imagination of listeners. Indeed, against those who believe classical music was once admired and is no longer, it is worth remembering that the works of composers like Beethoven and Igor Stravinsky were not always considered either classical or classy by those who heard them at the time of their premieres.

Amid all the change that classical music and popular culture have undergone, and amid all the hand-wringing that has resulted, what seems ever-resilient are the assumptions that we attach to the music. Most basically, adults tend to believe that it is somehow a "good thing" to encourage young children to learn to play difficult instruments. The broad acceptance that the Suzuki Method appears to enjoy in the US homeschooling community attests to this point most eloquently. As one homeschool blogger writes, the Suzuki Method trains her children to set realizable goals and work hard for them, while improving their concentration and instilling habits of discipline that can be applied to other tasks. What is delineated here is a set of transferable skills—one might even call them life skills—that seem worthwhile to acquire at a young age and that cannot be taken away even long after one stops learning music. Too, many adults crave the musical proficiency that eluded them, whether because they did not have the opportunity to take lessons, or because they did not know how to manage their time and put in the necessary daily practice, or because their parents were not committed to their success. These wistful adults hope the Suzuki Method might give their children a head start in developing musical talent, or, at the very least, an interesting and useful skill that could bring so much pleasure for a lifetime.[8]

The higher are such hopes, and the more they reside in parents as opposed to their children, the more easily they can backfire. This is true regardless of pedagogical approach, whether a traditional method, the Suzuki Method, or some other innovative system. In the wrong hands, the Suzuki Method can turn music-making into a kind of competitive after-school sport or martial art, in which passing from one level to the next becomes the main goal of committing a child to a difficult pursuit. "Tiger parents" with no previous love of classical music suddenly become experts, at least in the limited world of Suzuki music, and they focus on the pace at which their children progress through the instruction books, convinced that this is an absolute indicator of their kids' musical talent or lack thereof. Such parents are not much interested in Suzuki's central claim of "every child can." Music then becomes a site for misplaced projection, unrealistic expectations, even social ambition—and, more often than not, disappointment.

Suzuki himself recognized this alarming pattern early on. In a 1956 article for instructors and parents following his approach, he elaborated on this topic thoughtfully, albeit obliquely. "Having realized that all children on this earth had great potential to learn," he wrote, he decided to launch his "social movement," aided by "the high musical senses of Bach, Beethoven, and Mozart." To his dismay, however, he soon realized that his biggest challenge rested with parents, "who unknowingly made their children miserable." Rather than guide their children to become the best people they could be—in other words, people possessing kindness, patience, sensitivity, and what Suzuki called "noble hearts"— those parents became narrowly focused on raising "skilled violin players." This was a result, he believed, of a lack of self-reflection on the part of adults, who lost sight of why they wanted their children to learn to play musical instruments in the first place.[9]

Indeed, why did those parents want their children to learn classical music anyway? Did they truly understand and share in Suzuki's grand ambition for social transformation through holistic, child-centric education? If they did understand, what made them forget? Or did Suzuki's vision get the better of him? His desire to build a gentler society filled with high ideals and musical senses was a sign that, in the real world, those very things were woefully lacking. The headwinds he faced were not just foreseeable but also implicit in his efforts toward social change. And so we must ask: What is it about children's classical music education that makes adults lose perspective—or even their heads? What do we hope music will do for them, and for us? What do we want from music?

Because my childhood experience with classical music was a mildly unhappy one, I have often wondered if learning classical instruments at an early age is overrated. For me, classical music was always simply there, neither welcome nor unwelcome—at our home in Tokyo, at school, on the car radio, and, inescapably, in the piano practice that became part of my daily routine when I was four years old. This was not unusual for a child growing up in the increasingly affluent Japanese society of the 1970s and 1980s. I did not, however, learn to play the Suzuki way, which begins with a child listening repeatedly to the same recordings of the repertoire pieces even before she is considered ready to touch an actual instrument. Whereas Suzuki's approach emphasizes listening, then playing, and often much later reading—a process that traces the natural pattern whereby a child learns to use her mother tongue—I went about my piano education in the traditional way, by learning to play and read music at the same time. For my two siblings and me, half-hearted students of music, all those hours spent at the piano under the vigilant eyes of our mother, and even more hours spent trying unsuccessfully to avoid them, are not our fondest childhood memories.[10]

Nonetheless, when I became a parent myself, I did not think twice about signing my daughter up for violin lessons. I was in fact rather keen to have her pick up a 1/16th-sized instrument. That was because, as a teenager, I had come across Suzuki's autobiographical 1969 book *Nurtured by Love*. When I read it, his philosophy captivated me. I cannot deny that I felt sorry for myself. I regretted, with a teenager's self-righteous rage, that I did not have an informed parent who understood and appreciated the Suzuki Method, who could have approached music education with enough love. I willfully ignored the facts that my mother actually had started me on the piano at an early enough age, comparable to a Suzuki child, and that in her persistence and consistency she was again comparable to the most committed Suzuki parents. I faulted my exposure to the traditional way of teaching and conveniently concluded that my lackluster efforts could be attributed to my parents' failure to motivate me properly. That was how I had become determined that any child of mine would be a Suzuki student. So my daughter's association with the violin had been determined long before she was born.

I no longer believe that, had I been taught the Suzuki way, I would have automatically had a closer, more intense connection with music. I now know more about how the Suzuki Method works, or does not work, as I have struggled my way through enough Suzuki books with my daughter. She received her first four years of instruction in Suzuki programs in New York and Tokyo. When she started, I was not at all ready for the difficulty of home practice, which is the key to a successful collaboration with a Suzuki teacher, whom the child meets only once a week. On the whole, I was perhaps too naive in accepting Suzuki's vision of love guiding us through practical challenges. In reality, patience, restraint, flexibility, and good judgment are as important as love. And, to be fair,

Suzuki never actually said that love would solve everything, but that was how I chose to interpret his philosophy as a teenager.

The gap between Suzuki's professed ideals and the difficulty of everyday practice aside, there are further criticisms of the approach itself. The most common complaint is that the Suzuki Method relies too heavily on learning by ear, which has resulted in some unusual creatures: fine young classical instrumentalists whose music-reading skills lag far behind their performance ability. But this does not seem like such a grave problem as long as music-reading skills are introduced at an appropriate stage. After all, we never think of discouraging very young children, before they can read, from learning to recite the Mother Goose rhymes, and we would surely be impressed and pleased if they could recite longer verses—say, Shakespeare's sonnets—only from listening to them. Besides, a noncontrived, natural connection with music is an advantage for a professional musician. Andrew Bird, a highly successful multi-instrumentalist who learned to play the violin the Suzuki way from age four, claims that learning by ear, via the so-called mother-tongue approach, made him the artist he is today:

> If reading [scores] were the emphasis, I think I would've turned out different. The notes were there in front of us but they were just kind of part of the ceremony of playing. . . . Musically, what is most important about it is that, since I didn't learn to read music right away, I made a direct connection to what was in my head. That allows the music to not just go in my ear but also come out of my head and onto my instrument. And as a writer, composer and improviser—when I made that leap from classical rep[ertoire] to folk music or jazz over the years, it was not a big leap. And I saw other musicians around—people at conservatory—that couldn't move left or right without the written notes. . . . If I hear it, I can play it—just like if you hear it you can sing or whistle it. It's just second nature.[11]

Similar sentiments are echoed by Suzuki-trained classical musicians, who perform within stricter confines than those playing folk music or jazz. Arabella Steinbacher notes, "My father always played pieces over to me on the piano, and then I had to repeat them . . . It was only much later that I learned to read music." To this day, the quickest way for her to learn pieces is to "play them through and hear them." Kyoko Takezawa feels fortunate that, thanks to her Suzuki training, "music was already inside me before I learned to study notes." Later, with great surprise, she came to see that not all musicians were accustomed to paying attention to the sound of music itself.[12]

Yet even successful Suzuki musicians are tempted to find faults in their training. Takezawa switched from Suzuki's approach to a more orthodox style of violin study in the last years of elementary school, before going to a conservatory. She suddenly faced music scores, scales, and etudes for the first time, and, to her mind, regrettably late. She is also wary of listening excessively to one recording of a piece—as Suzuki students might be accused of doing—without knowing the score. The thinking goes that any one recording might present an interpretation very different from what the composer has written.

But those are technical criticisms. A far larger problem facing the Suzuki Method, as far as I am concerned, is its built-in, unrealistic expectations about what it could lead children to achieve. The Suzuki Method, or any other musical method, is not by itself enough to make its practitioner a musical person, let alone a beautiful and morally righteous one. It would be presumptuous to expect a method to provide a universal formula for cultivating the capacity to appreciate and respond to music. Developing such sensitivity—one might call it musicality, for want of a better word—is bound to be an intensely private affair, beyond the realm of mastering techniques, mimicking good sounds, and tapping into a reservoir of ready-made emotions. But because Suzuki suggested that the tasks of raising a beautiful human being and developing a child's musicality are somehow tightly linked, we are tempted to dream that the Suzuki Method might endow our children with good character and profound musicality at the same time. That might be the outcome in some fortunate cases, but it goes without saying that listening to or playing beautiful music does not turn human beings into angels.

And then there is another problem—still more serious—of execution. Even as a teenager, I sensed that Suzuki's grand desire to see "all the children around the world shine like little stars" was highly unlikely to be realized. How could we ensure that all children have equal opportunities in their earliest education, whether in music, math, drawing, or sports? Suzuki was not oblivious to this challenge. He knew that his ambition for educational reform could be carried out only with institutional support from the government. That is why in his early years of teaching, on the eve of the Pacific War, he became an advocate for a massive overhaul of public schools, whereby the Japanese state would ensure equal opportunities for early childhood education, regardless of parents' financial situation and ability to support learning. But his proposal was never taken up by the Japanese government in the sweeping way that he envisioned, either before or after the war.

What if Suzuki's approach had become incorporated into Japanese public education? One might not agree with all aspects of his highly idealistic philosophy. But it is hard to dispute the social utility of an educational system that prevents the creation of "dropped-outs" and fosters individual potential, increasing opportunities for as many children as possible. What if Japan had taken that road—especially right after the war, when the education system, like so many other things, could have been rebuilt from scratch? Perhaps Japan could have become a very different place. Could Japan have had a different experience of the dizzying miracle years of postwar economic growth, the intoxicating bubble years, and more recently the somber lost decades of stagnation? Could Japan have become a model for other countries? The answer is as elusive as music.

Music—in Stravinsky's words, "the best means we have of digesting time"—is a fleeting art. A good live recording might be made and then mixed and mastered to near-perfection by a skillful engineer. But, strictly speaking, that is no longer the art that was experienced by the musicians and their audience in that never-to-be-repeated original performance. The great twentieth-century Romanian conductor Sergiu Celibidache often resisted having his performances recorded and instead tried to make each concert what he called a "transcendental experience," convinced as he was that those magical moments could never be reproduced. There is a reason singing and other forms of music-making have been an integral part of religious ceremonies throughout history. Because it provides pleasure, excitement, comfort, and strength to those who make and hear it, music, particularly classical music, has acquired the reputation of

Suzuki leads a group of young violinists at Matsumoto Castle, circa 1967. *Talent Education Research Institute*

being spiritually enriching and elevating, especially but not exclusively in live performance. This was certainly Suzuki's view.[13]

The writer Alexander Waugh brilliantly makes the case for music's seemingly metaphysical power over us. Today he is a self-described "piano junkie," but he was also once a violinist growing up in rural England, whose lifelong association with music began with the Suzuki Method. (During a conversation over dinner, he told me he quit violin for piano because he could not stand the awful sounds he heard in Suzuki group lessons, which invariably came out of the students' factory-manufactured violins, often sold in a bundle with a bow and essential accessories like a cake of rosin.) Waugh is skeptical of the view that music is good for "the soul," but he knows that making music gets him "as close as I can get to the feeling of otherworldliness—that hyperstatic, dangling state, that is impossible to cast into words." Whatever our views on the soul, perhaps we can all agree that it is exhilarating to be able to get to a place where words fail us. Suzuki, directly and indirectly, has helped a great many people achieve that state.[14]

History, like music, is temporal and fleeting, and despite the common adage, it never quite repeats itself. Could not the task of a historian, then, be likened to that of a music producer or a studio engineer, who tinkers with the recorded sounds of a musical piece so that many listeners get a sense of the moment, despite not having been there? A historian, too, collects and interprets the facts of the past to construct a story that is broadly intelligible, and even tries to carry the reader to some other place through the power of that retelling. In a dialogue between the past and the present that is about to take place, I, as the chronicler of Suzuki's twentieth century, cannot remain an independent bystander. Rather, I will have to become a part of that story. Either implicitly or explicitly, my perspectives and experiences are bound to be interwoven, especially as Suzuki's story begins to overlap my own lifetime in later chapters. This is my retelling of the life of Shinichi Suzuki, and his dream to teach the children of the world.

1

NO ORDINARY CHILDHOOD,
NO ORDINARY ENVIRONMENT

MARCH 27, 1955, WAS A SUNDAY. By early afternoon, the morning clouds had dispersed, and Tokyo was basking in sunlight. That day, on the cusp of spring, the Tokyo Metropolitan Gymnasium became the venue for the First National Convention of the Talent Education Research Institute. The highlight of the event was to be the Grand Concert, with the institute's founder and leader, Shinichi Suzuki, conducting 1,200 performers brought from different parts of the country and ranging in age from three years old to fifteen. They were all studying with Suzuki or with instructors directly trained by him. On the program were fifteen pieces of violin music, including works by George Frederic Handel, Antonio Vivaldi, and Johann Sebastian Bach. A crowd of 20,000 gathered to listen, among them Crown Prince Akihito and other high-born personages and dignitaries.

The previous year, Jascha Heifetz had made his third, hugely successful concert tour of Japan. And just a month earlier, another violin giant, David Oistrakh, had made his first, equally successful tour. None of the young violinists in the gymnasium approached either Heifetz's or Oistrakh's superlative mastery of the instrument, of course. And yet, when the musicians started playing, the audience was deeply moved. To hear such young children—and so many of them!—play the violin in an unclouded, confident tone, as if they were singing the music, was nothing short of a religious experience. "We see here before us a miracle!" exclaimed one of the luminaries in attendance—Father Sauveur Antoine

Candau, a missionary of long standing and well respected by Catholics and non-Catholics alike, was in a position to know.[1]

The dazzling effect of the concert had been predicted by Oistrakh, who in Tokyo witnessed a smaller but still impressive performance of 200 Suzuki violinists. In a report on his Japanese tour for the official journal of VOKS, the Soviet-led All-Union Society for Cultural Relations with Foreign Countries, he wrote that his youngest musical colleague in the country was a three-year-old child taught by Suzuki. Oistrakh "regretted very much" that his schedule did not permit him to stay on to attend the upcoming Grand Concert. The 1955 Grand Concert was not the last, however, and Oistrakh would attend another twelve years later.[2]

Thanks to a team of documentary filmmakers, who employed five 35-millimeter movie cameras, we can readily see with our own eyes the historic spectacle that eluded Oistrakh. There is something intensely affecting about this black-and-white footage. In it, Suzuki, a wiry fifty-seven-year-old in a tailcoat, waves his arms briskly from a simple makeshift podium in the middle of the arena. The podium rises from an elevated stage, which Suzuki shares with a grand piano, the accompanist, and her page turner. The young violinists stand in neat rows, forming concentric rectangles around that stage. When the camera zooms in on the faces of some of the young performers, we sense their good cheer, despite the minor key of the piece they are playing—Bach's Double Concerto for Two Violins, the "Bach Double," for short. In their calm coordination, they appear to have been enchanted by their master-teacher. Their expressions reveal no hint of the nervousness that we naturally imagine attends such a formal and public performance in a huge venue. The musicians' easy confidence is evident, as their nimble fingers trail up and down their fingerboards. The bows move effortlessly, as if they were organic extensions of the performers' right arms. In spite of their youth, they are clearly veterans of this sort of group-playing.[3]

Though by no means easy, the first movement of the double concerto, consisting of two solo violin parts accompanied by strings and basso continuo—in this case, a reduction played on the piano—is not the most demanding of Suzuki's teaching repertoire. It falls somewhere in the middle, in the advanced-intermediate category, and as such, 800 of the 1,200 children were able to take part in this ensemble. Yet the Bach Double was a bold choice for so large a group. The work derives its beauty and excitement from the unceasing tension created by its two distinct voices. Each part must make room for the other, neither overwhelming it in volume nor engaging in some interpretive fancy that the other does not also pursue. But this is not all. To politely respect one another's voice is not enough to make a successful marriage: each part also must keep challenging, even provoking, the other to reveal its deep color. Only then do the two voices weave into one plausible musical fabric. The great English mystery writer Dorothy L. Sayers once had her fictional sleuth Lord Peter Wimsey listen to the piece at a concert. During the performance, he appears engrossed in its "whole intricate pattern, every part separately and simultaneously, each independent and equal, separate but inseparable, moving over and under and through, ravishing heart and mind together." After the concert is over, Whimsey concurs with his companion, who observes that to play something like the Bach Double, one has to be "more than a fiddler," one has to be "a musician."[4]

If a fine rendition of the double concerto is no mean feat for two experienced violinists, it is that much more challenging for 800 children. Suzuki divided the group into two, each playing one of the violin parts in a giant unison. As the conductor, he had to make sure that each group was internally in agreement and that neither group lagged the other. To preserve the subtleties of the piece, every child had to keep the continuous flow of all-consuming, singing notes. "Any child can" and "no children left behind"—the hallmarks of Suzuki's pedagogical mission—were on full display.

The footage of Suzuki's pupils playing the Bach Double would go on to astound music educators in the United States, paving a global path for his innovative teaching style. Symbolically speaking, it made sense that this collective performance would gain Suzuki and his methods worldwide attention. In March 1955, when the Grand Concert was held, Japanese society was undergoing rapid change and taking on the sort of heightened contrasts that mark the double concerto itself. The children's vivace-paced rendition of the first movement was of a piece with the relentless energy Japan brought to its own rehabilitation as a benign, peace-loving nation. Only a decade before, the country had been utterly

The first Grand Concert, March 27, 1955. *Talent Education Research Institute*

vanquished in World War II, with most of its major cities literally "ground to ashes," as Winston Churchill had accurately foretold at the war's beginning. It would be another sixteen months before Japan's Economic Planning Agency, judging solely from a material standpoint, announced, "It is now safe to say that we no longer live in the post-war era." The monochrome film emphasizes not only the juxtaposition of the two musical voices but also the disjuncture between what Japan had been and what it was becoming—between light and dark, between imperialist delusion and a chastened people reintroducing itself to the world.[5]

Simply by looking at photographs and footage of the concert, we can feel that the effects of the war lingered. True, the gymnasium, located centrally in the district of Sendagaya, was remarkable in its size. But it was also still under construction. Besides, the arena's clay surface, easily disturbed whenever people moved around, was not ideal for musical performances. If the camera had not captured the high dome of the roof, one might have concluded that the children were playing outdoors on some bare field, most likely a bombed-out plot left from the final year of the war. It's hard to imagine now, but Tokyo still had plenty of vacant lots then.

In so many ways, the ground under the children's feet attested to the unsettled dust of history. That very land in Sendagaya had previously belonged to the Tokugawas, the formidable samurai clan that ruled Japan in relative peace from 1603 to 1868. When the Tokugawa Shogunate fell to ambitious, reform-minded young samurai from the southwest, backed by British war technology, the fifteenth and final Tokugawa shogun vacated Edo Castle. It was a gesture that announced to the world a transfer of power, if not exactly the birth of a new kind of regime. For centuries, Japan had effectively been ruled by the shoguns, military dictators who were nominally appointed by the emperor. In order to legitimize their newfound power, the winners of 1868 also looked to the emperor—then only fifteen years old and residing in the ancient capital of Kyoto—for his blessing. But they did not stop there. They made the boy-emperor Mutsuhito into the ultimate symbol of Japanese nationalism, literally parading him across the country as the face of new Japan. Their goal was to build a modern nation-state that could hold its own against Western imperialism, united as one with the emperor—a sort of priest-king presiding over the Japanese nation as its pater familias. Among their first acts in power, these founding fathers relocated the young emperor from Kyoto to Edo Castle, renaming it the Imperial Palace and renaming the city of Edo as well. Now it would be called Tokyo, or Eastern Capital. This revolution from above became known as the Meiji Restoration, *meiji* meaning "enlightened rule" and the notion of imperial revival clearly suggesting that the fallen shogunate had illegitimately usurped the emperor's authority. Displaced from both their position and their court, the Tokugawas resided in their mansion in Sendagaya, three miles west of the Imperial Palace. The boy who would have become the sixteenth shogun was sent to England to attend Eton College, eventually becoming one of Japan's top diplomats.

The Sendagaya mansion was lost to the Tokugawa family in 1943, when the Tokyo city government bought the property to create an exercise hall. The government's stated purpose for the new facility was to "raise the nation's morale" by means of physical fitness. What this really meant was that an Allied breach of the homeland was imminent, and Tokyo residents, including women and small children, were going to be trained to fight the invaders—if they were lucky enough to survive the air raids.

At the end of the war, the Tokugawas' former property again changed hands, seized by the US occupying forces who converted its building complex into dormitories and an officers' club. After the Allied occupation ended and Japan's sovereignty was reinstated in 1952, ownership of the land reverted to the city of Tokyo. Soon enough there arose the idea to build a large-scale gymnasium, the biggest in Asia, which would enable Japan to host international sporting competitions and thereby reclaim its long-lost respectability and membership in the fair-playing, law-abiding international society. (Previously Tokyo was named the host of the 1940 Olympics, but the intensification of Japan's ill-planned war in China starting in 1937 prevented the games from taking place.) Old buildings were swiftly demolished, and the construction of the gymnasium began in October 1953, lasting until August 1956.

So it was that in March 1955 Suzuki and his young violinists turned a construction site into a theater of the most arresting scale. The kids met the moment in their Sunday best. In the footage, many girls wear huge ribbons in their hair, although their clothes are a far cry from the puffed-up dresses we often associate with children's music recitals nowadays. Quite a few of the young musicians have donned school uniforms as a substitute for formal attire. In fact, most of the clothes do not look new. Likely they are hand-me-downs that have already gone through several cycles of alterations to fit their new wearers, adding to the air of simplicity and frugality filling the unpaved gymnasium.

The children's energetic playing amid the relative desolation of a rebuilding state suggested the arrival of a long-overdue springtime. It was to be Suzuki's springtime as well. Fifty-seven years old, he was already two years over the retirement age instituted by most Japanese companies and public organizations at the time. What would be for most people a winding-down period proved to be the midpoint in Suzuki's career. His spirited conducting of the Bach Double was emblematic. Here was an old man, at least in official terms, seemingly as lithe and animated as his young charges. In his own person, he debunked the myth of talent. His belief in the capacity of all children extended as well to those with severe mental and physical handicaps, and while Suzuki was no longer a child, and while he was not handicapped, he was not supposed to be so vigorous, either. He was supposed to be past his prime.[6]

When the footage of the Bach Double reached the United States in 1958, the small group of musical professionals and educators who saw it were at first more incredulous than astonished. One of them, John Kendall, who studied at the Oberlin Conservatory of Music and Columbia's Teachers College, was deeply "skeptical" and refused to accept the footage at face value. The music could have been dubbed. The children, quite a few of whom seemed too young to even pick up a violin, could have been play-acting in some kind of theatrical performance. And even if they conceded that the footage was authentic, the disbelieving Americans could have wondered if the children were made to practice twenty hours a day, or if their skill was the product of some kind of Japanese or Asian magic so foreign as to be beyond their comprehension.[7]

I begin Suzuki's life with a snapshot of a concert held at the midpoint of his career because it helps us to appreciate what came before and after. Had they been born just a bit sooner, those violin-playing children, embodiments of a brighter future, might instead have been wielding guns or bamboo spears, mobilized for Japan's destructive and self-destructive war. It is a chilling thought. Yet, without those dark years, Suzuki might not have felt the same keen sense of urgency to perfect and promote his social movement.

Suzuki's insistence that talents were not fixed at birth, and that a nurturing environment could bring out enormous potential in all, was a vehement rejection of the broader fatalism to which many ordinary Japanese had succumbed during World War II. Still, in hindsight, elements of his unique life appear almost predestined by the circumstances of his origin. He was born into a remarkable and eccentric family, in a city full of entrepreneurs, in a country undergoing massive change. Suzuki's inquisitiveness and maverick spirit cannot be fully appreciated without knowing this background, which also tells us a great deal about Japan's relationship with Western classical music in general and with the violin in particular.

Shinichi Suzuki was born on October 17, 1898, in Nagoya, now the fourth most populous city in Japan. Because of its central location on Honshu, the largest of Japan's main islands, Nagoya has long been a significant place. During the Age of Civil Wars, which saw warrior clans vying for control of the country between the late fifteenth and late sixteenth centuries, Nagoya's strategic value was obvious. The eventual winner, Ieyasu, who founded the Tokugawa Shogunate in 1603, moved the Owari Tokugawa branch of his family to present-day Nagoya City in order to consolidate his rule there. As an Owari domain, Nagoya was an important stop for travelers on the Eastern Sea Road or *Tokaido,* a famous 320-mile route whose fifty-three scenic views are memorialized in Hiroshige's woodblock prints. Miyashuku, a neighborhood of Nagoya, was the largest inn town on the route, with a population over 10,000 by the middle of the nineteenth century. It was seen as a critical point of connection between the new Tokugawa capital of Edo in the east and the ancient capital of Kyoto in the west. Nagoya was well-placed to absorb a constant flow of information, money, culture, technologies, and new ideas.

But if Nagoya benefited from its position as a node in a larger network, that network was constrained almost entirely to Japan itself. For more than two centuries preceding the Meiji period, Japan existed in self-imposed isolation. Fearing the destabilizing potential of outside influences, the Tokugawas had allowed only limited trade with Chinese, Koreans, and a handful of Dutch merchants. It was under what were essentially protectionist conditions that Nagoya had thrived.

Japan's forced opening to the wider world in the second half of the nineteenth century might have upset this favorable status quo. In the 1850s and 1860s, the Tokugawa Shogunate reluctantly signed a series of unequal treaties with the Western great powers, agreeing to allow foreigners many new rights in the country—including trading rights. In exchange, Japan escaped formal colonization, but the treaties nonetheless were in many respects imperial instruments: their terms were thoroughly humiliating for Japan, robbing the country of sovereignty in key areas. Japan was required to grant previously prohibited traders access to a number of ports and to provide extraterritorial standing to foreigners, meaning that they would not be subject to Japanese law even when residing on Japanese soil. Such residence was also new: suddenly Japanese cities that had never known immigration would have to welcome foreigners. In addition, foreign powers took control of Japan's import tariffs. Together, these changes decisively undermined the political authority of the Tokugawas while dramatically altering the social and economic landscape in which cities like Nagoya had flourished.

With the fall of the Tokugawas, the treaties became a thankless inheritance for the Meiji government. Its urgent goal was to reverse the agreements and to protect Japan from outside influence by strengthening it militarily and economically. (The longest-lasting treaty, with the United States, expired in 1911.) Now the organizing principle of Japanese politics became, "If you can't beat them, join them." Japan would try to become one of those Western great powers; the patriotic slogan of the Meiji period—*Bunmei Kaika,* "Civilization and Enlightenment"—bespoke the desire to graft Western knowledge and ways of life onto Japanese society, in order to become a respectable and respected modern power. This would not just be a political and military transformation: Japanese diets changed, incorporating more meat and dairy products believed to promote physical strength and growth; Western-style clothes came into fashion; elementary-school education became compulsory; and the government established secure postal networks. Newspapers blossomed. So did railroads and new industries based on the latest technological advances. Alongside legal and policy changes, the Japanese people were asked to adopt new attitudes, new perspectives on what their society should be.

Nagoya, always adept at taking in fresh ideas, managed a successful transition. The city might have lacked something in glamor and sophistication, but it was also better prepared than most to take up the challenges of modernization. For one thing, it was free from the intense pressures that plagued Tokyo's complicated high politics. For another, it was more open to novel approaches than was Osaka, a major center of commerce but beset by a cutthroat business climate that favored large incumbents committed to protecting their investments. Under these circumstances, Nagoya came to be known for innovation in the couple of decades straddling Suzuki's birth.

Particularly noteworthy were a group of Nagoyaites who developed top global brands that we still recognize today. Names like Sakichi Toyoda, Ichizaemon Morimura, and Kenkichi Yasui might not mean much to most of us, but their corporate legacies are known the world over: Toyota (first a producer of automatic textile looms, later the world's biggest auto maker), Brother (originally a manufacturer of sewing machines, then copiers and printers), and Noritake (a maker of fine bone china). Nagoya's turn-of-the-century entrepreneurs prided themselves on high-quality craftsmanship, mastery of advanced technologies, and unapologetic ambitions for social and commercial success. The goal was not to produce good imitations of Western products but to create even better and more affordable versions of them, in quantities large enough to cater to growing mass markets at home and around the globe. And what drove that sense of purpose was not just pride in one's work but also in one's nation, a people who understood themselves as the equals of any yet who were also playing catch-up. They had to work that much harder than everyone else.

Shinichi Suzuki's father was an integral part of this upwardly mobile class. Born in 1859 to a modest samurai family in the service of the Owari Tokugawa domain, Masakichi Suzuki plied several trades before stumbling upon his calling as a violin maker. His education had been inconsistent and haphazard at best, but a yearning to be near some kind of music was a recurring theme from early childhood onward. As a boy, Masakichi was recruited to be a drummer for the band that accompanied the domain's rapidly Westernizing armed forces; he attended the military music school until the drummer's post was cut to make room for trumpets. A two-year stint at another domain-sponsored school, this one specializing in the acquisition of Western knowledge, especially English-language skills, ended when his scholarship was discontinued, prompted by a policy change initiated by the new Meiji government. His family then sent him to Tokyo to apprentice with a relative who was a lacquerware merchant. There he put in long hours of menial labor, only to see the shop fold after a few years.[8]

Masakichi returned to Nagoya, where his parents had opened a small workshop producing shamisen, three-stringed instruments used in a variety of traditional musical forms. (Earlier, Masakichi's grandfather had started making the instruments on the side to supplement his income from the domain.) For a family that had long produced guardsmen for the formidable Owari Tokugawa clan, this career switch must have seemed like a wretched one. But rather than dwell on their decline, Masakichi's parents swiftly and stoically adapted, using their paltry pension money to open the shop. Masakichi, too, learned to make the instrument. In his spare time, to train his ear, he took lessons in *nagauta*, Japanese epic songs sung to the accompaniment of the shamisen, which was originally featured in the kabuki theater.

After his father's death, Masakichi contemplated another occupational change. In 1887, aged twenty-eight, newly married, and barely making ends meet as a shamisen maker, he decided to become an elementary school music teacher. With some years of nagauta vocal training under his belt, Masakichi knew he could sing, and that was a prized asset. At the time, Japan's elementary music curriculum was largely focused on a new and unique vocal genre, in which children sang Japanese lyrics to Western melodies—part of the Civilization-and-Enlightenment effort, which presumed that the more children were exposed to Western culture, the more Japan would advance. True, catching up in the areas of natural sciences, engineering, military science, law, and medicine was the more urgent task, but Japan's nation-builders thought music sufficiently important that they hired a number of foreign teachers as special government advisers. These outsiders devised a universal education program—the program that Masakichi Suzuki sought to learn and implement. And the government eventually started sending Japanese students abroad so that they could study in the world's top music schools, then return to Japan and teach there. The first of these students was one Nobu Koda, a violinist and pianist who in 1889 matriculated at the New England Conservatory of Music in Boston and then at the Vienna Conservatory. She would later play a decisive role in Shinichi Suzuki's life.[9]

Before that, Masakichi, rightly detecting the government's growing interest in music education, must have concluded that, as a music teacher, he would be assured a stable, respectable position and a salary adequate to support a family. To be certified in his new trade, he took lessons with a professor at Nagoya's Teachers' College twice a week. Masakichi was expecting a crash course that would leave him with an adequate middle-class job as a vocal instructor. Instead, a chance encounter during the lessons changed his life. One month in, he saw and touched a violin for the first time. It was a domestically produced instrument belonging to a fellow student. (The first Japanese violin was probably made in 1880, by the Tokyo luthier Teijiro Matsunaga. Seven years on, according to records from a Tokyo craftsmen's exposition, there were at least four luthiers making violins in Japan.)

The author Satsuki Inoue reconstructs Masakichi Suzuki's first contact with the violin in her biography of the man. Knowing that Masakichi made shamisen, the violin's owner asked him, "Mr. Suzuki, why not make one of these yourself?" At first glance, it seemed a simple enough instrument to replicate. "What if I did?" Masakichi wondered. "Would it sell?" The violinist was optimistic: "There is a huge demand for it," he said, "so if you make it, it will sell." Seeing that Masakichi remained skeptical, he added, "This, you see, is a highly respected instrument in the West. It's been that way for more than two hundred years. If you can make it, it will be a great hit." Masakichi was intrigued. He begged the owner to lend him the violin so that he could study its structure. This, however, was not what the owner had bargained for, and he was reluctant to part with his possession. But he eventually relented on the condition that Masakichi borrow the instrument for only one night, while its owner was asleep.

Unbeknownst to Masakichi then, the violin was the very embodiment of what Japan had missed out on during its years of isolation. While Tokugawa Japan looked inward, the violin took off in a major way in Europe. Before the birth of the violin, many types of bowed and stringed instruments had existed around the world, including the ancient Greek lyre, the North African and Middle Eastern rebab, and medieval European rebec. But the violin, more so than any predecessor, became a distinctive social phenomenon. The instrument emerged in Cremona, Italy, in the middle of the sixteenth century, when luthiers such as Nicola Amati, Antonio Stradivari, and Giuseppe Guarneri built what are now regarded as priceless (or else extremely pricey) old-master instruments. Since then, the violin has changed very little. True, modern violins have longer necks and fingerboards, accommodating higher notes, and some older instruments have been adjusted to modern playing requirements accordingly. But the violin, from the moment of its birth, was essentially complete. A huge evolutionary leap, it achieved a long-sought ideal, all at once putting an end to the centuries-old quest to create a bowed and stringed instrument sounding beautifully in its register. Other designs also remained popular for some time before giving way, but there would be no further significant development of violin alternatives. And, by coincidence, the violin's rapid spread across Europe happened to occur at just the point in history when Tokugawa Japan was withdrawing into its shell.

When Masakichi came face to face with this unfamiliar musical instrument, he realized that he could not have been more wrong about its structure. In fact, there was nothing simple about building such a thing. To begin with, he could not figure out what materials to use. He guessed that he would need a soft, pliable wood, and so turned to the Japanese Judas tree. (In Europe, maple, spruce, ebony, and boxwood were commonly used.) Unable to disassemble his borrowed instrument, he instead traced it, inspected the interior as best he could, and made careful notes before returning it to its owner the following day. He then proceeded to build something that matched his memory of a violin, with plausible pegs, a tailpiece, and a fingerboard. He did not neglect the sound post, hidden from view inside the instrument. No record of the strings remains, but it is probable that he used the silk strings found on shamisen. At the time, the gold standard in violin strings was sheep gut, which is still used by some players today, although many have switched to synthetic options.

Thus Masakichi's instrument looked like a violin, but appearance can be deceiving. Shinichi Suzuki later wrote of it:

> The nearly flat fingerboard is attached to the top panel of the violin, and the sound post—an octagonal stick—was fastened with glue to the top and bottom panels of the instrument. It should have been resting close to the bridge. But in this case, it was placed far towards the top [of the instrument], directly under the fingerboard, even though the real purpose of a sound post is to conduct the vibration of sound effectively, from the strings to the bridge, and then from the bridge to the back panel.[10]

In other words, Masakichi had gotten the sound post, which is vital in creating the violin's haunting resonance, quite wrong. The importance of the sound post cannot be overstated—as the French term for it, *âme*, suggests, the sound post is the soul of the instrument. Its improper placement and the use of vibration-deadening glue decisively sabotaged its sound-conducting properties. Masakichi's first violin could make very little noise, let alone a pleasing sound. The instrument, completed in early 1888, was unsalable.

Undeterred, Masakichi vowed to make a better violin. Fortunately for him, he was soon asked to repair a violin with a broken neck. The job should have taken him only a day, but he held onto the instrument for three days, the better to study it. As he repaired the broken instrument, he built his second violin. This was a major improvement on the first and was immediately snatched up by a buyer. Now purchase orders began to flow in. Though still a luxury item, Masakichi's violins were priced competitively, costing less than half of Western imports. As he worked on more instruments, he continued to experiment with different combinations of indigenous varieties of maple, spruce, pine, and horse chestnut, while constantly trying to improve the quality of his varnish. After selling about thirty violins, he believed that he had found his calling. He got rid of his shamisen-making tools and invested all his capital in a violin workshop.[11]

From early on, Masakichi was not satisfied with the prospect of being a skilled artisan. Rather, he dreamed of a business following the model of semi-industrialized Western luthiery. Beginning in the second half of the nineteenth century, the mechanization of tools and increasingly rationalized division of labor had enabled some European instrument manufacturers, most famously in German, Bohemian, and French towns, to produce violins in large quantities. Builders in Mittenwald, Markneukirchen, Klingenthal, Adorf, Graslitz, and Mirecourt all thrived on a semi-industrial approach to violin-making. The move from intensive craftsmanship to time-, material-, and labor-saving production happened just as demand for the instrument was rising in global markets, especially the United States. Today, the products of these early mechanized workshops, while not on par with their entirely handbuilt predecessors, are highly valued, a reflection of their quality and of the workshops' eventual supplanting by large-scale assembly lines mass-producing low-cost plywood instruments. Only in the second half of the twentieth century was the time-honored art of Cremonese violin-making revitalized by luthiers toiling carefully, often alone, with hand tools.

Masakichi Suzuki, photographed in 1921 with a violin he built in
1888—the first of many. *Talent Education Research Institute*

By modeling his own production methods on those of modern European makers—in particular, those of Markneukirchen, who were the world's foremost builders at the time—Masakichi would gain a leg up. Other fledgling Japanese luthiers tended to approach violin-making more in the spirit of artisanal craftsmanship and so would be left in his dust. Despite some serious financial setbacks, in 1890 Masakichi realized his vision, establishing a small factory and employing seven or eight workers. The workers mostly came from samurai backgrounds similar to Masakichi's: all were descended from former retainers of the Owari Tokugawa domain, and they shared his strong work ethic.

But Masakichi was not just a follower of Western ways. He was also, in keeping with other Nagoya businessmen, an innovator. "Even though he never studied mechanical engineering as such," Shinichi Suzuki would write in 1960, "my father held twenty-one patents for his inventions." These included machines that could cut violin scrolls and back panels, enabling the partial mechanization Masakichi sought. Until his death at the age of eighty-six, his passion for research and improvement never ceased. The younger Suzuki said his father's drive impressed him greatly "from an early age, in everyday life." Built on these foundations of hard work and forward-thinking, the Suzuki Violin Company is still in operation today.[12]

If Masakichi was ambitious, he also was stubborn, so much so that Shinichi and others of his family did not bother arguing with the patriarch even when he was clearly in the wrong. Masakichi himself explained how he survived the financially challenging early days of his violin business: "Once I am convinced that I am right, I charge ahead no matter what others might say. I cannot do otherwise. I think that has actually been my strength." Having enormous self-confidence and no room for second guesses apparently paid off. Within five years of producing his first, greatly flawed instrument, Masakichi was exhibiting his violins in domestic and international expositions, including the Chicago World's Fair of 1893. The high regard his violins earned there was a great boon to business.[13]

By 1898, when Shinichi was born, Masakichi's violins had cornered Japan's midrange market. Another musical innovator, Torakusu Yamaha, had come to dominate the domestic market in reed organs and later pianos. Masakichi Suzuki and Yamaha became such intimate friends that they had a gentleman's agreement not to infringe on each other's instrumental territory—a promise kept well beyond their deaths, until the Yamaha Corporation finally began selling acoustic student violins in 2000. But compared to Yamaha's organs and pianos, which enjoyed considerable demand for classroom use all across Japan, violins had a limited customer base. Though local demand was growing, Masakichi understood that he would have to look beyond Japanese shores in order to achieve the scale of his ambition. Given the dominance of Germans in the violin-making industry, cultivating international markets was sure to be a formidable task.

At the same time, Japanese power was maturing. In 1896, Japan won an imperialist war with China and gained its first colony, the island of Formosa (Taiwan). More important than territorial aggrandizement, however, was the symbolism of China's defeat. For much of East Asia's recorded history, China had been indomitable—the Central Kingdom that Japan could only hope to emulate. But by the late nineteenth century, China's Qing Dynasty was beset by Western colonial encroachment and a scourge of opium addiction. Newly vulnerable, China proved incapable of defending itself against Japan's modernizing armed forces. The Sino-Japanese War made clear that there was another regional leader in East Asia, with aspirations for more. Ever since the forced opening of the country, Japan had despised Western colonialism, which discriminated against nonwhite peoples and cultures foreign to the Euro-American world. But once Japan began to see itself as a potential member of the exclusive, light-skinned nations, it became imperialism's most ardent advocate and practitioner.

Yet the timing of Japan's ascent, at the close of the era of imperial great powers, was not optimal for an aspiring empire. For one thing, competition for colonial gains was fierce, as the field was already crowded and little undominated territory remained. What is more, an emerging superpower, the United States, was beginning to promote successfully a different kind of imperialism, one that deemphasized territorial domination— albeit that the United States had spent the nineteenth century conquering its own land empire in North America and would, a few years after the Sino-Japanese War, take overseas possessions in the Pacific and

Caribbean. Even so, Washington was winning allies and gaining influence by preaching cultural imperialism via the global spread of egalitarian and democratic ideals that it failed to practice among its own racial minorities or in its colonial and de facto colonial territories, whether Puerto Rico or Hawai'i, the Philippines or American Indian reservations.

In Japan, where homegrown democratic activism struggled to make headway against the rigidly hierarchical political culture set in place by the Meiji founding fathers, egalitarian messages from the United States had little immediate impact. But alongside its professed political ideals, the United States was also spreading its influence by promoting its economic and educational paradigms, and these found greater purchase in Japan. For both Masakichi and Shinichi Suzuki, the extension of US culture and consumerism would prove critical in the long run. For the father, the American campaign to propagate free-market, capitalist-backed culture created opportunities to sell instruments on a mass scale. For the son, the US-influenced trend toward including classical music training and appreciation in public school programs would mean greater receptivity for his approach to music education long before the arrival of the Suzuki Method.

By the end of the nineteenth century, Americans were increasingly interested in violin instruction as a vector for social reform. Like US movements for abolition, temperance, and suffrage, the effort toward uplift via music was greatly inspired by antecedents in Britain. There, wealthy philanthropists and social reformers had ventured to remedy the ills of the Industrial Revolution by using music to enlighten, educate, placate, and entertain the increasingly unhappy working class. For instance, mechanics' institutes, often funded by industrialists, acted as learning centers for the working class in major cities. Many institutes focused on the arts, and some offered adult sight-singing classes. Sight-singing became so popular that it was added to Britain's state school curriculum in 1872. At about the same time, inexpensive "Concerts for the People" were gaining popularity in British cities.

By the early 1880s, British adults could enroll in violin courses for minimal fees. The classes attracted considerable interest but achieved limited success because students had to put up with sharing a small number of violins. However, similar group violin classes for children took off, thanks largely to the ingenuity of a certain Thomas Mee Pattison, an advisor to the London music publisher John G. Murdoch & Co. Pattison devised a program in which underprivileged children, who had hitherto been unable to afford expensive private tuition, let alone good violins, were given group instruction in their regular schools. The company provided instruction books, instructors, and plenty of decent rental instruments imported in large quantities from Germany and Bohemia. Fees were affordable, all-inclusive, and could be paid in monthly installments. This socially conscious yet sufficiently business-minded musical enterprise came to be known as the Maidstone Movement, after the first school in Kent to take up the program. Through the Murdoch-sponsored Maidstone School Orchestra Association, founded in 1897, the program became widely known for its ensemble "festival" performances in famous venues like London's Crystal Palace, Royal Albert Hall, and Alexandra Palace. (Shinichi Suzuki would later put on concerts in the same spirit at Tokyo's Budokan and New York's Carnegie Hall.) Maidstone-affiliated programs were eventually said to have touched 400,000 schoolchildren, amounting to one in every ten students enrolled in Britain's state-run school system. This now largely forgotten social movement, which preceded the Suzuki Method by half a century, lasted until the eve of the Second World War.[14]

Contemporaneous American music educators took note and began experimenting with their own versions of group-based violin instruction. By the 1920s, group violin classes either directly or indirectly inspired by the Maidstone Movement, and equally propelled by the movement's core idea that music-making should be available to every child, had become widespread in the United States. The result was a profusion of public school orchestra programs, with violins and other string instruments enjoying a central place in large group instruction. Recalling his musical boyhood in 1940s Milwaukee, where he started playing the violin as an eight-year-old in a public school orchestra, historian David Schoenbaum notes that, in those days, the city "took its public school[s] seriously, and the public schools took their music programs seriously." He continues, "Like any city in those days, there was a series of orchestras, beginning with the school orchestra and working up to a city youth orchestra," with instruments and lessons made widely available.[15]

The proliferation of affordable children's music programs in the first half of the twentieth century in the United States was remarkable. It was born of the hopeful notion that music could somehow increase opportunities and improve lives. This was hardly a niche idea; it was, in fact, so compelling that it seeped deeply into the popular culture and arguably has never receded. Even Hollywood seized on it. The tale of socially disadvantaged youths successfully finding a better future through the violin is told, most famously, in the 1939 film *They Shall Have Music*. The script follows Frankie, a New York street urchin blessed with the gift of perfect pitch. With fortuitous help from Jascha Heifetz, played by himself, Frankie is able to save a financially strapped music school for the poor, where he ends up receiving free violin lessons. Music, it is suggested, not only helps Frankie rise above a life of petty criminality but also saves all the downtrodden kids enrolled in the school. Given the allegedly obvious relationship between musicality and virtue portrayed in such a story, it is hardly surprising that many parents embraced the Suzuki Method when it came to the United States two decades later. What might it do for their own wayward, or potentially wayward, children?

That kind of hope has proved extraordinarily resilient. The same formula seen in *They Shall Have Music* was recycled, with a heavy dose of the Suzuki Method, in 1999's *Music of the Heart*, inspired by the true story of an East Harlem teacher played in the film by Meryl Streep. The movie chronicles her struggle to establish a Suzuki-based strings program for underprivileged students in New York, culminating in her ensemble's triumphant performance at Carnegie Hall. Similarly the 2015 Brazilian film *The Violin Teacher* is an account of a young professional violinist who stumbles into teaching at a public school in a São Paulo slum. At first the students, all troubled teens, do not trust their instructor, but little by little he gains their acceptance. The first piece the class plays together, at a rundown open-air basketball court, is Suzuki's Book 1 composition "Allegro."

The global vogue for music instruction generally and violin instruction in particular, and the idealism that underlay it, was greatly to Masakichi's advantage. So much the better because he had a lot on the line. The growing violin business was not just a matter of personal and national pride but was also the means by which Masakichi supported a large and exceptional family.

Undated portrait of Suzuki's mother, Ryo. *Talent Education Research Institute*

Shinichi's mother was not Masakichi's legal wife, but a geisha called Ryo. That Shinichi was born out of wedlock was not so rare by the standards of the time; it merely suggested that Masakichi had arrived and was sufficiently well off to keep a mistress. Still, the living arrangement Masakichi made for his family *was* rather unusual. He brought his wife Nobu and mistress Ryo into a single household, where all the children he fathered with both women—nine sons and four daughters— were raised as siblings. (Two of the nine sons, however, died young.)

This spared his illegitimate children stigmatization and feelings of inferiority. However unconventional, the arrangement must at the very least have been workable: Shinichi would later work closely and equally with his full and half brothers to form a successful chamber music group.

When I bring this large family into focus in my imagination, the picture looks something like a caricature of a religious commune, with a loyal flock of women and children devoting themselves to the charismatic guru, Masakichi, who has in turn sworn allegiance to his own higher calling—the art, craft, and business of violin-making. The violin factory next door to their family home was both their source of income and their holy temple.

Despite the seriousness with which the Suzukis took the violin industry, playing the instrument was not a significant part of their family life. Masakichi did eventually learn to play the violin well enough to demonstrate his instruments in public and to write a teach-yourself manual in 1902. One of the older sons took private lessons from a violinist who boarded with the family at one point. But, according to Shinichi Suzuki, he himself did not take up the instrument in earnest until the age of seventeen. And, as a boy, he felt little affinity for violin music.[16]

That said, he was certainly exposed to the instrument. "Whenever I think of my elementary-school years," Suzuki wrote, "I remember them fondly, always against the background of the factory." Right after finishing his dinner, little Shinichi would dash over to the handicraft division of the factory, where "about fifty to sixty people were busy finishing, among other things, violin surfaces in one big room." In those days, the employees of Suzuki Violin worked late to meet burgeoning demand for their product. Since there was no electricity, each craftsman's work was illuminated by an overhead oil lamp. The motive behind this nightly visit was not to lend a tiny helping hand, though Suzuki would start helping out soon enough. Rather, it was to listen to the workers recite tales of legendary samurai heroes. "It occurs to me only now that they were actually quite expert story-tellers," Suzuki recalled in 1960. "They would narrate, like real professionals, long stories, all the while shaving off the outer surfaces of violins." Under the flickering light, the young boy became "simply absorbed by the world of those tales."[17]

But just when a story was about to reach its climax, the narrator would always stop and say, "Let's grill some mochi." A dutiful errand boy, Suzuki would run home, grab some of the rectangular, snow-white rice cakes kept in the kitchen, and run back to the factory, eager to hear the rest of the story. The storyteller would then recommence, at once moving his hands on the violin and keeping a watchful eye on the well-earned nighttime snack grilling on a small charcoal stove next to his worktable.

These evening hours spent with the craftsmen shaped young Suzuki considerably. As a boy, he saw firsthand that even repetitive, seemingly tedious tasks could be approached with a sense of fun as much as persistence. Eventually he would apply that lesson to his teaching, combining playfulness with children's everyday violin practice. Perhaps it was also in the factory that he came to appreciate the power of repetition, as he listened to those samurai stories night after night. His insistence that his students listen over and over to the same recordings, until they had internalized them completely, might have had deep roots in this early childhood routine.

Whatever the case may be, Suzuki's memory of the factory was steeped in "sheer beauty and fondness." When he proceeded to secondary school and was old enough to help out at the factory in his spare time, he did so happily. He became well-versed in the mechanics of the violin. Hard work and compulsive inquisitiveness marked him as much as they had his father.

During Suzuki's childhood, Nagoya's transformation was in full swing. New industries including textiles, watch-making, and pottery started to take over traditional ones such as plant-oil expression, lacquerware production, and fan-making. The city was wired for telephones. Its dark streets were lit by electric lights. To Nagoyaites' delight, in 1898 they began riding Japan's second public tram system. The city's population was just short of 160,000 at the turn of the century; within thirty-five years, it would grow to a million. Western-style theaters, banks, and department stores sprang up throughout the old castle town.

It was not just Japan's fast-growing cities like Nagoya that began to look markedly different. Its people did too. Though many still wore kimonos, Western sartorial style was no longer a rarity, and more and more people effortlessly switched back and forth between Western and Japanese clothes or mixed the two. Kinnosuke Natsume, affectionately referred to by his pen-name Soseki and considered by many to be Japan's first and finest modern writer, often featured characters wearing Inverness capes. This quintessential Victorian outerwear, today commonly associated with Sherlock Holmes, became a popular item among Japanese gentlemen. It was often worn not with a western suit but with a kimono, as the cape's free-flowing design accommodated the traditional attire's baggy sleeves.

Such experiments in fashion were in sync with Japan's developing love of the violin. *I Am a Cat,* a 1905 novel by Soseki, provides a glimpse into this world of eclectic tastes, where the violin was a marker of modernity's imprint on Japan. The work is a satirical gem told from the viewpoint of a domesticated cat, who is "yet to be named." Its characters are amusing, especially the cat's owner, Sneaze, a hypochondriacal and socially awkward professor of English presumably modeled on Soseki himself.

One of the novel's most hilarious passages concerns the professor's acolyte Avalon Coldmoon, a young scientist with an artistic temperament. A great violin enthusiast, Coldmoon recounts to the professor and his friends his frustrating quest to purchase his first violin, when he was a student. "The streets these days are chock-a-block with bright, young men walking along with violin cases in their hands," Coldmoon says. "But when I was a high school lad, very few of us could play any Western instrument whatsoever." Since he attended a country school, "nary a student played the violin"—that is, except for girls studying at a local boarding school. This is a telling irony, bespeaking Japan's adaptation of Western custom rather than its wholesale importation, for it was in fact men who predominated among violinists in Europe into the twentieth century. But Coldmoon would not be caught dead carrying a violin in his small rural community, lest he be perceived as other than masculine. All the same, he secretly pined for the instrument, so much so that, at one point, he peered through a shop window to catch, in his words, "a faint reflection of that glare shining from the polished body of a violin," with "its pinched-in waist."[18]

Having taken the trouble of disguising his identity, one late evening Coldmoon finally manages to buy a domestically made, relatively inexpensive violin—the very kind Masakichi Suzuki was then producing. Indeed, Torahiko Terada, a physicist who served as a model for the character of Coldmoon, purchased a Masakichi Suzuki violin in his student days, in 1898, Shinichi Suzuki's birth year. Even Terada's low-end instrument cost almost nine yen, consuming nearly his entire monthly stipend of eleven yen. It is no wonder that the character of Coldmoon hangs on to his violin with the zeal of a jealous lover, taking it with him wherever he goes and even sleeping with it.[19]

Like the violin, Western classical music was at the turn of the century quickly becoming a sign of acculturation to the modern world, at least in Soseki's urbane, educated circles. It appealed to them for the same reasons that Romantic literature and visual arts did: all these forms were characterized by a surplus of intense and private emotions that had been less overtly expressed in traditional Japanese music. (Think, for example, Johannes Brahms' 1878 violin concerto.) And, of course, the violin had become one of the most dominant voices of classical music, owing in no small part to its most successful promoter, Niccolò Paganini. Thus, to the extent that Western classical music was a symbol of progress in Japan, a cultural wonder that could accomplish what local equivalents could not, so too was the violin. And so young men in Soseki's times might carry violin cases in public to advertise their own enlightenment and sophistication, even if just a few years earlier the instrument was seen as effete.

Soseki started writing *I Am a Cat* during the Russo-Japanese War and published it soon after the two countries reached a truce, mediated by US president Theodore Roosevelt, in 1905. This was a moment in the sun for Japan. The Sino-Japanese War had shown that Japan could be a regional leader. Now the fledgling empire was emerging as a confident, even hubristic, great power. Crucially, Japan's victory over Tsarist Russia defied the notion of White superiority. Suzuki was growing up in a society that assiduously proved the point, so dear to him later in life, that environment and effort matter more than biology. Japan did not have to be White; it had to cultivate war-making technology and train its soldiers. Its people could become strong by learning Western ways and eating the "correct" diet, regardless of their endowments at birth. The war was a victory not only over Russia but also over the colonial notion that people's worth was determined by their skin color and everything they inherited along with it. Roosevelt, a convinced social Darwinist who did not doubt the racial superiority of Whites, nonetheless admired Japan's military ascent and offered the Japanese the highest praise by agreeing to broker the peace with a White adversary.

Japan's victory over Russia inspired millions of colonized people the world over. India's first prime minister, Jawaharlal Nehru, was a teenager when "Japanese victories stirred up [his] enthusiasm." He later recalled waiting "eagerly for the papers for fresh news daily." He even "invested in a large number of books on Japan." True, luck and good timing had a lot to do with the war's outcome; Japan's resources were stretched to their limit, and the country might have capitulated had Russia not been preoccupied with its own domestic instability. But what military exploit is untouched by luck and timing? Victory was victory, and this one had tremendous consequences that shone brightly in a world of empires. Japan took over Russian railway interests in Manchuria—China's northeast—and greatly expanded its influence over Korea, which it would annex in 1910.[20]

Nationalistic pride swelled even the minds of small children. A famous play song that young girls sang while bouncing balls went like this: "Negotiations broke down/The Russo-Japanese War began/Russian soldiers fled quickly/While our Japanese soldiers served the empire till they perished." The song continues along this line until victory is secured, at which point the girls exalt Admiral Heihachiro Togo, commander-in-chief of the Combined Fleet. Finally, the children scream, "Long live the emperor!" It is said that the song was so popular that everyone in pre-WWII Japan knew it, demonstrating the successful use of music in early childhood education, at least in instilling a sense of martial patriotism.

Suzuki appears to have been largely unmoved by the music of his own youth, however. He was seven years old when the Russo-Japanese War ended, but his writing about his childhood does not mention any popular songs. In his telling, music, if not the violin business, had a minimal role in his upbringing. An energetic boy, he preferred to play outdoors rather than sing or learn instruments. He regarded the violins lying around his house as no more than useful props for sword fights with his equally rambunctious brothers.

According to Suzuki's autobiographical writings, it was a seemingly incidental exchange with his mother that put him on a new path, a path that eventually brought him to a serious engagement with music. One day around dusk, little Shinichi, aged nine or ten, sat face to face with his mother in a small, dimly lit room near the front door. He had been summoned there because he had misbehaved, though years later he could not remember his exact offense. As he prattled away in self-defense, she listened silently. After a while, he noticed that tears were trickling down her cheeks. Without uttering a word, she left the room, walked out the front door, and disappeared into the twilight. Suzuki recalled feeling "waves of terrible remorse engulfing my heart." Contrite and worried, he ran after her, and when he finally found her by the river, he was able to say, simply and sincerely, "I am sorry."

"My mother's tears achieved far more than any loud scoldings could ever have done," he wrote. Suzuki credited his mother with giving him, right there and then, the greatest gift in life: "the power of self-reflection." He was forever grateful to her, for he believed that "without the power to reflect . . . there would be no room for a person to grow," and if a person cannot grow, "there would be no room for education." This moment, in retrospect, was a new beginning. "On that quiet, early evening, my mother opened doors for my personal development—with those silent tears of hers."[21]

There is no way to verify the validity of such private memories. Besides, reminiscences are necessarily subjective and unreliable. That is especially so if they are written after substantial time has elapsed since the events that inspired them, as is often the case of Suzuki's writings. After all, he lived a long time and had much to remember. Where there is no possibility of cross-checking, no one will ever know for sure which memories are accurate, which are selective, and which are simply in error. And yet, absolute accuracy is not the main concern here. On the whole, Suzuki wrote to enlighten and instruct, and to make a larger philosophical point. Because of this, his life stories have an air of doctrine—even religious catechism—from which practitioners of his approach are expected to draw their own lessons. The story of a mother's wordless admonition that moves a young heart is no exception. It is, true or false, a parable whereby Suzuki illustrates the importance of self-awareness and self-improvement. His ardent desire to be a better and more reflective individual, ignited, according to him, on that long-ago evening, would only grow more powerful as he approached his adolescent years.

2

FORMATIVE ENCOUNTERS

IN APRIL 1910, AT THE AGE OF ELEVEN, Suzuki enrolled in Nagoya's Commercial Academy. Founded as an all-boys public school in 1884, its purpose was to educate the new kind of Japanese, confident navigators of global trade and industry. Masakichi Suzuki's company was yearly becoming more international in its market reach, and he hoped his son would be well prepared to follow him and continue growing the business.

The Commercial Academy was a forward-looking, congenial place to study. One of its most notable graduates was Suzuki's contemporary Shotaro Kamiya, who helped Kiichiro Toyoda—son of Sakichi Toyoda, the founder of Toyota Industries—make Toyota Motors into a formidable global corporation. Kamiya credited the school with helping him develop the international perspective that underlay his eventual career, first as a steel trader in London, then as a sales executive at General Motors Japan, and finally in his critical role making Toyota not only Japan's, but also the world's, top automobile manufacturer.

Both Kamiya and Suzuki attended an academy run by Principal Yoshiki Ichimura, a progressive educator and pioneer in business training. Ichimura was a patriot whose personal goals aligned precisely with his country's: he demanded of himself that his own work build up Japan as a respected member of the club of modern states. Thus he insisted to his students—which included boys and girls at various points—that Japan become a viable, independent trading nation. Now that Japan had demonstrated its military might against Qing China and Tsarist Russia, the country's next mission should be one of proving its soft power.

Over the school's entrance hung a sign bearing the motto, "The World Is My Marketplace."

In photographs, the bespectacled and mustachioed Ichimura wears a Western schoolmaster's suit, resembling a character out of Heinrich Mann's 1905 novel *Professor Unrat*. But unlike Professor Unrat, who was ridiculed for his pomposity, Ichimura endeared himself to his students. They could feel that he wanted more for them than practical training; his leadership had a humanistic dimension. Ichimura preached that a commercial education could not end with teaching the technical aspects of industry and trade. Rather, a student of business was also learning to be a decent person. After all, he reasoned, commerce boiled down to negotiations between human beings. He also stressed that in order to grow "vertically," people should reflect on their own efforts and accomplishments instead of comparing themselves to others. Only by gauging our own progress would we stretch our abilities and reach our full potential.

This philosophy clearly influenced Suzuki. During his time at the Commercial Academy, he came to appreciate that the purpose of education is not the cultivation of specific skills, whether in mathematics or languages or another discipline, but instead the development of morally upright individuals sensitive to each other and to all peoples as they struggled to live and grow together in a complex and interconnected world. Four decades later, Suzuki would claim this same goal for his talent education movement. After the 1955 Grand Concert Suzuki wrote, "We are not raising miniature violinists. We are trying to raise worthy citizens while proving that talents are not inborn, . . . that great sensibilities and talents can be nurtured in any human being." Evidently it was these ideals, not the Commercial Academy's applied teachings, that stuck with Suzuki. As an adult, he proved utterly incapable of dealing with money.[1]

It is unsurprising that Suzuki's formal education had a decidedly moral component. The fact is that, for centuries, merchants had not been well regarded in Japanese society, and they had to work to earn the population's trust. Today this can be hard to fathom, given the esteem granted Japan's later titans of business at home and abroad. But in the preindustrial era, Japanese traders occupied a lowly social stratum. The samurai class—just 6 percent of the population—were at the top, setting the rules for the rest. Immediately below were farmers, who provided the population's indispensable sustenance. Then came artisans, who had attained skills through years of hard work and proper training. Just above the bottom of this feudal hierarchy, which was the province of hereditary social outcasts, were merchants. Merchants were commonly viewed as at best a necessary evil. Yes, people desired goods they could not easily produce themselves, but merchants were understood as having no special skills and were associated with greed, corruption, and mundane temptations. In reality, in feudal Japan as elsewhere, money meant power. Despite their official position of inferiority, merchants often became influential figures—and the social elite sometimes became merchants. One cannot live on honor alone, so members of the samurai class, including Suzuki's own ancestors, supplemented their income by venturing into commerce.

In the fledgling years of modern Japan, this dynamic was spun on its head, as the country's modernization depended on developing economic resilience. This did not mean that businessmen were suddenly celebrated; long-standing social structures, and the prejudices attached to them, do not topple overnight. Merchants sought rehabilitation in the eyes of the public, so that the nation would stand behind them as they carried the burden of Japan's future. Eiichi Shibusawa—the Meiji era's foremost a businessman, credited with having introduced Western-style capitalism to Japan—was emblematic of the socially conscious modern Japanese industrialist. "Through industry I thought I could discharge my obligation to my country," Shibusawa explained.

> My personal fame and my family's wealth had never entered into my thoughts from the very start of my career. My burning desire was to promote the application of the collective welfare of the country; the development of Japan's industry; the increase of the public wealth; and to elevate the status of merchants and businessmen so that they could be placed on an equal footing with those of Europe and America.[2]

For Suzuki's samurai family, earning a living through commerce rather than service to the feudal domain was a definite step down in traditional terms. But their timing could not have been better.

A psychologically sensitive individual, Suzuki imbibed the communal appeals of the Commercial Academy under Ichimura. Indeed, several moments during his high school years illustrate his powerful moral feeling. One of these moments came when he was seventeen and was nearing the end of his studies at the academy. After school one day, he stopped by his father's violin factory to help out, as he often did. In the administrative office, an English-language typewriter caught his eye. Such a gadget was still a rarity in Japan; its presence indicated that Suzuki Violin's overseas business was flourishing, since the typewriter was primarily used to prepare export invoices. Like a child drawn to a new toy, he started typing at the keyboard, even though there was no paper on the black rubber roller. A Mr. Yamazaki, who headed the company's export division, appeared. "Master Shinichi," he admonished, "you shouldn't tap an empty typewriter," which would wear out the parts. Suzuki hesitated, then said he was just pretending. "Is that right?" the older man asked, before leaving the office. But this episode was not over for Suzuki. "Perhaps caught red-handed, my true nature revealed itself," he later wrote. He felt deeply uneasy that he had lied instead of apologizing, almost like "my heart was being crushed." By not taking responsibility for his actions, he was wasting his mother's invaluable lesson in self-reflection. Though he had committed only a trivial wrong by misusing the typewriter, the act of lying cut to his core. Unable to compose himself, he left the factory and set out for home.

By this time, the family was no longer living next door to the factory. Suzuki spent the twenty-minute walk home perseverating about his lie. When he reached his destination, he decided to keep moving. After some wandering, he ended up on the town's main street, where he entered a bookstore and started browsing. A small volume entitled *The Diary of Tolstoy* attracted his attention. He took it out and opened at random to this passage: "To deceive oneself is worse than to deceive others." It was the stuff of epiphany. In an instant—at least, according to his recollection— Suzuki understood that all people were responsible to themselves, and that he owed it to himself to keep striving to become a better person. "I could barely contain myself from shaking," he wrote, "and felt thankful that those pages that I opened by chance contained those words." He purchased the Tolstoy diary, went home, and devoured it.

From then on, he carried it with him everywhere he went, eventually reading it to pieces.

Suzuki read other works by Leo Tolstoy as well, and he was hardly alone in his appreciation for the Russian master. In fact, Tolstoy was one of the most admired and widely read foreign authors in early twentieth-century Japan; his works had been available in translation since 1886. Tolstoy's literary, religious, and political oeuvre provided a language in which educated Japanese could express themselves, whether they were novelists, artists, playwrights, or social and political activists. By the time Suzuki picked up the diary, five years after the author's death, Tolstoy's pacifism and egalitarian humanism had seeped into the Japanese psyche, in large part owing to his vocal opposition to the Russo-Japanese War. Tolstoy's pacifism resonated in Japan even as the country's official self-image relied heavily on building a strong modern army.

One example of this reflective side of Japan was Akiko Yosano, a leading poet who would collaborate creatively with Suzuki in the 1930s. Yosano wrote a famous verse in 1904, in the middle of the war with Russia, entitled "Please Do Not Die in Vain" (*Kimi Shinitamo koto Nakare*). The poem is a heart-wrenching plea addressed to Yosano's younger brother serving in the Imperial Army, whom she feared might die needlessly in an impulsive act of self-sacrifice. "Dear young brother, I cry for you. Please do not die," she implores, reminding him that "your parents did not raise you to be a man of twenty-four so that you can kill and be killed."

A mere child during the Russo-Japanese War, Suzuki was drawn to Tolstoy for his philosophical, rather than his political, beliefs. After Tolstoy, Suzuki discovered the pioneering seventeenth-century empiricist Francis Bacon, as well as the sutra *Shushogi,* which explains the teachings of the thirteenth-century Zen Buddhist monk Dogen. This was, in Suzuki's words, an intellectual and spiritual coming of age, as he "embarked on a pilgrimage to trace the footsteps of those wise men of the past." Later, Suzuki would promote the idea that he had been guided by life rather than by books. He even declared in a lecture once that he "hardly read books" because he knew he could learn more from observation and experience. While it is true that his educational methods and the philosophy underlying them did not draw systematically on existing literature, their development owed much to his late teenage years, when he read voraciously in search of guidance and concluded that he had to arrive at his own answers.[3]

Constant reflection and reading did not render Suzuki an introvert. Quite the opposite. His open temperament and his desire to learn from his surroundings—likely encouraged by Bacon's empiricism—meant he would never be bookish and withdrawn. His intensifying desire for self-improvement brings to mind Benjamin Franklin, whose *Autobiography* famously presents a regimen of personal reforms intended to foster virtuous living. Whereas most teens can hardly be roused, Suzuki started waking up at the crack of dawn, a habit he would keep for the rest of his life, sometimes to the dismay of those around him. Years later, on tour, Suzuki's secretary bade the composer and Cambridge professor Alexander Goehr to meet her boss at 5 a.m., an invitation that Goehr politely but firmly declined. (Even more years later, when Goehr told me this story, he remained highly bemused and amused by the episode.) As for the teenage Suzuki, he made use of every waking hour, helping out at home and at the violin factory and taking care of his younger siblings and other neighborhood children.

It was also around his seventeenth year that Suzuki grew to be fascinated by those young children. He wrote in his memoir of feeling particularly happy whenever he would come home, either from school or from the factory, to a welcoming flock of kids. Eventually he realized why he enjoyed their company so much: "Children of five or six never lie to themselves." With this insight in mind, he would engage children with a humble awareness that they were his teachers. Why, he wondered, did the honesty of children disappear as they aged? Why was it not nurtured in school and by society generally? He was disturbed that conventional education seemed to do more harm than good, molding honest, spirited children into unhappy, calculating adults. An important question was beginning to dominate Suzuki's thinking: What is education? At the very least, it should not be a means of diminishing what was best in children. For his own benefit, he pledged to try to preserve within himself "the natural, unaffected ways of five- and six-year-olds."[4]

It would be hard to overstate the ferment induced by these adolescent discoveries—Tolstoy and Bacon, Zen, the moral learning provided by his formal education and interactions with adults, and a budding philosophical and critical posture fostered by time spent with children. Yet this was not all. At the same time, another external stimulus was increasing Suzuki's sensitivity to and awareness of the world: music.

Music entered Suzuki's life not through his fingers on a violin but through phonograph recordings. The phonograph had been introduced to Japan in 1879, just two years after it was invented in New Jersey by Thomas Edison. But its high price prevented it becoming a household item right away. The following decades instead gave rise to the business of *chikuonkiya*, literally "phonographers," who were rather like organ-grinders in European cities. They would walk the streets playing record-ings of popular songs, political speeches, traditional folk songs, and the like for a small fee. A 1901 illustrated magazine article entitled "Find-ings from the Street" depicts a phonographer hawking their services in a "unique, half-high-brow, half-popular tone" of voice. Those interested would pay for the use of a stethoscope-like earplug—it sounded only in one ear—through which they heard a famous geisha singing or an actor reciting his lines. Besides providing entertainment, those traveling pho-nographers played an important role in spreading urban culture to remote corners of Japan. They remained prominent until more affordable, often domestically produced phonographs became available for home use, starting in the second half of the 1910s.[5]

The availability of this new technology also spurred new forms of music, for instance, "The Song of Katyusha," a huge hit from 1914 to 1915. The song, whose tune was drawn from Japanese folk music and German lieder for hummable effect, was composed for stage and film adaptations of Tolstoy's 1899 novel *Resurrection*. Sung by the theater star Sumako Matsui, it is considered Japan's first pop song, having sold, purportedly, more than 20,000 records. At this point, bulky early pho-nographs, which recorded sounds as etchings in wax cylinders, were being replaced by a new standard—flat shellac discs. It was these that took off, thanks to their smaller size and reduced cost. It is most likely this type of phonograph that came to Suzuki's household. He recalls the appearance of their family machine:

> Back then, a record player, unlike today's electronic player, was
> a very old-fashioned contraption . . . in order to produce a sound,
> you had to grind the handle with your own hand. And the horn

that acted as a speaker had a flaring shape that looked like a morning glory flower. It was so large that a child's head could have easily fit into it.

Eager to try the phonograph, Suzuki bought the violinist Mischa Elman's recording of Franz Schubert's *Ave Maria*. He cranked up the machine and was stunned by the sound it produced. A "dream-like melody" came with "soul-shaking sweetness." It felt as if he was being "wrapped around in velvety softness." That a violin could sound so beautiful was an especially shocking, and embarrassing, discovery for Suzuki: he had grown up surrounded by violins without ever appreciating what they were capable of. His oldest brother, Umeo, eight years his senior, played a little bit of violin at home. But the sound emerging from the morning glory-shaped horn was something altogether different. It was unearthly.

Why then—why was the seventeen-year-old Suzuki suddenly moved by the sound of an instrument that could have captivated him so much earlier? Perhaps he had first to be open to the depths of feeling he encountered in the Elman recording. It was thanks to Tolstoy and other readings, he later explained, that he was able to perceive something personally meaningful in *Ave Maria* and the instrument that sang it. And so, just as playing with young children made him wonder about education, listening to music made him wonder, "What is art?"[6]

The Elman *Ave Maria* that so affected Suzuki was probably recorded in 1913 with the Victrola label. Listening to that performance now, I am struck by what feels like the exaggerated timbre and phrasings of Elman's violin playing. What sounded sweet and velvety to Suzuki's ear feels almost too sweet, sticky, even sentimental to mine. It conjures up the style of playing that one associates with table-hopping violinists who try to sell "romantic" tunes to couples dining in a restaurant—perhaps themselves a dying breed of musicians. The culprit here must be the generous use of glissandos, for which Elman is particularly noted. He slides his left fingers from one position to another while vibrating the string continuously, dramatically inflecting his music in a manner that recalls the exaggerated Shakespeare performances of his time. But after several listenings, I am more convinced of the beauty of Elman's tone, which shines through the hefty dose of slides and accents. Did my own idée fixe about what an acceptable interpretation of *Ave Maria* should sound like initially obstruct my appreciation of this recording? It is at least plausible. I have a very clear opinion of what *Ave Maria* sounds like, because, as a child, I listened every day to an orchestral arrangement of this very piece, which was broadcast throughout my school for a five-minute reflection before homeroom began. Was my adult self now approaching classical music in a dogmatic, unimaginative, and methodical way?

Indeed, such inflexibility is widespread in the classical music world. In Bruno Monsaingeon's documentary *The Art of Violin: The Devil's Instrument* (2000), the master violinist of our time, Itzhak Perlman, wonders about this exact point. "If you compare violinists of today, and violinists of let's say the 1920s, '30s, '40s, and '50s"—Kreisler, Elman, Enescu, Heifetz, Francescatti, Szigeti, Milstein, Menuhin, Oistrakh, Stern—you will note a dramatic change. Today's violinists aim for comparable brilliance, producing, more often than not, results that fall within the expected range of sounds, whereas none of their predecessors, Perlman believes, "sounded like the other." He attributes this to the great technical and musical leeway violinists once enjoyed in creating their own individual voices. If one tries to pull off similar tricks today, Perlman is certain, "you'll be called 'old-fashioned.'" Lamenting the disappearance of the soloist's glaring individuality, he remarks, "I wish I had more of those old-fashioned things!" I wonder, assuming Perlman's assertion is valid, if the disappearance of the "old-fashioned things" has also left audiences less able to accept pronounced individuality when they do hear it—on old records or from those rare eccentric performers who still find work. To take the question further, I wonder if the prevalence of a musical method like Suzuki's, which undoubtedly expanded opportunities for many a youngster, has also contributed to the homogenization of what was once fascinatingly varied.

In any case, Suzuki's encounter with Elman's playing left him yearning to play the violin himself. He brought one home from the factory and started "scraping at it" every day. Soon he picked up another of Elman's recordings, this time a Haydn minuet, which he felt he might be able to learn more easily than *Ave Maria*. Although Suzuki does not specify which of Haydn's minuets this was, it was most likely the Minuet in D

Major, arranged by the German violinist Willy Burmester and recorded in 1911 or 1913. Without a written score, Suzuki attempted to emulate what he was hearing from the phonograph. He explained that he does not remember how long it took, but after a period of trial and error, he managed to learn the whole piece. It was a moment when he demonstrated the same single-minded persistence his father had brought to building his first violin nearly three decades earlier. Shinichi Suzuki was getting hooked. Playing the violin gave him "great comfort" and he became "increasingly attached to music." His love of philosophical books was being supplanted by a love of listening to music and learning to play it.[7]

It was an exciting time for an impressionable Japanese youth to be introduced to Western classical music. Suzuki's discovery of Elman's recordings came at the zenith of classical music's globalization, democratization, and popularization. Technological advancements made recordings of great musical performances more widely available. This in turn fed the popular desire not only to listen to music but also to play musical instruments, accounting for at least some of the success of Masakichi Suzuki's affordable violins in Japan and abroad. And abroad was becoming ever closer, owing to revolutionary changes in how people traveled. This was especially thrilling for classical music lovers in Japan, as easier travel—by rail, ship, and soon air—allowed musicians to circle the globe and deliver live performances to their adoring audiences. Suzuki's first idol, Elman, made three visits to Japan to give recitals, the first in 1921.

Violinists were at the crest of the classical wave. With so many people taking up the instrument, there was huge demand for recital materials and pieces that hobbyists could play by themselves at home. In the late nineteenth and early twentieth centuries, the solo repertoire expanded and diversified in the hands of marquis players like the Austrian-born virtuoso Fritz Kreisler, who would eventually replace Elman as Suzuki's favorite violinist. Kreisler composed and arranged the kinds of pieces he wanted to play himself, pieces that would become a staple violin repertoire. (Doubting that his compositions could attract attention, Kreisler attributed them to famous composers in history. He kept the secret until he turned sixty, in 1935, by which point his reputation as one of the world's most revered violinists was secure.) Burmester, who arranged the Handel piece that was likely the first Suzuki learned, was also a highly accomplished violinist. His arrangements—published under such titles as *Pieces by Old Masters* and including solo violin renditions of works by Rameau, Lully, J. S. Bach, Martini, and Beethoven, in addition to Handel—have enjoyed enduring popularity. Many would later find their way into Suzuki's method books, most recognizably perhaps Gossec's Gavotte, featured at the end of Violin Book 1. Even more explicitly pronounced among Suzuki's influences is the Hungarian violinist Tivadar Nachéz. His arrangement of the Vivaldi concertos has been a milestone of Suzuki studies for generations.[8]

Not long after Suzuki began his private course of self-improvement with reading and music, his moral character was to be tested in a very public way by a seemingly insignificant incident that developed into a local scandal. On December 8, 1915, Suzuki was at school taking an exam in abacus calculations. During the exam, a student named Fujita caught a classmate cheating. Fujita reported the scofflaw, which prompted the teacher to dismiss him from the classroom. The boy, devastated, took his leave. It was his final year, and it was unlikely that he would be allowed to graduate. The rest of the class kept working the abacus beads until the exam was over.[9]

Once they finished, the students flooded into the hallway. Just as the informer Fujita came out, a group of eight to ten students encircled him. "Fujita, what a fine friend you are!" one jeered. Then the boys descended on him, punching his face and dislodging his glasses. Fujita, though well-built, was overpowered and fled in tears. Suzuki, who exited the classroom later, did not take part in this mob "punishment." But he did feel "furious at Fujita for his unfriendly gesture."

Soon Suzuki was fully embroiled in the affair. By virtue of his position as class president, he was summoned to the teacher's lounge to report what happened. Suzuki was not a top student, but that had not stopped him from being elected class president two years in a row. Charming and pleasant, with dreamy eyes that would remain strikingly unchanged throughout his long life, Suzuki put peers and teachers at ease. He made friends effortlessly and had no enemies. But on that winter day, Suzuki knew he had some serious explaining to do. When he went into the lounge, four or five grim, glaring teachers were waiting around a charcoal heater. His conversation with them was to be a precarious balancing act between his sense of solidarity with classmates and his nascent Tolostoyan zeal for truth.

Mr. Kikuchi, an English and homeroom teacher, sat in the middle. Ordinarily mild-tempered and gentle, he did not mask his displeasure as he began firing questions at Suzuki. Asked if he knew anything about the incident, Suzuki answered that he did, and that he had joined his classmates in beating up the tattletale. And no, he did not think it was the right thing to do, but snitching had also been wrong. It showed "a regrettable lack of friendship." "Among us friends, we live by our own rules," he added. "For instance, even if we catch a friend stealing something, we would not dream of turning him in to the police right away. That is not something we call friendship. Real friends would try to talk to that friend, and convince him never to steal again . . . friends should defend their own first." Mr. Kikuchi responded, "Enough of your theory on friendship, which does not make the beating right." Suzuki agreed and proposed that the class be punished collectively.

Back in the classroom, Suzuki explained to his classmates what he had told the teachers: that the whole class had beaten Fujita and that everyone deserved to be punished. This, in his mind, was the whitest of white lies. He pleaded with the class to accept shared responsibility and, in the worst case, repeat the final grade the following year. He must have been quite persuasive, as the whole homeroom class of around forty students quickly agreed to stand by his version of the story, join the minority who had actually taken part in Fujita's pounding, and risk being unable to graduate at year's end.

The next morning, the school administration announced its decision. It named only ten students, including Suzuki, to be "indefinitely suspended." Another ten received milder reprimands. The students made a huge fuss, angry that the administration had ignored their collective acceptance of blame. Word of the treatment of Suzuki's class got around, and students gathered after school to plan a protest. When Suzuki went home, late at night, he related the whole story to his father and apologized for likely having to repeat his final year. Masakichi laughed it off, saying, "I suppose it cannot be helped." The following day, the whole student school, led by Suzuki's class, went on strike.

Parents and local media took note. The paper featured the news under the headline, "Students Strike Back at the Commercial Academy."[10] The matter remained unresolved for several days. On December 13, Principal Ichimura assembled the entire student body of about 1,700. As his eyes filled with tears, he offered that there had been mistakes made on all sides, including his own. After thorough deliberation, he had decided that the school should rescind its previous punishment and instead readminister the exam to make a fresh start for everyone.

This is how the strike came to an end. On March 15, 1916, everyone in Suzuki's class—which, according to the newspaper article, "never had a good reputation to begin with," and according to Suzuki, was "not a particularly distinguished group"—managed to graduate together. No students were left behind. Looking back, Suzuki said the incident taught him the same lesson Tolstoy had, that the utmost obligation was to be truthful to oneself. When first called to the teachers, he stayed true to his heart by protecting his classmates, even though he did not tell the objective truth about what had happened. He had nothing to regret. Rather, he felt reassured to have acted according to his own truth, guided by feelings of friendship and loyalty.

Suzuki's keen sense of moral responsibility was in keeping with the spirit of the age. The student protest at the Commercial Academy happened in 1915, the fourth year of the reign of Emperor Yoshihito, who succeeded the Meiji emperor, Mutsuhito. Yoshihito's reign, from 1912 to 1926, came to be called Taisho, or "Great Righteousness," in light of the enormous social and political changes Japan was undergoing. So-called Taisho Democracy, much like Germany's Weimar Republic between the two World Wars, now evokes a sense of nostalgia for a time of abundant hope and optimism—a longing for what could have been, had the nation continued a worthy political journey.

The Taisho era was marked by increased popular participation in politics. For instance, in 1913, large-scale protests in Tokyo objecting to autocratic government prompted the prime minister to resign. It was also during the Taisho period that Japan began to experiment seriously with a multiparty political system. The seeds of this moment had been planted earlier by the Freedom and People's Rights Movement of the 1870s. Inspired by the likes of Jean-Jacques Rousseau and the nineteenth-century Scottish reformer Samuel Smiles, the movement argued that the Meiji

Restoration went neither far nor deep enough in ensuring a society that guaranteed equal rights for all its members. Proponents decried the authoritarian, neo-Confucianist, quasimartial regime, which was run by a small group of elites with samurai backgrounds, and accused it of overlooking women and social outcasts. These sentiments swelled during the imperialist wars with China and Russia and flowered in the Taisho years.

The transformative quality of the Taisho period is indexed by political achievements, like those mentioned above. But there was more to it than new laws, leaders, and governing structures. Nor was it tied exclusively to official politics and mass mobilization. Taisho Democracy was a daily, civic exploration in cohabitation through which, ideally, all could learn to live with one another more respectfully. It reflected a conviction that society in general gained when each individual thought carefully about their responsibility to the community and to others. The willingness of Suzuki and his classmates to defy school authorities by organizing around what they believed to be a righteous cause was a manifestation of the Taisho mood, and so was the school administration's willingness to listen to the other, weaker side.

After graduation, Suzuki did not question the plans his father had made for him; he eagerly began working full-time at Suzuki Violin. To meet his own exacting standards, he carefully avoided falling back on his status as the boss's son. It disturbed him that others in his family working at the factory started later than ordinary employees, who all began their days at 7:30 a.m. By his own account, he rose at 5 a.m., woke his younger brothers and sisters, and took them to a park some miles away by train. There they engaged in morning exercises and fed koi, the distinctive and colorful Japanese carp, at a pond. Then they came home for a quick breakfast, and Suzuki was at the factory gates well before they opened, where he milled with other employees waiting to get inside.

Suzuki Violin was busier than ever, racing to keep up with the deluge of foreign orders resulting from the outbreak of World War I in Europe in the summer of 1914. German violin makers had until then dominated the world market but were unable to meet international demand in wartime. Suzuki Violin was prepared to fill the vacuum. The company had been building its reputation steadily through international exhibitions, like the 1915 Panama-Pacific International Exposition in San Francisco, a celebration of the city's recovery from the 1906 earthquake and the completion of the Panama Canal, connecting the Atlantic and Pacific Oceans. Masakichi Suzuki's violins won the expo's gold medal.

The first significant wave of international orders had come over the wire within a week of the United Kingdom's declaration of war on Germany—from John G. Murdoch & Co., the publisher responsible for orchestrating the Maidstone Movement in British state-run schools. More orders would follow from France, North and South America, Australia, Southeast Asia, South Asia, and China. Many of the warring countries tried to finance their military efforts by controlling the import of luxury items, the better to keep cash in domestic coffers. Yet orders still poured in. At its peak during the war, Suzuki Violin employed more than 1,000 workers, as well as two 5-horsepower generators that drove Masakichi's woodworking machines. The factory produced as many as 500 violins a day, along with violas, mandolins, guitars, violin bows, strings, and instrument cases. Between 1915 and 1924, this Eastern maker of Western musical instruments exported 521,467 stringed instruments and 2,498,004 bows.[11]

Suzuki Violin's booming trade was, of course, just a fraction of the larger national growth, variously called the Great War Prosperity or the Taisho Economic Bubble. From 1915 to the early 1920s, the Japanese economy shifted its focus from imports to exports, as foreign powers came looking for supplies. Military purchases from the United Kingdom and Russia, Japan's allies, resulted in the dramatic expansion of Japanese mineral mines, ship-building, and commodities-trading houses. The volume of exports quadrupled in those years, transforming what was once a debtor nation into an international creditor.

Principal Ichimura's dream of seeing Japan as a first-class trading nation was being realized within his lifetime—alas, on account of a devastating and prolonged war whose casualties were not confined to the trenches of Europe. Having entered the conflict on the Allied side, Japan too was at war as of August 1914. Japanese forces marched into and conquered the German leasehold of Shandong Peninsula in eastern China. And while the alliance with Great Britain did not oblige Japan to dispatch troops to Europe, from 1917 onward the Imperial Japanese

Undated, but most likely Taisho-era (1912–1926), photo of Suzuki Violin. Workers are cutting violin panels with the aid of mechanized tools. *Talent Education Research Institute*

Navy did the perilous work of escorting Allied ships in the Indian Ocean and the Mediterranean, completing 348 missions, convoying 750,000 Allied personnel, and at times rescuing sailors stranded by enemy submarines. Japan's naval ships themselves were targeted, as when an Austro-Hungarian U-Boat attacked a Japanese destroyer off the coast of Malta, resulting in casualties. Nevertheless, World War I was an important opportunity for Japan to further its national ambition, economically and politically.

Meanwhile, Suzuki mostly worked in the export division of his father's business. He performed a variety of tasks, from packing shipments to keeping books. After about two years, he thought he had learned the ropes. But just as work was beginning to get comfortable, his body was feeling otherwise. For no clear reason, he was constantly lethargic. And early every evening, he developed a slight temperature—never a full-blown fever, but not a normal state either. It was precisely the kind of mildly unhealthy, hazy condition that Hans Castorp, the unassuming young hero of Thomas Mann's *The Magic Mountain* (1924), feels throughout the epic novel. In it, Castorp visits his cousin in a luxury sanatorium in the Swiss Alps before World War I. What is intended as a brief stop turns into a seven-year stay, on account of possible tuberculosis, until Castorp finally descends the mountain to enlist in the German army, his prospects shadowed by death.

In the fall of 1918, the twenty-year-old Suzuki was given an identical diagnosis. His doctor warned that he might develop "catarrh of the pulmonary apex," a euphemism for tuberculosis. Code words were necessary because consumption, as it was also known, was regarded as a death sentence. It was an "industrial" or "urban" disease, whose rise coincided with Japan's high-speed modernization. Crowded living and working conditions in silk mills caused an outburst of the disease among workers, mostly girls and young women, around 1910. And as the sick were sent home to their villages to recuperate, tuberculosis spread across the countryside. Japan's tuberculosis mortality rate was never higher than in 1918, when the disease caused 2.57 deaths per 1,000 people. Only that year's global flu pandemic, the so-called Spanish flu, killed more Japanese.[12]

Urged by his father to rest, Suzuki set off to the seaside town of Okitsu in neighboring Shizuoka Prefecture, about 120 miles west of Nagoya City. His travel companions were *The Diary of Tolstoy* and his violin. Little did he know that an encounter there would dramatically alter the course of his life.

3

ENCHANTED CIRCLES

Suzuki recuperated at Okitsu for three months, beginning in late autumn 1918. The location of his respite could not have been more agreeable. During the Edo period, before Japan's opening to the West, the town on Suruga Bay had been one of the scenic stops on the Tokaido, the route connecting Kyoto and Tokyo. Okitsu's centuries-old inns had provided lodging for the retinues of feudal lords as they made their way to and from the capital, where they were required to reside on a regular basis and pay fealty to the Tokugawa shoguns. After the Meiji Restoration, Okitsu reinvented itself as an elegant resort with easy access to beaches. The bay was particularly famous for an optical illusion whereby the water and sky become indistinguishable, blending into each other as a wash of cobalt blue. And from the bay one could experience a stunning view of the perpetually snow-capped Mount Fuji, Japan's spiritual center located some forty miles to the northeast.

While regaining his strength, Suzuki befriended two young siblings who were also guests at his inn. Exactly what drew the three together is unclear, but there was something of the Pied Piper of Hamelin in Suzuki. Throughout his life, observers noted his magnetism in the presence of children. William Starr, a pioneering Suzuki Method instructor from the United States, remembered sitting outside with Suzuki one sunny day when a small girl passed by, stopped, and turned to him. After a chat, the girl went away beaming. The American was surprised to learn that she was not one of Suzuki's students, and indeed that they had not met before. "I had already greeted her wonderful living soul as she approached me," Suzuki explained. "She caught my greeting and came over to say

'Hello.'" Such an inexplicable power aside, it's easy to see why children gravitated toward Suzuki. He never ran out of playful ideas and never talked down to them. One student remembered how Suzuki made even a potentially stressful recital tour an occasion for fun and enrichment beyond music, teaching the kids how to skip a stone on a river, to draw landscapes with droplets of his fountain pen ink, and to race carrying pebbles with chopsticks (his version of the egg-and-spoon race). Even when the children had to sit still for eight hours on a train, Suzuki never let them get bored. He would invent one game after another. It is no wonder that Suzuki came to know the two children in Okitsu first, and then their parents, Mr. and Mrs. Ichiro Yanagida.[1]

The Yanagidas were longtime residents of Tokyo, but the husband originally came from an extremely wealthy family in Hokkaido, the northernmost of the five main Japanese islands. In Nemuro, on the east of the island, the Yanagida family had made its name and fortune in fishery, forestry, and farming as well as banking and education. Suzuki did not have much in common with them, but the children brought them together.

From the beach where Suzuki and the young family spent many a pleasant winter day, a construction site would have been visible. There, carpenters were erecting a simple yet impeccably executed wooden cottage that would become a key setting in Japanese politics over the next two decades. Zagyoso (Sit and Fish Cottage), as it would be named, was meant as a retirement retreat for Prince Kinmochi Saionji, a leading politician and the last surviving Meiji founding father. A classical liberal, Saionji had studied law and politics in France for ten years; his stay there began while Paris was under the Commune, a left-leaning revolutionary government that came to power by force in March 1871 and lasted only until May of that year. Back in Japan, he was appointed prime minister twice and even while out of office wielded enormous influence, almost as though he was a second emperor. As it turned out, life in Okitsu would not be so quiet. Right up until his death in 1940 at the age of ninety, Saionji would attract a steady stream of visitors seeking his help, advice, and blessing.

When Suzuki and the Yanagidas were in Okitsu, Saionji was preparing for his final public duty: leading the Japanese delegation to the Paris Peace Conference at Versailles, which decided post–World War I settlements. Saionji's villa was finished in February of 1919, shortly after Suzuki bade farewell to the Yanagidas and returned to Nagoya. His fever had gone and he was feeling much improved. He recommended his life at Suzuki Violin full of energy.

But that spring, he would hear from Ichiro Yanagida again, with an invitation that turned out to be critical for Suzuki's future. Yanagida asked Suzuki to join him and some friends for a trip to the Kuril Islands, located north of Nemuro. The islands, which were taken by the USSR after World War II and are now administered by Russia, constituted Japan's northern extremity. The trip was not a holiday but an expedition. Utterly unlike Okitsu, the Kuril Islands are rough and sparsely populated, their natural beauty largely untouched by human hands. The journey was to take place in the summer and would be led by Marquis Yoshichika Tokugawa, an eccentric aristocrat and Yanagida's old schoolmate, who was also a member of the old ruling Tokugawa clan. In fact, had the Meiji Restoration not occurred, Marquis Tokugawa would have become the lord of the Owari Tokugawa domain and therefore the Suzuki family's master. The invitation was a humbling honor, especially from Masakichi's perspective. Despite his modern, entrepreneurial outlook on business, Suzuki's father retained a strong attachment to feudal decorum; declining the invitation was inconceivable. Furthermore, the fresh northern climate would benefit the recently compromised health of his son, who was eager to embark on the adventure. And so Suzuki's participation was confirmed without reservations.

Later Suzuki would describe Marquis Tokugawa as his "second most important influence," after Tolstoy. The marquis was thirty-two years old when he met Suzuki and had lived through some of modern Japan's most dramatic changes. He would experience many more, too. Tokugawa was variously identified as a politician, military advisor, patron of the arts, and philanthropist; he was especially generous when it came to the education of the deaf. But he was most famous as an adventurer. Like a Japanese Teddy Roosevelt, he traveled extensively so that he could hunt bears in the north and tigers in the south. And he was a university-trained botanist whose love of plants and the natural sciences led him to found the Tokugawa Biological Institute. (In 1970, the institute would be handed over to Yakult, a manufacturer of probiotic drinks that are hugely popular in Japan and throughout Asia and now increasingly in Europe.)

Tokugawa's political ideas were conflicted to say the least. Fundamentally he was a social democrat, who thought that aristocratic privileges were detrimental to humanity. As a parliamentarian in the hereditary House of Peers in the 1920s, he proposed curbing the influence of politicians who were not popularly elected. He urged the granting of female suffrage, much to the chagrin of his mostly conservative colleagues. He would, however, also display an imperialist side in the 1930s, supporting military-led reforms and later actively participating in Japan's wartime occupation of Southeast Asia, during which he was stationed in Singapore. There he played an instrumental role in preserving the botanical and zoological collections of the fallen British colonial institutions.

When World War II ended, American efforts to democratize Japan greatly diminished the Tokugawa family fortune, and the marquis was stripped of his title, which he had been ready to give up in any case. Now he openly espoused socialism. Ironically, even in this new incarnation, it was the fact of his blue-blooded pedigree that gave weight to his activities, including his eventual support of Suzuki's educational endeavors. Perhaps Tokugawa is best understood as a man of the Enlightenment, though born almost two centuries later and far from Europe.

It was Tokugawa's passion for collecting, organizing, and analyzing scientific specimens that led him to plan the expedition to Japan's northern frontier, with its vast open spaces and relatively minimal human imprint. He also had something of a tribal attachment to Hokkaido, where some of the former samurai retainers of the Owari Tokugawas had made a permanent home. In 1878, with the domain's financial backing, those settlers established a community called Yagumo. In the generations since, Yagumo had been frozen in time. Its founders were poor, their samurai pensions cut off by the Meiji government, and ill-equipped to spur local development in a modernizing age. Over the course of nearly 270 years of relative tranquility during the Tokugawa Shogunate, many samurai had grown accustomed to their hereditary privileges, losing sight of practical skills.

Tokugawa and Yanagida often traveled together to the north to satisfy their adventurous spirit and anthropological curiosity. Only the

Scholar-adventurer Marquis Yoshichika Tokugawa on a bear-hunting trip in Hokkaido, likely March 1918. *The Mainichi Newspapers Co.*

year before their excursion with Suzuki, they had gone up to hunt hibernating bears and were accompanied by Ainus, indigenous people who live on Hokkaido and the island of Sakhalin. Ippei Okamoto, a popular painter and caricaturist, tagged along and produced an illustrated report for the national newspaper *Asahi*. The piece earned Tokugawa the nickname Bear-Hunting Lord. The striking gap between the nobleman's polished, scholarly appearance and his audacious exploits could not go unnoticed.

Now Tokugawa and Yanagida would venture even farther north, to the Kuril Islands, with Suzuki and eleven other travelers. Most were Tokugawa intimates and family, including the marquis's wife Yoneko, his older sister, and his nephews. Others came from his biological research institute, to collect plant samples. There was, too, a middle-aged woman, Tokugawa's friend Nobu Koda, whom we met briefly in chapter 2. Earlier in her life, she had been the first music student sent abroad by the Japanese government to study in the world's great conservatories. By 1919, she was known as the first Japanese composer of Western-style classical music.

Koda had a personal reason for joining the expedition. One of her elder brothers was a naval officer and celebrated adventurer who, in 1893, had begun a movement for permanent Japanese settlement on the Kuril Islands. His was a perilous, patriotic scheme. Countless early settlers, many of them destitute former samurai, died. A few small communities managed to stay afloat through the turn of the century, but in the long run and on balance, the project was a failure. Koda apparently wanted to pay her respects at the sites of her brother's ill-fated movement.

Suzuki's few written recollections of the trip are warm. He describes playing the violin every evening to Koda's piano accompaniment, helping the scientists collect rare plants growing on a steep cliff, and contemplating the rugged, romantic landscape around him.[2] In 1921, Marquis Tokugawa published his own travelogue, a fine, entertaining work that might best be described as part *Moby Dick* and part P. G. Wodehouse. Tokugawa's book is highly detailed, providing a striking look at the group's experiences. They traveled on a modest Japanese Postal Service ship, whose critical mission was to deliver food, timber, and fuel to the islands' inhabitants. Success was a matter of life and death; Kuril islanders would be shut off from all forms of communication during the long, ice-locked winter months, so they needed supplies ahead of time. Even during summer, when Suzuki's group made the journey, the northern sea was freezing. Tokugawa recounts witnessing the rescue of stranded Japanese fishermen, one of whom, exhausted and delirious, fell off his boat the moment he registered that help had arrived. Tales of island life included illness, acute hunger, and even alleged cannibalism within settlement communities.

Tokugawa leavens such dark accounts with self-deprecating, light-hearted stories about his unsuccessful attempts to hunt seals and more successful episodes of fishing cod and salmon and shooting crested puffins. He refers appreciatively to young Suzuki, "the favorite child of Mr. Suzuki, known for the violins he makes," whose music gave the group joy during their voyage in close quarters. Suzuki amused his companions with musical improvisations, composing melodies and accompanying their singing. Aside from music, the personal quality Tokugawa found delightful in Suzuki was his naivete. One day, while the group was fishing, Tokugawa noticed that Suzuki had landed a huge sculpin, a big-mouthed, sharp-rayed fish. This one measured easily more than twenty inches, whereas most species of sculpin are shorter than five inches. "Look at this centipede!" Suzuki proudly announced.[3]

Noting Suzuki's obvious love of music and his starry-eyed quality, Tokugawa felt that his young friend's vocation might not be making and selling violins. Toward the end of the month-long voyage, Tokugawa came straight to the point. "My dear Shinichi, why work at the violin factory? Why not study music formally?" Koda enthusiastically seconded the idea. Suzuki was bewildered at first; he had never considered becoming a professional musician. He was just beginning to discover the world of art and enjoyed pondering this open-ended endeavor that gave so much pleasure and comfort. Playing violin occupied but a fraction of Suzuki's fledgling, private explorations; he found joy and purpose in many activities. At work, he went beyond the call of duty to teach himself the niceties of machine operations and handicrafts, becoming well-versed in the entire process of violin-building. Outside work, he cherished his time playing and conversing with young children. Furthermore, he doubted that his father would allow him to pursue music full time. "Why keep bowing in front of people?" his father would say of professional musicians. "If you want to hear music," he had told his son, you should make enough money "so that you can have someone else play for you." This was not some idle meanness; Masakichi was true to his word, sponsoring recitals in Nagoya for great violinists like Elman, Kreisler, Heifetz, and the Russian-born master Efrem Zimbalist. Doubtful that his father could be persuaded, Suzuki told Tokugawa that he would give his prospects as a musician due consideration, all the while intending to let the matter drop.[4]

With the expedition completed, Suzuki returned to Nagoya and his work at the violin factory. After his lengthy illness and recuperation, followed by the substantial journey north, it was time to settle down again. But then, in the autumn, Tokugawa came to visit, and not for a simple social call. He wanted to have a heart-to-heart with Masakichi about his son's future. Tokugawa was much younger than Masakichi, who was at this point well-known and highly respected. On these terms, Tokugawa was rather brazen to advise the elder Suzuki on what he should do with his own family. But then, Masakichi was the son of Owari Tokugawa vassals, and he felt the tremendous pull of the marquis's feudal charisma. Soon enough, the matter was settled: come spring, Suzuki would be sent to Tokyo for formal instruction in the violin and other musical subjects. When Suzuki's Tokyo lodging plans fell through, Tokugawa came to the rescue, boarding the student at his grand family residence. And so, during the cherry blossom season of 1920, the twenty-one-year-old Suzuki began his life in the capital in high style.

In those days, Tokyo was a rising megalopolis. This was at the tail-end of the Taisho Economic Bubble, the boom years brought on by World War I. Politically, Taisho Democracy was in full swing. Takashi Hara—a long-time champion of popular elections and a tireless advocate for political parties, as against Japan's traditions of nepotism and factionalism—had become prime minister in 1918. A member of the House of Representatives and the head of its majority party, he was the first elected legislator to hold the country's top political post, which previously had been held by noblemen, top-echelon military commanders, and others who could not claim a mandate from the voters. Hara was known for his frugal lifestyle and for vehemently rejecting an aristocratic title when it was offered to him and was admiringly nicknamed the Commoner Premier.

The political mood of the moment was inclusive, as movements urging social, labor, and gender equality gained momentum. Shortly after Suzuki's arrival in Tokyo, Japan's first May Day celebration was held in the city's Ueno Park. Prompted by the labor organization Yuaikai—literally, the Association for Love and Friendship—approximately 10,000 people gathered to demand eight-hour shifts, measures to prevent unemployment, the establishment of minimum wages, and other worker protections. Ueno Park was a meaningful place for Suzuki. One of the country's first Western-style parks, it was home to museums and other cultural institutions, including a concert hall and fine arts schools. After a course of private study, Suzuki hoped to gain admission to Tokyo Music School (now the Tokyo University of the Arts), located at Ueno.

Japan's changing landscape of popular entertainment was especially vivid in the capital. Shochiku, a company producing kabuki and other traditional and modern theater, established a film studio in Tokyo in

1920. The studio would go on to propel the careers of such notable directors as Yasujiro Ozu and Mikio Naruse, both of whom are known for their postwar masterpieces yet had already made cinematic treasures before World War II. Movie houses playing Japanese and foreign films, department stores, dance halls, and cafes flourished in the city. Tokyo's print publishers put out numerous magazines, increasingly geared toward mass culture and attracting the kinds of audiences fostered by modern market segmentation—children, housewives, automobile aficionados, literature enthusiasts, and so on. Trend-conscious young men and women with disposable income competed to make an impression as they strutted through the fashionable Ginza district. These classy urbanites were called *mobo* (modern boys) and *moga* (modern girls), adapted from the English terms of the Roaring Twenties. The telltale signs of a mobo included a pair of Harold Lloyd glasses, loose-fitting sailor pants, and a narrow walking stick. A moga would have walked by in a flowing skirt or even trousers, a cloud of François Coty perfume wafting around her. With hair bobbed and a proud smile on her carefully made-up face, she was the equal of any Western flapper.

The dizzying liveliness of Suzuki's Tokyo seems all the more remarkable with the benefit of hindsight. The "Dark Valley" of the 1930s, with its political unrest, xenophobia, and strident militarism lay not too far ahead, and even as the capital grew and partied through the 1920s, discontent was brewing. Japan had benefitted from World War I enormously in material terms, yet there was a feeling that the country had been shortchanged, victimized by the racism of the great powers. A major source of agita was the League of Nations, the forerunner of the United Nations, founded at the Paris Peace Conference. This multilateral framework for intergovernmental cooperation and dispute arbitration was proposed just as Japan thought it had mastered the art of Western imperialism. The right of conquest, Social Darwinism, spheres of influence—all of these had been the intellectual underpinnings of power, the justification Earth's masters had called upon when exploiting the weak. No sooner had Japan grasped these concepts for itself than the West claimed to have discarded them in favor of international law, sovereignty, and national self-determination. Gallingly for Japan, it was Americans at the head of the charge, with President Woodrow Wilson the league's loudest defender. Now the same people who had imperiously demanded Japan follow their tune were insisting that states hew to Lockean notions of the public good and that this would pave the way for a peaceful world. Wilson's idealistic proclamation that Europe had just experienced "the war to end all wars" did not sit well in Japan, as it seemed to sell out Japan's commitment to military strength for purposes of both self-defense and power projection.

Some prominent Japanese publicly joined other "have-not" powers such as Germany and Italy in suspecting that the United States and Britain had conceived the league primarily as a sinister tool to freeze the world political map in their favor. On the eve of the peace conference, Prince Fumimaro Konoe, a young nobleman and a member of the House of Peers, spoke out against this "conspiracy." Writing in a nationalist magazine, he urged Japan to "reject the Anglo-American Peace" proposed at Versailles. Konoe would eventually serve as prime minister three times, presiding over the country, on and off, for most of the four years leading up to Japan's attack on Pearl Harbor in December 1941. To the disgruntled nationalists among his countrymen, Prince Konoe's views were confirmed when Japan's proposed inclusion of principles of racial equality and religious freedom in the League of Nations' Covenant was rejected by the Western powers, chiefly the United States and Australia. (Fumimaro Konoe was, incidentally, the elder brother of Hidemaro Konoe, the founder of the New Symphony Orchestra of Tokyo and the person who introduced Japanese audiences to the work of Gustav Mahler. Today the New Symphony has become the NHK Symphony, Japan's foremost philharmonic orchestra.)[5]

Officially, though, the Japanese government expressed no resentment, instead subscribing enthusiastically to the idea of liberal internationalism as embodied in the league and other intergovernmental bodies that emerged in this period, such as the Permanent Court of International Justice at the Hague and the Health Organization, which later became the World Health Organization, a United Nations agency. Japan agreed to join the League of Nations, and for more than a decade sent financial contributions and its ablest bureaucrats and diplomats to Geneva, where the organization was headquartered. As much as Japanese chauvinists and populists questioned the global trend toward liberal internationalism, it was felt at various levels of society, a partner to the ideals of Taisho Democracy.

Suzuki in 1920. *Talent Education Research Institute*

Suzuki thrived in this atmosphere of optimism, cooperation, and Western charms. Indeed, his Tokyo environs brimmed with all of these. The Tokugawa household in Tokyo was then located in the neighborhood of Fujimicho, one of the leafiest parts of town, on land now occupied by the French Embassy. The main building was a light-colored, two-story Western-style structure, decorated with some Japanese details, such as window shutters framed in carved woodwork. In those days, most Japanese did not know what Christmas was, but Marquis Tokugawa celebrated the holiday with gusto by opening his house to the children of tradesmen and artisans from the neighborhood. The master put on theatrical entertainments and treated guests to Christmas cakes. More than sixty years later, one attendee nostalgically recalled how the chandeliers hanging from the high ceiling glowed and how spacious the rooms were. He also remembered his first Christmas cake. The sights, the warmth, the taste, the whole experience of this alien world rendered his younger self speechless. What was a fantastical stage for Christmas visitors became Suzuki's daily milieu.[6]

An important feature of Suzuki's life in Tokyo was dinner with Tokugawa. When the marquis had company, which was often, his guests made for stimulating conversation. To Suzuki's delight, one evening's guests included Torahiko Terada, the violin-playing physicist immortalized by Soseki as Avalon Coldmoon. Reveling with a carousel of highly accomplished people from different fields gave Suzuki ample opportunity to reflect on the nature of talent. By taking the young Suzuki under his wing and exposing him to his circle of friends, Tokugawa had put himself in charge of Suzuki's intellectual formation.

As for Suzuki's musical formation, he took private lessons in music theory, ear-training, and, of course, violin performance. His most important influence was his violin teacher, Ko Ando, the younger sister of Nobu Koda and herself an accomplished musician by the Japanese standard of the time. Ando had studied with the virtuoso Joseph Joachim in Berlin and had risen to become a professor at Tokyo Music School. As Suzuki's private instructor, she did her best to prepare him for the school's highly competitive entrance examination.

Suzuki devoted himself to improving his score reading and other exam skills—until he heard what the students at the prestigious academy actually sounded like. When Suzuki attended the conservatory's graduation recital, his expectations were dashed in an instant. He never wrote down what he heard or why specifically the pieces were unappealing to him, but what little he did say was damning. "Up until then, I studied by listening to the records of the world's top musicians," he explained. In contrast to what he heard from the players he admired, the students' performance sounded "forlorn" and "unmoving." It was "a world apart from the great performances of great musicians." Suzuki's mind was made up. The day after the recital, he told Ando that none of the performances had touched his heart and that he thought "it would be pitiful if I sounded like that when I graduate." He would not take the entrance exam but hoped to continue private lessons with her. Ando chuckled, perhaps amused by Suzuki's forthrightness. Some would have called him impudent, but honesty of that sort must have been refreshingly rare in her teaching experience. She then said, according to Suzuki, that she did not care either way because as long as he truly applied himself, she knew he would land on his feet no matter what he did. She also must have been well aware by then of Suzuki's stubbornness, and of the fact that his family could afford private lessons while he refused the state-subsidized conservatory.

And so the routine of private lessons continued past the second spring. That same state of affairs might have persisted indefinitely had another opportunity not presented itself. One evening, Suzuki was having dinner with Tokugawa when his benefactor declared: "Let us go together. Let us go around the world." But Suzuki, though he possessed an element of the marquis's wanderlust, felt that his musical studies had barely begun and so declined.

Still he did tell his father of Tokugawa's invitation. "That sounds interesting," Masakichi said, which counted as a firm endorsement. To see the world would be a good education for his son, he thought, and moreover, he was willing to give him 15,000 yen to cover the grand tour. Suzuki could not help feeling that it was wrong to accept such a huge stipend, which was twenty or thirty times the starting annual salary of a university graduate. He was nonetheless struck by his father's enthusiasm and relayed the episode to Tokugawa. The marquis, entertained, mischievously suggested that Suzuki accept the 15,000 yen from his father and see the world after all. If he felt so bad about spending the money loafing around, Suzuki could study the violin abroad, Tokugawa added. This was a proposal even the determinedly principled young man could not resist. Having recently realized that Japan's top conservatory would be unable to meet his expectations, he was tempted by the prospect of seeking musical instruction elsewhere. In mid-September 1921, he made the decision to go. The party was to set sail for Europe at the end of October. Trunks had to be packed and a passport swiftly obtained. There was no time to develop cold feet.

Suzuki, now twenty-three years old, joined Tokugawa's entourage on the maiden voyage of the luxury liner *Hakone-maru*. Exhausted by the weeks of frenzied preparations, he felt relief more than anything else when the ship left the port. He intended to stay in Germany for one year. In fact, he would spend the rest of his twenties there.

4

BERLIN, THE GOLDEN CITY

SUZUKI FOUND HIS SEA LEGS on the expedition to the Kuril Islands, but Germany was to be an adventure of a different order. When the enormity of the step he was taking began to sink in, he felt a mixture of "intense expectations for the unknown world, and inevitably, a little bit of anxiety." As the *Hakone-maru* sailed on, however, the sheer excitement of all the new things he was seeing—Shanghai, Singapore, the Indian Ocean—eased his nerves. He was quite enjoying himself by the time the ship reached Marseille, where he parted company with Tokugawa and his companions. Suzuki headed for Berlin, where he hoped to find a master-teacher.[1]

Upon arrival, he chose the Hotel Excelsior as his lodging. Located in a bustling area on Königgrätzer Straße, the hotel was one of the most fashionable spots in Berlin. Its fame would only be magnified with Vicki Baum's 1929 novel *Grand Hotel,* set at the Excelsior, which provided the basis for a Hollywood movie starring Greta Garbo three years later. But when Suzuki appeared there in late 1921, the Excelsior was already a hub of aristocrats and film stars. Even Kaiser Wilhelm II, before the war, was known to drop in for a cup of coffee. No doubt the Excelsior was a fortress of creature comforts. It was equipped with gas heating, superior plumbing, and electricity, and it boasted six hundred rooms, nine restaurants, a spa, and an array of shops. It might seem excessive that Suzuki, or any student trying to stretch a year's stipend, should decide on a luxury hotel. But it was also a practical choice. Suzuki did not know how long he would stay in town, and the hotel's convenient location—right across from the grand train station Anhalter Bahnhof—made it an ideal home base.

Berlin, with its thriving art schools and performance culture, was a natural choice for a violinist seeking exposure to the best in classical music. But Germany then was not a simple place to be. World War I had decimated the country's political order; the flight of the kaiser and the army high command had left the Social Democrats, led by Friedrich Ebert, to deal with the mess and humiliation of postwar settlements. The goal of the new government, formed in Weimar, was stability. Though the Social Democrats were broadly driven by Marxist principles, and though they had done much to develop Germany's labor organizations in the previous decades, they were by no means revolutionaries in the Leninist sense. Rather, the Social Democratic Party positioned itself in the middle of the road and was highly suspicious of the Bolshevist doctrine that had driven Russia's October 1917 revolution. All the same, the Social Democrats were despised by Germany's right, represented by landowning Junkers—hereditary Prussian nobility—and military officers.

Later, of course, it would be the discontented right that rose to confront and eject the Weimar Republic. But in the early 1920s, Social Democrats were more worried about the radical left, which had shown itself to be their immediate enemy. In January 1919, members of the Communist Party of Germany, led by Karl Liebknecht and Rosa Luxemburg, had orchestrated the Spartacist Uprising. In fact, it was at the Hotel Excelsior that the group met and decided to incite a revolution. The rebellion was a disaster—for the left and for Germany. Ebert authorized the Freikorps, a right-leaning paramilitary unit, to quell the unrest, leading to the arrest and murder of the Spartacist leaders. In the short term, the Social Democrats managed to contain a political adversary, but only at the great long-term cost of accommodating the far right. The moderate leaders decisively alienated the left while making a pragmatic but ultimately fatal deal with a clutch of disenfranchised soldiers who would never be completely satisfied with their subordinate position in the post–World War I order. Many Nazis of rank high and low did their own stints in the Freikorps, and although they would not take over the government for some time, they were emboldened by the suppression of the Spartacists. Throughout the 1920s, German right-wingers acted out violently against democratic principles, plaguing the country's political life and helping to foment the fanatical nationalism and militarism that underlay Nazi power.[2]

Exacerbating the environment of political upheaval was Germany's postwar economy, which was spiraling into an abyss just as Suzuki arrived in Berlin. The kaiser had financed the war through heavy borrowing, believing that Germany would easily repay its loans once it had won. Instead, defeated Germany's debt burden increased with the reparation payments imposed by the Treaty of Versailles. As the Weimar treasury desperately printed more and more bank notes to buy the foreign currencies in which indemnities had to be paid, the value of the German mark depreciated precipitously, leading to hyperinflation from the summer of 1921 onward. In January 1923, France and Belgium occupied the Ruhr Valley and refused to leave until Germany paid off its arrears. But the occupation only intensified Germany's economic chaos, further undermining its ability to pay. Rejecting the bellicose foreign demands, German workers called a general strike, and the resulting stagnation compelled the government to print even more notes. At the height of hyperinflation in late 1923, the mark traded against the US dollar at one-trillionth of its prewar value.[3]

This trying period for Germany was in some ways a boon for Suzuki and other visitors, as the weakness of the mark made life there extremely affordable for those possessing foreign currency. During the Weimar period, Germany overtook other European countries and the United States as the most popular destination for young Japanese elites. The Japanese government could easily fund students, civil servants, military officers, and researchers heading to Germany, alongside a smaller number of musicians and other artists. In 1926, Japan's Ministry of Education sent 351 scholars abroad: 100 went to Germany, 53 to the United Kingdom, 34 to France, and 30 to the United States. Even those initially sent elsewhere often ended up spending time in Germany on the way home. It is likely that 80 percent of Japan's state-funded scholars in the late 1920s had some direct exposure to the Weimar Republic. And there were Japanese visitors of private means, like Suzuki. Collectively they made for a substantial expat community. Suzuki's intended year in Berlin turned into six in part because he ended up "not having to spend much," though Masakichi did send more money after the original 15,000 yen was gone.[4]

Suzuki's first three months in Berlin did not portend such a long stay, as he used those early days trying, and failing, to find a master-teacher.

He took an unusual path. Instead of seeking an instructor from one of the city's conservatories—someone with an established teaching reputation—he attended recitals every night and let his ear be his guide. He heard the most sought-after violinists of the time, such as Bronisław Huberman, Gustav Havemann, Carl Flesch, and Henri Marteau, as well as lesser-known ones, and hoped to ask for lessons from whomever demonstrated the tone he admired most. Yet, while he enjoyed many of the performances, he was not convinced by what he heard. None of them played in a way that sufficiently appealed to his sensibilities.[5]

Perhaps, Suzuki thought, he would have better luck in Vienna. But then a German acquaintance invited him to an all-Beethoven program by the Klingler Quartet at the Singakademie, one of Berlin's renowned music societies. That night at the concert, Suzuki experienced another musical epiphany, much as he had as a seventeen-year-old listening to Elman's recording. What Suzuki heard this time was, he later wrote, "music of the soul"—music that spoke to him quietly and beautifully, with "unwavering, secure, and restrained technique." He was especially captivated by the playing of the quartet's leader, the Strasbourg-born violinist and composer Karl Klingler. Klingler's music-making was exactly what Suzuki had been looking for. The young man went home in a state of trance, and immediately wrote a letter—in English, as he did not then know enough German—beseeching Klingler to bring him on as his pupil. As Suzuki awaited Klingler's reply, another Japanese musician in Berlin warned him that the maestro did not take private students. Suzuki was therefore surprised when the reply came: he was instructed to come to No. 11 Sophienstraße, Klingler's home, at one o'clock the following afternoon.

To be sure he was on time, Suzuki took a taxi. But when he gave Klingler's address, the driver asked which Sophienstraße he meant. Puzzled, oblivious to the fact that there were at least two Sophienstraßes in town, Suzuki replied "the one in Berlin." The driver either guessed wrong or was taking advantage of Suzuki's ignorance; he headed off to the outskirts of the city and deposited his passenger in front of a shabby, four-story building with an off-kilter staircase. Taking in its terrible state, Suzuki reasoned that Klingler, like many other Germans, was suffering financially. But a search for Klingler's apartment proved fruitless, so Suzuki gave up and hailed another taxi.

An hour later, he finally reached the right house on Sophienstraße, centrally located near Alexanderplatz, Germany's largest urban square. Klingler's elegant home was a far cry from the dump his prospective student had just seen. The habitually punctual Suzuki was mortified to arrive so far behind schedule, but Klingler, a well-built, gentle-looking man in his early forties, received him cordially and tried to put him at ease. He invited Suzuki to play something; he chose a concerto by the French composer and violinist Pierre Rode. In the middle of the piece, Suzuki made a mistake. Between that and his tardiness, he assumed that he had squandered his chance. But when Klingler spoke, he seemed, to Suzuki's translating ears, to be asking when the young man would come see him next.[6]

A cynic might wonder if Klingler was just looking for regular payments in a stable foreign currency, but there is little reason to believe that money was his primary concern. His fine home attested to the wealth he already possessed, thanks to his artistic success and, probably just as importantly, his marriage to Margarethe von Gwinner, a daughter of the extremely wealthy and aristocratic banker-politician Arthur von Gwinner. So when Suzuki asked Klingler about a fee for lessons, the master violinist was at a loss, muttering that he had no idea what to charge. Klingler had no other private students, and evidently need for money was no guide. After reflecting for a while, he asked how much Suzuki had paid Professor Ando in Tokyo. The amount had been ten yen; Klingler suggested simply doubling it, and that was that.

These lesson fees constituted the bulk of Suzuki's expenses in Berlin, as the cost of basic subsistence was "absurdly low," in his words. A high-quality necktie could be had for 0.1 yen, while a proper restaurant course of soup, fish, and meat was a mere 0.14 yen. Attending concerts was also remarkably cheap. For instance, over two weekends, the pianist Artur Schnabel played a program of Beethoven sonatas for a pittance, which was both a deliberate choice to ensure that ordinary Germans could attend and a reflection of the weakness of the German mark. Suzuki considered listening to music a critical part of his studies, and he attended all the events he wanted, often five a week. In light of everything else, Klingler's fee of twenty yen—which was in 1922 approximately

$40 US—was indeed disproportionate. But it was much less than Suzuki had expected; he had heard that Leopold Auer, the Hungarian-born star violin pedagogue then teaching in the United States, charged up to $100 per lesson.[7]

Had Klingler been cash-strapped, or mercenary, he could have charged more, and Suzuki would have obliged. Klingler's credentials would have justified higher fees; in every respect, he was a cultural luminary. Like Suzuki's former teacher Ando, Klingler had been a student of the great violinist Joseph Joachim at the Berlin Hochschule, where Klingler had also studied composition under Max Bruch and won a prestigious composition prize while still in his teens. Klingler started teaching at the conservatory before even completing his studies, and within ten years he ascended to Joachim's professorial chair. As a performer, he played the viola in the Joachim Quartet and became deputy concertmaster of the Berlin Philharmonic in 1904. In 1905, Klingler formed his own quartet, a musical heir to his teacher's group. The Klingler Quartet survived World War I to enchant Suzuki on that fateful evening at Singakademie. It is fair to conclude that Klingler was intrigued and charmed by the young man from the East who suddenly turned up at his door, whose hunger for music moved him. Suzuki was a special case.

After the first six months of lessons with Klingler, Suzuki sent his oldest brother a postcard. Dated October 21, 1922, the message describes the already-falling snow. Suzuki also mentions the generally unpleasant atmosphere caused by deteriorating economic conditions. The front of the postcard is a headshot of "my sensei Professor Klingler." In interwar Berlin, classical musicians were so admired that they could be postcard icons, figures who represented to the world a place and its people. In his later recollection, Suzuki called his teacher "a man of fine principles" who tried to impart to him, "in every lesson, the essence of music." When Suzuki was studying Handel's Violin Sonata in D Major, Klingler explained the composer's acute religiosity and then demonstrated on his violin—a Stradivarius formerly owned by Joachim—how awareness of that context might translate into certain tonal characteristics. Having gotten a late start, Suzuki had much to learn on the technical side, but Klingler never talked of technique as something dissociated from music itself. "He took my hand and guided me, so to speak, on my journey to locate the sources of art and the men who made it," Suzuki wrote.

Suzuki with his teacher, Karl Klingler. Berlin, 1922. *Talent Education Research Institute*

This particular Handel sonata was a critical feature of Suzuki's early studies with Klingler. In spring 1923, Suzuki played the piece for an entrance examination at the Hochschule. Twelve out of forty-four candidates passed; Suzuki was waitlisted. We have no way of knowing whether and to what extent this outcome discouraged him, as it is not discussed in his memoirs or in surviving contemporaneous documents. Since he did not try for the Hochschule a second time, it seems safe to say that both Suzuki and Klingler were content to continue with their private arrangement.[8]

There remains at this point less documentation of Klingler's and Suzuki's relationship than one might expect, but what we know suggests a warmth shared between the two. One postcard, dated January 22, 1925, asks Suzuki to come for a lesson the following week and "recommends" that the young man have a look at Henri Vieuxtemps's "Ballad and Polonaise." It is notable that Klingler did not heavy-handedly require that Suzuki learn a specific piece; the trust between them was such that the teacher allowed the pupil to make some of his own decisions. Another letter, on Klingler's personal letterhead and dated September 27, 1927, informs Suzuki that Klingler had been traveling and eagerly suggests that the pair meet within two days. By the time this letter was written, the men had known each other for some years; their time together must have been a high priority for Klingler, something he looked forward to while they were apart.[9]

Klingler's lessons usually lasted three times longer than the one hour he and Suzuki agreed to, as the teacher patiently and conscientiously walked through every problem he recognized in the student's playing. Suzuki credits Klingler's teaching style, which saw Suzuki correcting bad habits not by mindlessly ploughing through etude books but by playing a multifaceted assortment of pieces selected to tackle a certain technique—a thoughtful and motivational approach that honors the joyous spirit of music-making. Klingler's lessons followed Suzuki's interests. Thus, after Suzuki tired of concertos and sonatas—the focus of his first few years of study—he switched to a blooming passion: chamber music. Suzuki was enthralled by the intimacy and depth of the playing he heard in salons and concerts and asked Klingler, a foremost practitioner of the form, to teach him chamber repertoire. This became his project until he returned to Japan. With no specific career goals in mind, Suzuki wanted to explore and make sense of the universe of art.[10]

In Suzuki's account, the association with his teacher went well beyond lessons. Klingler invited him to musical gatherings in his home with friends and colleagues, and through these social encounters Suzuki witnessed in action the lifestyle perfected by Germany's upper bourgeoisie—the *Bildungsbürgertum*. Central to this way of life was a commitment to the Enlightenment and Romantic beliefs that education and the arts, especially music, contributed to character formation, or *Bildung*. This outlook would shape Suzuki's view of music's role as a foundation of virtue. At that time, there was probably no better place than Berlin for such a high-minded dedication to the arts. As chronicled by foreign writers such as Christopher Isherwood and Vladimir Nabokov, interwar Berlin was a one-of-a-kind city. It was rich in music, literature, as well as experimental art and theater and was home to a vibrant film industry spearheaded by the giant studio UFA. The city's educated class welcomed visitors like Suzuki who tried to absorb their moral and intellectual sensibility and their creative spirit.

Suzuki's later writings recall "unforgettable musical performances" he enjoyed in Berlin. He was not exaggerating; any lover of classical music past and present would be envious of the concerts Suzuki attended. Great soloists like Schnabel and the violinist Fritz Kreisler could be heard easily, and the Berlin Philharmonic proudly stood as one of the world's foremost orchestras under the baton of Wilhelm Furtwängler. Suzuki also heard composers such as Alexander Glazunov, Richard Strauss, and Pietro Mascagni conducting their own works. Whoever was conducting and whatever the style of delivery, Weimar Berlin's symphonic concerts were often epic in scale. Mascagni, for instance, conducted a choir of a thousand, followed by the intermezzo of his most renowned opera, *Cavalleria Rusticana*. It was an era when composers of grandeur, composers like Strauss, Anton Bruckner, and Gustav Mahler, were in vogue, their pieces commanding bigger sounds, which in turn required bigger orchestras and performance spaces.

While music of the late Romantic, Baroque, and Classical eras dominated Berlin's classical concert scene, Suzuki sought out contemporary music as well—music now broadly considered modernist. Berlin's International Society for Contemporary Music, founded in 1922, introduced this brand of new classical music to the city. The society was championed by the charismatic pianist and composer Ferruccio Busoni, who taught Kurt Weill, among others. Suzuki was particularly taken by Furtwängler conducting a symphonic poem by Arnold Schoenberg, *Pelleas und Melisande*. Not everything Suzuki heard was to his liking, but he knew that it was a privilege to be exposed to contemporary works firsthand, almost as they were being created.

Attending musical events also gave Suzuki ample opportunities to observe the lives and attitudes of the people around him. He came to appreciate what he thought of as their straightforward, unapologetic practicality and dignity. One telling instance came during an evening at the opera. Left with an extra ticket when his companion cancelled at the last minute, Suzuki approached a long line of people waiting at the box office to purchase the cheapest seats available in the house. He offered his extra ticket to one of them at no charge. Still, the lucky person in line asked how much Suzuki was selling it for. Thinking he had been misunderstood, Suzuki insisted that he had no intention of being paid. The person still demanded that Suzuki name a price. Exasperated, he went on to someone else and said, "I purchased this ticket for a friend, who cannot make it this evening. Could you please take it, as a favor for me?" This next potential beneficiary was also adamant about paying something, and Suzuki just as stubbornly refused. He tried one more person before giving up. "What an obstinate, bone-headed people they are!" he thought. After some reflection, though, he felt that he had been in the wrong. He realized he had been immature for failing to realize that his well-intended gesture would hurt these people's pride. Had he named a price, however little, perhaps any one of them would have snatched up the ticket. Besides, he concluded, they probably preferred a clear-cut economic transaction, especially when dealing with a complete stranger.

Suzuki thought Germans rather uncompromising, given to drawing sharp boundaries and refusing on principle to cross them, come what may. That suited his own temperament just fine. He saw the same tendency reflected even in Germans' appreciation for music, as demonstrated by their reactions to the many concerts he attended. In Japan, it was customary for audiences to clap at the end of any piece, no matter their true impressions; even a mediocre performance was guaranteed, at minimum, a polite response. In contrast, Berlin audiences did not respond unthinkingly or unfeelingly. Their reception conveyed their honest collective assessment and therefore ranged from stern silence to rapture. On two occasions, both at contemporary music concerts, Suzuki began to clap, only to be shushed by other audience members who apparently hated what they had just heard. But when enough of an audience wholeheartedly enjoyed a piece, the clapping would not stop, and listeners would call for encore after encore. Whether or not he agreed with their verdicts, Suzuki remembered fondly Berlin audiences and their unyielding standards.[11]

It was during one of these musical evenings that Suzuki met the woman who would become his wife. Waltraud Prange hailed from a respectable middle-class family of musicians. She was seven years Suzuki's junior when they met during his third year in Berlin, at a concert in a private home. The courtship began immediately. While escorting Waltraud home, Suzuki expressed interest in meeting her family and was introduced to her mother and siblings. She wrote in her memoir that he came back for a visit the following day, and the day after, "then nearly every day." He would play music with the family and soon was taking Waltraud to recitals and concerts.

Waltraud's physical beauty was as Teutonic as her name. She had large, solemn eyes and a head of wavy blonde hair. Although her family was struggling financially when Suzuki met her, its mores were firmly in line with that of the Bildungsbürgertum. After her father, an executive at a chocolate manufacturer, succumbed to illness during World War I, her brother Albert, a violinist, founded a small orchestra to provide for the family. Eventually they took in lodgers as well. Rather than move into a smaller home, they opted to have strangers under their roof so that they could continue their family concerts. The extra income enabled Waltraud, who had been forced to quit her piano lessons during the privation of war, to resume them at the Stern'sches Konservatorium. (Today, along with the Hochschule, the Konservatorium is part of the Berlin University of the Arts.) She also took voice lessons and was a soloist in a church choir.

For families like the Pranges, music was a coping mechanism in hard times—a means, in Waltraud's words, of rising above "all the upheavals and materialism outside." In this respect she was a perfect match for Suzuki. Though well off, Suzuki was not much interested in a life of luxury; for example, after finding his master-teacher in Klingler, he economized by moving out of the Excelsior and into a more modest rental apartment. He lived comfortably but not ostentatiously. And Suzuki, too, loved and cherished music simply for what it was; he was less focused on attaining skill and reputation than on the way that music made him feel. He was compelled by the beauty of finely crafted sound. It brought him to a place of emotional fulfilment, providing what nothing beyond music could.[12]

Suzuki had a charmed life abroad. He found love, and he had the attention and friendship of a dedicated, expert teacher. He had a niche in the cultural elite and could attend any concert he wished to, thanks to his father's money. Suzuki was enormously privileged. At one point he turned down an opportunity to buy a five-story building, though with his ample supply of dependable Japanese yen, he could have afforded it.

It is in the nature of privilege that its possessor fails to notice it. Such was the case for the young Suzuki, at least at first. Against the grotesque economic realities of Weimar Germany, he brought to bear the naivete of a fortunate son. In one instance, he gave a substantial loan to an anxious Japanese university professor who came to his door pleading that he needed to sail home with his wife due to an emergency. After handing over enough for two first-class fares, Suzuki wrote proudly to his father of his good deed. Masakichi's shocking reply: "How dare you assume that the money I send belongs to you!" Like Polonius advising Laertes, Masakichi warned his son against lending money. When he was self-sufficient, he could help anyone he wanted—by giving his money freely rather than lending it. "If you ever find yourself in a position of being able to help others," Masakichi told him, "if you ever come to have that kind of money, you should then be prepared to give it to people in need, and moreover to share in their hardships."

Masakichi's strong words affected his son, who resolved never to lend money. Instead he would put aside a monthly budget, and whatever he did not exhaust, he willed himself to give to those around him who seemed to need it more. The determinedly disinterested manner in which Suzuki would dispense money on what he regarded as worthy causes later in life confirms that he learned his father's lesson well and never forgot it. Such self-discipline was closely connected with a sense of communal obligation. In his personal financial choices, Suzuki tried to act according to the creed preached by modern Japan's pioneering industrialists, sharing their conviction that the ethical accumulation of money lay in its use for the social good.[13]

Suzuki may have turned down Berlin real estate, but there was another case in which he did take advantage of Germany's economic plight. This too would be an occasion for reflecting and learning. In 1922, not long after he had begun lessons with Klingler, Suzuki was presented with a violin belonging to a certain elderly woman. It had been passed down in her family. Suzuki was immediately enthralled by the instrument; the scroll, in particular, was beautifully carved. Though fully aware that the label stuck inside an allegedly priceless instrument was often fake, he checked it anyway. He saw the label of Joseph Guarnerius and the date of 1725, leading more naïve observers to expect that it could be a work of the legendary Giuseppe (Joseph) Guarneri "del Gesù" of Cremona. Suzuki was sure that the label was fraudulent. Yet, it was an exquisite instrument all the same. With it was a certificate of authenticity signed by Otto Möckel, a Berlin luthier active in Charlottenburg, renowned for his Guarneri-style instruments. In Möckel's opinion, the violin in question was built by another member of the Guarneri family, Pietro Guarneri, an older brother of Giuseppe Guarneri del Gesù, during the time when he worked in his father's workshop as an assistant. Pietro Guarneri was a master luthier in his own right, and his instruments have been played by virtuosos such as Kreisler and Joseph Szigeti. In a 2020 auction, a Pietro Guarneri violin sold for $892,685.

In 1922, the seller was asking for 2 million marks, the equivalent of 4,000 yen, or approximately $8,300. This called for more than Suzuki had on hand, but he knew where to find the funds. At the time, there was no possibility of wiring a sufficient sum from Japan, so he contacted Marquis Tokugawa, then in London, who promptly agreed to lend the money. Once Suzuki had received the cash, he advised that the seller take payment in yen or US dollars rather than volatile German marks, but she was oblivious to the workings of foreign exchange and would not listen. So he went to the bank to turn his yen into 2 million marks. But, it being a Saturday, the bank had closed early. By the time Suzuki returned on Monday morning, he was astounded to see that the value of the mark had been cut in half. He ended up paying only 2,000 yen for the precious instrument.

Years down the line, Suzuki did not look back on the episode proudly. "I know it was not a good thing that I bought a Guarnerius for a paltry 2,000 yen," he wrote. The feeling of guilt stuck with him. True, others tried more thoroughly to exploit Germany's economic disadvantage; Suzuki didn't see in the disaster an opportunity to vacuum up property or corporate stocks. But by purchasing the Guarnerius, which presumably had been in the same German family for generations, he helped to drain the nation's wealth and cultural inheritance. In his later reflections, he wondered if activities like this, added up across the scale of the country, had not stoked popular discontent that paved the way for Hitler's rise.

At the moment of acquisition, however, excitement prevailed. Two days after the purchase, Suzuki had a lesson with Klingler. When Suzuki opened the violin case, his teacher rushed over. "Where on earth did you manage to get such a remarkable instrument?" he asked. He took it out of the case and started inspecting it. Suzuki recounted the story, and the price. "I wouldn't call that a price," Klingler replied. "That's nothing." When, in the summer of 1925, Suzuki returned to Japan for a stay that lasted about a year, he took the violin with him and presented it to his father. The Guarnerius inspired the elder Suzuki. After years working from the proverbial corner office, offering affordable products to customers around the world, Masakichi would take to his workbench for a final project: a high-end, entirely handcrafted master instrument.[14]

Then, too, there were times when having money—and being conspicuously foreign—did not play in Suzuki's favor. In one such encounter, he was window-shopping with three Japanese friends at the Tauentzienstraße, one of Berlin's liveliest boulevards, when the police unleashed a so-called *Schieber*-hunt. A Schieber was a black marketeer who traded marks for foreign currencies at greater than the official exchange rate. Suzuki's three friends were swept up by a police cordon—one only had to look suspicious. Suzuki happened to be a few steps ahead of his group and managed to escape. He helplessly watched his friends being loaded into a police truck and then, coming to his senses, went to the police station to help negotiate their release.

There was no evidence of wrongdoing, and eventually the men were released. It was, however, a chilling premonition of Germany's future.

Amid the economic downturn, outsiders were objects of skepticism, profiled as enemies of a people struggling to rebuild. It was a sign that even before the Nazis were in power, German officials were racializing the agents of their national suffering. Among the detainees that day was Matasuke Kawamura, a constitutional law scholar who would become one of Japan's first Supreme Court justices after World War II. It is inconceivable that he was involved in illicit dealmaking. But moral integrity did not necessarily spare a Japanese persecution in Germany, and soon enough it would be wholly irrelevant. Alas, in Japan as well.[15]

During his hiatus back home, Suzuki made a few notable appearances as a violinist. In November 1925, he played Tokyo's Hogakuza (the present-day Marunouchi Piccadilly), a brand-new theater that featured in the city's rebuilding effort following the Great Kanto Earthquake of September 1923. The 7.9-magnitude quake wrought devastation of a kind unthinkable today. It leveled portions of Tokyo and Yokohama at midday, while residents were cooking their lunches, resulting in fires that engulfed both cities. Almost 150,000 people were killed. Music became a source of solace for a grieving Japan. Only two months after the quake, Jascha Heifetz played outdoors in Hibiya Park, just south of the Imperial Palace, as a fundraiser for disaster relief.

At another recital, on March 30, 1926, in Nagoya, Suzuki was accompanied by the pianist Leonor Michaelis. The multitalented Michaelis was moonlighting. A Berliner who worked in Japan between 1922 and 1926, Michaelis was a professor of biochemistry and biophysics who headed a medical school, which is now the medical faculty of the University of Nagoya.[16]

Suzuki noted that it was through Michaelis that he became acquainted with Albert Einstein, sparking a relationship that is central to the Suzuki legend. Later in his career, Suzuki recalled a warm bond between the two and described the profound influence that Einstein, who was also a violinist, left on his ideas and his work as an educator. And yet, there are factual gaps in the stories that Suzuki and those close to him have told. Some have doubted whether the two men ever knew each other.

We do know that Michaelis had accompanied Einstein's violin in 1923, during the great scientist's fantastically successful forty-three-day

Suzuki with Leonor (seated) and Hedwig Michaelis, 1925. *Talent Education Research Institute*

lecture tour of Japan. According to Morikatsu Inagaki, Einstein's interpreter, the sound of piano and violin always ended Einstein's hectic days; while in Nagoya, Einstein and Michaelis played some of their favorite pieces after dining together. They would perform again at least once more, in their adoptive home of the United States. Coincidentally, Marquis Tokugawa also became friendly with Einstein as they happened to sail on the same ship from Europe to Japan, a journey during which they played table games and suffered from the same stomach ailment. Tokugawa welcomed Einstein for dinner while he was in Tokyo, and Einstein thanked his host by performing Bach.[17]

In an autobiographical essay written in 1960, Suzuki explains that Michaelis introduced him to Einstein—not in Nagoya, but in Berlin. The historian Margaret Mehl, however, questions this recollection, and rightly so. Suzuki does not provide an exact date but mentions that, at the time, Michaelis was headed for the United States to teach at Johns Hopkins. But Michaelis took up his post in November 1926, after his time in Japan, and sailed from Yokohama to the United States via Vancouver. So Suzuki could not have spent time with Michaelis in Berlin in the fall of 1926. It is possible that Suzuki, writing decades after the fact, simply misremembered. After all, Michaelis had gone to the United States on another occasion, in May and June of 1924, and had visited Johns Hopkins during that trip. It is possible that Michaelis then stopped in Berlin on his way back to Nagoya from the United States, at which point he could have introduced Suzuki to Einstein. Still, it does seem highly unlikely that Michaelis, on his way to the United States, introduced Suzuki to Einstein in Berlin, in either 1924 or 1926.[18]

All that said, other evidence demonstrates indisputably that Suzuki was known to Einstein, whether they were introduced by Michaelis or by Tokugawa, or perhaps in some other way. The archives of the Talent Education Research Institute (TERI) include a playful self-portrait by Einstein with an inscription to Suzuki from the physicist, as well as a thank-you letter from Einstein to Masakichi Suzuki for the gift of a high-end violin from his workshop, which his sons, Umeo and Shinichi, personally delivered. Likewise, the Einstein Archive holds a letter from Michaelis to Einstein mentioning Suzuki. Besides, as we shall see, there are some details in Suzuki's autobiographical writings that have hitherto been overlooked and that only an insider in Einstein's social circle could have known, making the two men's association all but certain.[19]

Despite the documentary evidence, in 2014 the well-known American violinist and composer Mark O'Connor waged a bizarre campaign against Suzuki, claiming that he lied about having known Einstein. O'Connor, who markets his own "O'Connor Method" as "an American school of string playing," asserted in blogposts that Suzuki's essay collection *Nurtured by Love* contains numerous other fabrications as well. For instance, Suzuki is accused of lying about studying with Klingler and about hosting a postwar student concert attended by Pablo Casals. O'Connor's oddly impassioned claims—more accurately, slanders by innuendo—against a dead man he did not know created sufficient buzz that the *New York Times* followed up with its own investigation. The report concluded that O'Connor's chief allegations were spurious and compared him to a conspiracy theorist analyzing "the Zapruder film of the John F. Kennedy assassination." The article could not, however, get to the bottom of the Einstein question, or the precise nature of Suzuki's association with the physicist.[20]

This may be the true mystery. What exactly were these men to each other? Suzuki, in *Nurtured by Love,* calls Einstein his "guardian" (*kokennin*). Several layers of misleading exaggeration, not all of them Suzuki's fault, appear to surround this statement, so suggestive of fondness and intimacy. The original 1960 autobiographical essay that formed the basis of the Einstein material in *Nurtured by Love* never uses the term "guardian." The essay does state that young Suzuki was introduced to Einstein and was taken under his wing, accompanying the physicist to concerts and parties. The original Japanese edition of *Nurtured by Love* (*Ai ni Ikiru,* which is more accurately translated as *To Live for Love*), published in 1966, does use the term "guardian." But Suzuki did not have a direct hand in making the book. Rather, it was compiled by Tomio Sonehara, TERI's executive director at the time, working with an editor from the Tokyo publisher Kodansha. The pair drew on Suzuki's various autobiographical and anecdotal writings to assemble what would become the most widely read work under his name, both at home and abroad.[21]

That version of *Nurtured by Love* is the book that so moved me as a teenager. It is also nothing like the English-language version that most Americans are familiar with. Until a new edition was published in 2013, the only version of *Nurtured by Love* available in English was a stilted translation by Waltraud Suzuki, who was neither a native speaker of Japanese nor English. Not only that, this English version has both abridgments and insertions, made presumably at Waltraud's discretion, and so is not an accurate rendering. When I enrolled my daughter in the School for Strings, a Suzuki Method–based music school in New York City, I was handed this flimsy booklet (that's what it is) as required study material for aspiring Suzuki parents. I was astonished by what I read. Waltraud's edition has none of the absorbing power of the original.[22]

Between memory lapses, poor translations, incomplete editions, and the possible embellishments of editors, there were many opportunities to varnish the Einstein story with half-truths and fictions, or simply to get facts wrong. Equally, in light of the other evidence, we can be certain that Einstein and Suzuki did know each other, at least in some capacity. Meanwhile, O'Connor's charges are either unsupported or contradicted by evidence, and where there are gray areas, we have no reason to suspect Suzuki of the sort of self-aggrandizement that O'Connor accuses him of.

However unsubstantiated, O'Connor's assault has made very clear one thing, which is TERI's failure to rigorously archive historical records. There has been no systematic effort to keep Suzuki's correspondence after his death and make it available to researchers, and as a result, it is thought that some of his valuable papers were lost. Included in them, presumably, were letters and tape-recordings Suzuki received from Klingler, with whom he maintained contact until well after World War II. Indeed, in the early 1980s Klingler's daughter Marianne became one of the founding members of the European Suzuki Association and the association's first chairperson, making O'Connor's claim that Suzuki also faked his relationship with Klingler especially outlandish.[23]

We must, of course, take all memoir with a grain of salt. The balance of the evidence suggests that we should trust Suzuki's recollections in broad strokes, but not in every detail. And this much is all we really need in order to understand how Einstein affected Suzuki's evolution as a thinker and teacher. Einstein almost certainly associated with Suzuki and was unquestionably a philosophical North Star. Accordingly, in Suzuki's original essay discussing his experiences with Einstein, he mentions three seminal moments, each highlighting lessons learned from the physicist about the importance of humility, humanism, and human potential.

The first occasion came in Berlin. Einstein telephoned Suzuki to invite him to a concert, most likely a chamber program by the Busch Quartet, a group led by Einstein's violinist friend Adolf Busch. (Suzuki wrote elsewhere about a Busch Quartet performance at Singakademie he attended with Einstein, which may or may not be the same event. Suzuki's recollection from that occasion includes a conversation the two had with the master luthier Ernst Kessler, who spent the intermission reminiscing about his old friends Brahms and Joachim, citing specifics that seem difficult to make up.)[24] Suzuki and Einstein were to travel to the concert together by bus. When Suzuki arrived at the bus stop well before the appointed time, expecting to wait for Einstein, he was embarrassed to find that his host had arrived first. To show up ahead of schedule, so that one's companion need not linger alone, was a sign of humility; Suzuki made such hyperpunctuality a lifelong habit, even arriving early for lessons with his students. But surely if anyone could dispense with humility it was Einstein, whose very name is synonymous with genius. And yet Suzuki was profoundly impressed.[25]

On another occasion, Suzuki and Einstein were attending a house concert, and Suzuki was asked to play a concerto by Max Bruch, which he was studying with Klingler. Afterward, an old lady was overheard saying to Einstein, "I just don't understand why that Mr. Suzuki, who grew up entirely in Japan, could so clearly express the German-ness of Bruch. How is that possible?" Einstein paused pensively, then replied, "Madame, people are all the same." It was a statement of humanistic regard that inspired Suzuki for the rest of his long life, succinctly giving voice to his own convictions.

The third experience came at a dinner party at Einstein's house. Suzuki again relates the story using details he could not know were he not at the event—and, indeed, were he not a close acquaintance of Einstein's. The episode's authenticity is therefore hard to dispute.

At the party was a young composition student by the name of Kaufmann. An excellent improviser on the piano, Kaufmann was asked to amuse the other guests. Einstein first played a short melody on the piano himself, then urged Kaufmann to expand on the theme. Effortlessly, Kaufmann began to play a fugue in the style of J. S. Bach. Then came a nocturne in the style of Chopin, with all the melancholy characteristic of the composer. Brahms, Beethoven, Johann Strauss, and

Mahler followed. Suzuki was amazed that someone so young had internalized all those stylistic differences so exquisitely, and, moreover, was able to demonstrate them on the spot. The word that came to Suzuki's mind while witnessing this extraordinary entertainment was "fluency." Kaufmann, Suzuki felt, was not just conversant, but fluent in music. This impression portended the not-so-distant future in which Suzuki would find similarities between the acquisition of language and the cultivation of musical skills. Suzuki regretted, many years later, that he was unable to record Kaufmann's playing, not simply as a souvenir of a special evening but for purposes of his broader research on how talents develop. He further supposed that the kind of ability Kaufmann exhibited, without any hint of hesitation, must be rooted in the musician's childhood environment.

In Suzuki's account, Kaufmann appears briefly and disappears after uttering a line or two. He does not even have a first name. But Kaufmann had his own remarkable story. According to Suzuki, Kaufmann was eighteen years old at the time of the dinner party, a student of the Hochscule's director and dean of composition, Franz Schreker. We can use this fact and Kaufmann's correspondence with Einstein to deduce that the exceptional young man was Walter Kaufmann, born in 1907 in the Czech city of Karlovy Vary (also known by its German name, Karlsbad). After finishing his studies with Schreker in 1930, he got off to a successful early career as a composer and conductor. However, because of rising antisemitism, he was compelled to flee Europe. In 1934 he immigrated to India, mainly because it was easy to obtain a visa; his wife Gertrude, a niece of Franz Kafka, later joined him. While in India, he made a point of studying the country's music. Initially he was puzzled by the seemingly alien sounds, but he assumed his response was a product of his upbringing and training, not a function of the qualities of the music itself—after all, he explained, millions of Indians were "appreciating or in fact loving this music." He stayed in India for fourteen years and cofounded the Bombay Chamber Society, along with the violinist and conductor Mehli Mehta, father of star conductor Zubin Mehta. The lasting achievement of his Indian years was his composition of All India Radio's theme tune, still used to this day and loved by generations of listeners. After the war and a brief stint at the BBC in London, he left for Canada and eventually Bloomington, Indiana, where

Signed November 1926 self-portrait of Albert Einstein, inscribed, "Zum Shinichi Suzuki im freundliche Erinnerung" ("To Shinichi Suzuki in friendly memory"). *Talent Education Research Institute*

he became a professor of musicology at Indiana University. He died there in 1984.[26]

After their paths crossed at Einstein's dinner table in Berlin, Kaufmann's life encompassed the twentieth century just as Suzuki's did.

On February 8, 1928, Suzuki married Waltraud Prange. Masakichi raised no objections to the couple's betrothal, although he did send his eldest son Umeo to Berlin to assess the fiancée and her family. On Waltraud's

Suzuki and Waltraud's fairy-tale wedding in Berlin, February 8, 1928.
Talent Education Research Institute

side, however, there were obstacles. Her mother's relatives thought marriage to a Japanese inadvisable, considering Japan's geographic and cultural distance from Germany. These gulfs were on Suzuki's mind, too. To minimize the physical separation from Waltraud's family, he proposed that, after marrying, they settle in Switzerland. As for cultural differences, he was willing to adapt to any extent necessary. Suzuki even converted to Roman Catholicism, though he was not keen on any organized religion. Still, Waltraud describes relatives threatening that "no one will come to the wedding." But, when the day of the wedding arrived, her relatives "were all there!" The event was filled with the fairy-tale touches of "a bridal carriage, pulled by white horses," "two coachmen in livery," and "a red carpet [that] was rolled out from the altar."[27]

These were happy days for the young couple, not least because at around the same time as the wedding, Suzuki's art took a major step forward with his recording of César Franck's Sonata in A Major on the Deutsche Grammophon label. (Accompanying on piano was Manfred Gurlitt, who would later join the Nazi Party, then be ousted from the party on account of his partly Jewish heritage. He fled to Japan on the eve of World War II and spent the rest of his life there as a composer and music director.) There is unfortunately no existing documentation of the recording's reception, except one note from a student who happened to overhear the sonata flowing from the speaker of a phonograph and remarked on his delight at the performance. This student was a compatriot of Suzuki's who was also in Berlin to study alongside its musical masters, one Junichi Natsume. Not only that, but Natsume was a son of the great novelist Soseki. Like his father's fictional creation Avalon Coldmoon, he was in love with the violin.[28]

Suzuki's was the first recording by a Japanese violinist to be sold internationally. The recording, a movement from which was rereleased in 2018 on the occasion of Deutsche Grammophon's 120th anniversary, was a milestone for Suzuki, who at the time had no plans to become a professional musician and who considered himself less a performer than a seeker of the meaning of art. What did he intend to do after this huge leap? Whatever his plans, they did not come to pass. Only four months after the wedding, in June 1928, an urgent cable arrived: Suzuki's mother was dying. The fears of Waltraud's relatives were justified after all: the young couple had to travel to Japan immediately.[29]

5

FOR THE SAKE OF BEAUTIFUL TONE

IN LATE MAY 1928, Suzuki and Waltraud boarded the Trans-Siberian Railway. The journey covered 5,800 miles; the Moscow-Vladivostok leg alone took seven nights. And yet it was the quickest way from Berlin to Nagoya. When they arrived, Suzuki's mother, Ryo, was still hanging onto life, although she was too frail even to rise from her futon.

Waltraud was astonished by how small her husband's hometown was. Having grown up in Berlin, she could not recognize in Nagoya a proper city. Worse, she was unprepared for life as an outsider. The social, cultural, and linguistic gulf between her world and her husband's—which, in Berlin, had been obscured by their mutual love of music—suddenly became all too clear. But Waltraud found solace where she could. Every Sunday, she and her husband attended a Catholic church presided over by an old German priest. There were also visits to Marquis Tokugawa's Nagoya residence, where Waltraud was introduced to various traditional Japanese arts. And she could not complain about her in-laws' hospitality. Masakichi allowed her to use his chauffeur-driven Packard on a regular basis, an offer she happily accepted. But she soon grew tired of being stared at whenever she went out—the rare Westerner in town. Self-consciousness bred a degree of isolation.

The couple moved into a modest home across from Suzuki's parents' place. With no Western-style furniture to speak of, the house felt empty to Waltraud. To help her feel more at home, Suzuki bought a sofa, two chairs, and a table from a department store. This well-meaning gesture only exaggerated her feeling of alienation, as a few items were simply not enough to fill up the serene expanse of a tatami-floored Japanese sitting room. Desperate, she had all the furniture moved into a smaller room, where she ended up spending most of her time. Her days were almost as wide open as her house. Feeling she needed to do something, she decided to learn Japanese. But Suzuki saw no use for it; he was convinced that they would stay in Japan no longer than he needed in order to fulfill his filial duty. As far as he was concerned, this visit to Nagoya was a stop on their way to Switzerland.[1]

While Waltraud searched for ways to occupy herself, her husband formed a chamber music group with three of his brothers with a view to introducing the art of the small ensemble to a country where it was as yet largely unknown. Suzuki was the eldest of the group, suggesting that his younger brothers had been influenced by his example—Masakichi's boys no longer limited themselves to making and selling string instruments; they also played them. Suzuki played the first violin, Kikuo the second, Akira the viola, and Fumio the cello. Kikuo and Akira had studied in Tokyo with Ko Ando, Suzuki's first teacher. Fumio had also followed in his older brother's footsteps, studying in Germany under the cellist and composer Julius Klengel. Within a few months of its founding, the Suzuki Quartet was performing in notable venues in Nagoya and Tokyo, where they played their first recital in October 1928. The group was doing so well that it would have been a shame to disband it. By the time Ryo died after almost a year of illness, Suzuki decided he wished to stay in Japan after all and keep the quartet going. And so Waltraud and Suzuki set aside their plan to settle in Switzerland and moved to Tokyo in 1929. The rest of the quartet followed them.[2]

To Waltraud's relief, Tokyo proved a far more agreeable environment than Nagoya. She felt she belonged in its sizable expatriate community, which revolved around various educational institutions and business concerns, as well as the embassies dotting the capital city. It had been nearly a decade since Suzuki lived at the Tokugawa mansion in Fujimicho, but Tokyo was still riding high on the waves of cultural and political liberalism. While entertainment opportunities multiplied seemingly by the minute, classical music remained a central feature of Japan's accommodation of the West, ensuring that the Suzuki Quartet could readily find an audience. And though the Taisho Emperor Yoshihito had died at the end of 1926, political transformation kept pace under his son Hirohito. His reign was called Showa, or Enlightened Peace—a reflection of Japan's sustained growth as a global power in the modern mold. And in July 1929, the hugely popular Osachi Hamaguchi, leader of the Constitutional Liberal Democratic Party, became prime minister, a position from which he accelerated ongoing reforms. With his impressive head of white hair, Hamaguchi was nicknamed the Lion Premier, a fitting moniker for the king of Japan's political jungle. More than any of his predecessors, Hamaguchi was determined to stand up for the weak and underprivileged; his party pursued legislation to bolster labor unions and tenant farmers and instituted tax reforms aimed at equitable redistribution of the national wealth. Hamaguchi and his supporters also were committed democrats. With their leadership, Japan lowered the male voting age from twenty-five to twenty and came ever so close to enfranchising adult women in local elections. In global affairs, the Constitutional Liberal Democratic Party stood for peaceful cooperation, arms reduction, and free market economics. Japan in this period actively participated in internationalist projects and contained its own military buildup by ratifying the London Naval Treaty, which outlined the rules of naval engagement and capped the number of vessels to be maintained by major naval powers.

As the broader success of liberal politics suggests, change was not limited to the air of Tokyo, by far Japan's most cosmopolitan place. Cities all over Japan aspired to be like the capital and welcomed new art and new thought. The Suzuki brothers thus had a grand time traveling the country and performing together. Akira, Suzuki's gregarious, energetic half-brother, embodied the quartet's infectious spirit of joy. Both a natural-born clown and an intense musician, Akira was unaffected on stage, which is to say he was demonstrative. His mannerisms could provoke laughter among even the most uptight audience. In addition to their concert performances, the quartet played often for the fledgling NHK—Japan's national public radio service—helping to expand the chamber music audience.[3]

The brothers took their time studying the works of Haydn, Mozart, Beethoven, and Schubert, as well as arrangements of Scottish folk songs and African American spirituals that were already popular in Japan. The quartet also embraced newer compositions. In June 1932 it premiered a work by Kate Ingeborg Hansen, an American of Danish extraction who taught at a girls' school in the northeastern city of Sendai. A Christian

The Suzuki Quartet, featuring Shinichi (left, first violin) and his brothers Kikuo (second violin), Akira (viola), and Fumio (cello), enjoyed considerable success in the late 1920s and 1930s. *Talent Education Research Institute*

missionary and university-trained musician, Hansen had composed a four-movement piece inspired by her roots in Schleswig, which had been a Danish territory for centuries before its annexation by Prussia in 1864. The day after the quartet performed *Schlesvig* [*sic*], Hansen excitedly wrote to her family back home in Kansas. When she heard the piece for the first time in a rehearsal, she said, she was struck by how much better it sounded in real life than in her musical imagination. She also noted that the Suzuki brothers could "keep on pitch better than any other Japanese ensemble I have heard." They must have inherited their father's ear, she surmised. Masakichi Suzuki, his sons told her, had "a remarkable ear for music" and could "detect variations in pitch that even trained musicians like themselves fail to identify."[4]

The brothers also played music composed by their cellist, Fumio. Most notably, he wrote a suite based on the *Tale of Genji*, Lady Murasaki's eleventh-century masterpiece chronicling the life of a Don Juan–like prince. The novel was going through something of a revival in Japan at the time. Its popularity owed much to another female literary figure, the poet Akiko Yosano, who wrote the aforementioned antiwar verse for her brother fighting in the Russo-Japanese conflict. Yosano had taken on the momentous task of translating the classic work into modern Japanese. When the quartet recorded the suite with Nippon Columbia, an affiliate of the UK company Columbia Graphophone, she recited a portion of her modern text to accompany the overture.

Suzuki died believing that this was, regrettably, the only surviving recording by the quartet. However, a decade after his death, well-preserved recordings, totaling almost an hour of music, were discovered and released in their entirety. The violinist Koji Toyoda, a protégé of Suzuki's, praised his mentor's playing on this collection, describing "resilient, pure, and transparent" music, "free of all unnecessary properties." This spare treatment reflected Suzuki's personality, in Toyoda's opinion, even as he felt sure that Suzuki would have liked to emulate the "powerful, flexible, and far-reaching sounds" of his idols Fritz Kreisler and Jacques Thibaud. One way or another, Suzuki was no longer just a seeker; he was a musician, with his own artistic personality.[5]

The late 1920s and early 1930s were good for Suzuki artistically and professionally, but the rest of the world was not altogether sharing in his good fortune. The late 1920s brought economic decline to Japan, as the Taisho bubble burst. Then the worldwide Great Depression started in October 1929, only making matters worse. Tragically for Japanese democracy, the political fallout was absorbed by Lion Premier Hamaguchi's government, which would be blamed for everything that went wrong. On a global scale, the Depression prompted even the United States and Great Britain, erstwhile champions of liberal internationalism, to withdraw and look inward, creating self-sufficient economic blocs by restricting international trade. This had an immediate and crippling impact on Masakichi Suzuki's violin business. In 1920, at its most prosperous, Suzuki Violin produced 150,000 violins annually. In 1928, the number was down to 34,000, and in 1933 to just 13,000. The workforce shrank accordingly, from 905 employees in 1920 to 101 in 1930.[6]

The bad economy bred a volatile atmosphere. In late 1930, an ultranationalist opposed to Japan's signing of the London Naval Treaty shot Hamaguchi; he died from his wound the following year. Hamaguchi's death heralded the demise of Japan's era of progressive social reform.

In time, the democratic socialism that had shaped Taisho Democracy would be challenged by the radical right, a group most conspicuous within the military. The armed forces themselves faced serious internal divisions, but collectively men at arms regarded themselves as the rightful leaders of Japan's future. Militarists of different stripes, especially ideological young officers, demanded drastic changes. They envisioned the country operating under a kind of military junta, where democratic processes had no place and the Imperial Way of Japan, untainted by outside influences, prevailed. To legitimize their claims to power, officers invoked the martial glory of an imagined Japanese past and escalated the cult of emperor worship to an extreme. Like the Meiji generation before them, they saw in the emperor a route to their own political power, which in their view was perfectly aligned with Japan's national interest. Their adulation of the figure of the emperor was genuine—fanatical, really—although it had nothing to do with his personal beliefs. Hirohito is generally thought to have been a constitutional monarchist in the British vein, whereas the radicalized men in uniform and their supporters saw institutions like elected parliaments as obstacles to the empire they believed was Japan's destiny.

The early 1930s were marked by a string of further political assassinations by ultranationalists. The violence was of a piece with aggressive Japanese expansion on the Asian continent. Recall that in 1905, following the settlement of the Russo-Japanese War, Japan had taken Russian possessions in Manchuria. In 1931, these territories remained under military occupation by Japan. On September 18 of that year, a Japanese detachment in Manchuria attempted to expand its hold over China's northeastern provinces by manufacturing a pretext for invasion: the soldiers detonated a small explosive on a Japanese railway and blamed Chinese saboteurs. The so-called Manchurian Incident was not a reflection of official Japanese strategy; command staff had not authorized the plan, which had originated with radicalized middle-to-lower-echelon officers in the field. But once the scheme was carried out successfully, and the jingoistic media inflamed popular support, the Japanese army and government were compelled to double down on the soldiers' freelancing. The result was a further invasion of Manchuria—eventually with official approval. The conflict lasted until February 1932, culminating in the founding of the Japanese puppet state Manchukuo. These events also led to Japan's 1933 decision to withdraw from the League of Nations. A few years of surface calm ensued on the Chinese mainland, but in the summer of 1937 the Japanese army's ambition to conquer greater China finally exploded with a full-scale invasion. All in all, Japan spent the 1930s becoming increasingly undemocratic, helped along by a complicit news media. With limited access to information, the Japanese public was largely oblivious to the true extent of the country's aggressive and expansionist overseas activities.

Of course, amid the economic downturn, most Japanese people were preoccupied with everyday concerns. Suzuki was faced with the mundane reality of having to work for a living for the first time in his life. He had worked in his father's factory, but that was a matter of personal interest and devotion to family; need of money had not been a factor. And the quartet, for all its successes, did not generate enough money to live on. It, too, was a passion project. Waltraud, who was familiar with financial struggle, was never comfortable with the attitude that followed from such privilege. She felt her husband had grown to adulthood assuming that money would "always be there" and so spent unthinkingly, for example hailing taxis when he could have easily walked or taken public transportation, leaving them unable to pay their gas bill. In Waltraud's opinion, not just her husband but his whole family was "very impractical." For a time, they went on "living in the style they were accustomed to," even after the violin factory stopped laying golden eggs. Masakichi, a man of his word, continued giving his money to the needy until he joined their ranks. Eventually he had to cut off his grown son's allowance—a major blow to the young couple, given the high cost of living in Tokyo—and went into debt himself. To support his father, Suzuki sold one of his violins, a Vuillaume, while Waltraud sold her Bechstein piano.[7]

So Suzuki needed a job, and from necessity arose another transformation: he began to teach the violin. At first, he taught part-time at a private conservatory, while taking some pupils on the side. Then, in the spring of 1931, he was formally engaged as a member of the faculty at another private conservatory, located in Daida, a newly developing, prosperous suburb in Tokyo's Setagaya ward. At different times, the school was called Teikoku Ongaku Gakko (Imperial School of Music), Teikoku Koto Ongakugakuin (Advanced Imperial Academy of Music), and Teikoku

Koto Ongakugakko (Advanced Imperial School of Music), a reflection of the administrative complications and internal politics that plagued the institution from its founding in 1928 to its closure in 1943. Most refer to it by the abbreviation Teion.[8]

Teion had plenty of competition, thanks to the growing appeal of Western music in Japan during the first decades of the twentieth century. But it managed to stand out, and in a way that perfectly suited Suzuki's personality. A major feature of the school was its philosophy and policy of self-rule by the student body. This meant, for example, that the students were entitled to appoint faculty members by vote. As a result, the teaching staff tended to consist of publicly visible musicians. All of Suzuki's brothers in the quartet were recruited to teach at Teion as well, attesting to the group's popularity among aspiring young musicians. Most renowned among the faculty was the Russian violinist Alexander Mogilevsky, who settled in Tokyo after visiting the city on a concert tour. Mogilevsky has often erroneously been called Suzuki's teacher. In fact, on three separate occasions Mogilevsky refused Suzuki's entreaties for lessons, though he did agree to "study together" with his colleague.[9]

The school prided itself on its inclusiveness, in terms of both the breadth of subjects offered—Teion was home to Japan's first composition department, before the national conservatory in Ueno set up its own in 1931—and the diversity of students and faculty. With Russian expats on the faculty and with a substantial number of students coming from Taiwan, Korea, and China, Teion had a cosmopolitan atmosphere. At one point in the late 1930s, the student body of one hundred included about forty students from the Korean Peninsula. In addition, Teion offered continuing education opportunities for individuals who were not enrolled in its standard program.[10]

The school went out of its way to admit anyone with the capacity to succeed. To enroll, one had to pass an audition, and those who auditioned tended to be middle school and high school graduates. But the admission guidelines specified that "even without such qualifications," and thereby irrespective of age, "if one exhibits sufficient talent," one would be accepted. Suzuki's educational philosophy was only beginning to take shape in 1931, but it is easy to see how he would sympathize with this commitment to the wide accessibility of talent, equating it not with some innate,

Suzuki leads a string orchestra at Teion, 1931. The pianist is Motonari Iguchi, who would go on to establish an early childhood music program whose notable graduates include the conductor Seiji Ozawa. *Talent Education Research Institute*

exclusive property or with educational accomplishments but with concrete, demonstrable skills. What is more, the school's goal, as announced in its prospectus, was "to strive for the nurturing of character, as well as true musicianship." As such, the curriculum ranged far beyond lessons, ensembles, and composition. Students also studied music pedagogy, music theory, operatic theory, Japanese language, German (which Suzuki taught), aesthetics, and even ethics.[11]

Teion's humanistic coursework and democratic governance were strongly redolent of Taisho ideology. At the same time, its institutional principles dovetailed with the *Bildung* spirit that Suzuki had relished in Berlin: the conviction that art and culture could aid in a never-ending process of moral and intellectual improvement. Any art could, in Suzuki's view, serve this purpose, hence at one point in his writing he cites and rejects the English critic Walter Pater's proposition that "all art constantly aspires towards the condition of music." Nonetheless, Suzuki did think music unique in the way it connects the composer and the performer and the performer and the audience. Music served as a sort of medium, bringing these three groups of people into communion and raising all involved to an extraordinary plane of consciousness. As Suzuki established himself at Teion, he began to wonder about the effect on an individual of constant exposure, from an early age, to such a medium. Would it change one's character? Would it also affect one's talent?[12]

Conservatory life provided many occasions to ponder these questions, as Suzuki observed the learning and teaching going on around him. One Teion student stood out above all, and there are cogent reasons to believe that Suzuki's approach to teaching very young children was inspired by her example. Her name was Nejiko Suwa.

On June 14, 1932, Teion held a schoolwide concert at Nippon Seinenkan Hall, a prime venue where the Suzuki Quartet had made its Tokyo debut four years earlier. The program included solo, duo, chamber, chorus, and orchestral performances given by members of the faculty and student body. Under Mogilevsky's baton, Suzuki and others performed Handel's Concerto Grosso in D Minor and Edvard Grieg's Elegiac Melodies. But, as fine as those renditions must have been, the *pièce de résistance* and the pride of the school came later. Toward the end of the program, a twelve-year-old with the quiet intensity of a mature adult appeared with her violin.

Young as she was, Nejiko Suwa was deemed to have more than "sufficient talent" for admission to Teion. She studied with the great Mogilevsky himself. Only two months before the schoolwide concert, the "genius girl violinist," as she was identified in the media, had given her much-hyped first public recital, in which her teacher played second violin to her first in Vivaldi's Concerto for Two Violins in A Minor. For the school concert, Suwa performed two contrasting pieces, the lyrical Romanza Andaluza from Pablo de Sarasate's *Spanish Dances,* and Ferdinand Ries's up-tempo "Perpetual Motion." The pieces were well chosen to showcase both her interpretive and technical skills. Accompanying on piano was Nadezhda de Leuchtenberg, Mogilevsky's aristocratic wife, who was also on the Teion faculty.

By then, Suwa had surpassed most, if not all, of Japan's top violinists. Observing this phenomenal girl, whose family apparently did not have any money—which meant she had mostly been given free lessons—Suzuki must have wondered about the nature of her talent. Her environment and educational history provided some clues. Like countless Suzuki violinists to come, Suwa started listening to classical music long before she picked up a violin. Her father, Junjiro, came from a wealthy family, which had allowed him to acquire a certain amount of education and exposure to elite culture. Though he had lost his fortune, he retained an interest in music and took his daughter to her first violin recital, given by Efrem Zimbalist. It was then that she fell in love with the instrument. For her part, Suwa's mother, Taki, was a dedicated music lover. Before her marriage, she had dreamed of becoming a classical singer, and she made sure her daughter listened to the assorted virtuosi catalogued in Victor's Red Seal Records series. While also raising three younger children, Taki oversaw her eldest daughter's daily practice beginning at age four. Whatever her "natural" talent, Suwa's skill benefited greatly from parental investment.

She also had an able instructor. Anna Ono, née Bubnova, had studied in St. Petersburg with the world-renowned master-teacher Leopold Auer. In 1917, she married Shunichi Ono, a young Japanese biologist whom she met after giving a recital. Amid the revolutionary gunfire that soon overtook the city, they fled to Japan on the Trans-Siberian Railway, a decade before Waltraud and Suzuki traveled the same route. In the realm of early childhood violin education, too, Ono was about a decade ahead of Suzuki; she guided Nejiko Suwa and her own child Shuntaro so effectively that they became top performers before they hit their teens. Ono recognized how important Suwa's early immersion had been. "By the time she came to me, her ears had already been very well-trained," the teacher explained. Because of her thorough exposure to professional recordings, Suwa could identify various performers on records, differentiating among individual styles. More fundamentally, music was in her ears long before it was in her hands and her eyes, fixed on a score. Again, this approach was unusual at the time; only recently had it become possible, thanks to the technological changes that brought recorded music into the home. The similarities between the Suzuki Method and Suwa's musical upbringing are striking.[13]

Another similarity lies in Suwa's total embrace of music, which made the violin an essential component of her life. Practicing and playing the violin, as Suzuki would later tell his students and their families, should be approached as a part of one's daily routine, not as an extra effort—just as breathing, speaking, eating, and sleeping are natural and necessary motions we undertake without a second thought. And Suwa certainly approached her violin practice in a comparable way. According to this worldview, missing practice was not an option. Ono duly noted that her prized pupil never skipped lessons. On rainy days, Suwa would show up drenched in her tiny rubber boots, hefting her tiny instrument. The sight was at once moving and pitiful; it almost made Ono cry.

Suzuki would have heartily endorsed not only Suwa's determination but also her habit of always carrying her violin. Indeed, carrying one's own instrument, no matter one's age, would become a cardinal rule of the Suzuki Method. This is another way in which the violin becomes an indispensable part of the student's life. By the time beginning students are deemed ready to play on real instruments, they will have been eagerly anticipating the day they could carry their own violins, as they first work on basics such as standing and holding mock violins made of cardboard in the right position. The idea is that a child should develop a sense of pride, responsibility, and commitment to music before they even play a note, suggesting that the personal qualities of musicianship precede musical knowledge. By directing that students care for and respect their instruments, Suzuki made good on his humanism, for one need not carry one's own instrument to be able to play music, but doing so deepens one's connection to music and is a small lesson in being a decent person. I myself have found this proposition to be empirically sound. When my daughter started taking Suzuki lessons at age three, I recognized all those feelings of pride, responsibility, and commitment awakening in her as she navigated the crowded New York subway with her 1/16th-sized violin case strapped on her back. Some Suzuki parents will carry their kids' instruments as a matter of course, so that this practice becomes a telltale sign of which families are truly dedicated to the method as a source not just of musical training but also education in character.

Suzuki must have seen in Suwa what the wider public often did not. The press tended to emphasize inborn qualities—Suwa's "genius" and her photogenic face. Her family's relative poverty made for a fetching

Cinderella story as well, which helps to explain why Suwa, more than other young Japanese musicians of her era, became a sensation. Suzuki, however, would have been drawn not to what was innate or what Suwa's parents lacked but to what her parents gave her. They had a love of music, and they made sure to pass it along to their daughter thorough early immersion. Without this head start, no amount of hard work would have sufficed to create the phenomenon that was Nejiko Suwa. Her exposure to a range of excellent performance from an early age was the source of her great musical sensitivity; Suzuki would urge parents to create a similar home environment. From Suzuki's perspective, this was essential training, although it was not the source of musical sensibility in and of itself. Every child possesses musical sensibility, he thought, and it was up to adults either to nurture that sensibility or to waste it—or even abuse it, if unwittingly. A young child who was constantly exposed to out-of-tune lullabies would be an expert at singing out of tune, Suzuki argued. Such a child would sing badly not because she had "bad ears" but precisely because she had good ones, capable of internalizing whatever music she heard.

In the early 1930s, Japanese classical music lovers increasingly agreed that starting young was essential. At the time, early music instruction was still rare, but it was becoming something of a vogue in segments of urban Japan. This trend both fostered and was enabled by the influx of European musicians and pedagogues during the interwar period. Teachers like Anna Ono introduced Japan to systematic approaches to Western music-making. Such approaches, based on highly focused, conservatory-style training, catered to those who were deemed exceptional or precocious, and, as such, would not have suited every child. Suzuki's later innovations reflected his adjustments of these more traditional methods. But what mattered at this point was that some Japanese children were being exposed to music from a young age and were being well trained by European instructors. These émigrés—mostly Jews, many from Russia or Germany—did much to create a cadre of strong musicians in a relatively short time.

Suwa was among the best of them and was the first to receive intense media attention and achieve nationwide celebrity. It was not surprising that she had a key role in popularizing the early-start approach. Suzuki joined her in this respect. By 1933, he was publicly making the case for early immersion. In a newspaper interview, he said it was rather "unnatural like I did, to pick up Western music [later in life], go abroad, and become a musician." He thought it was the likes of Suwa as well as Miwako Kai and Chieko Hara—students of the foreign pianists Maxim Schapiro and Pedro Villaverde, respectively—"who have all been raised steeped in music since childhood" and could thus be called "true musicians." Soon enough, he predicted, early immersion would produce Japanese virtuosi in Western classical music.[14]

When Suzuki referred to early education, he meant three- and four-year-olds, which was unusual at the time. When, also in 1933, the national conservatory in Ueno launched a youth music program, it was geared toward children in the fourth grade and older. (Later, the age floor was lowered to accommodate third graders.) Suzuki would certainly have approved of the repertoire and quality of instruction: participants sang choral works and took instrumental lessons and counted among their teachers the German conductor Klaus Pringsheim, an influential émigré musician of the period. But, by Suzuki's standards, these students were not getting a head start. They were coming late to music, missing out on the opportunity to gain fluency.[15]

To be sure, Suzuki understood that fluency was not everything; it was a minimum requirement for becoming a "true musician." There is a huge gap between fluency and artistry, just as fluency in English does not automatically enable one to become a great orator or poet. Even a "girl genius" like Nejiko Suwa had to put in the work. As she herself would say many decades later, "There is no shortcut to art." She tried to find one, and she could not. "Though I tried to omit what was unnecessary, and to get there quickly," she concluded poignantly, "there was no such route."

It is worth dwelling for a moment on the hard work Suwa did, because it is closely related to Suzuki's development as an educator. When he first heard Suwa play, he had not been teaching long, and his ideas were still crystallizing. He was open to influence, and he must have been eagerly observing and reflecting on how Mogilevsky, his esteemed colleague and Suwa's instructor at Teion, went about guiding this extraordinary girl.

Anna Ono had provided Suwa the best foundational guidance then available in Japan, but when the young violinist switched to Mogilevsky at age ten or eleven—she could not remember precisely which—she realized that there was much more to learn about the instrument she thought she knew so well. The uncompromising Mogilevsky required of her a variety of technical skills she either had to acquire or relearn. According to him, her rhythm was off, her pitch was shaky, and the shifting of her left hand was clumsy. But most importantly, Mogilevsky directed that she change her bow hold. To those who have never played bowed string instruments, this may not seem like a major issue. But Mogilevsky was in fact turning his student's world upside down.[16]

Generally speaking, establishing a proper bow hold occupies an enormous amount of time, focus, and coordination, and the effort can dominate the initial stages of string studies. Asking a student to change the bow hold she grew up with is almost like asking a right-handed person to learn to write with her left. Mogilevsky, however, was insistent. Ono had taught Suwa the so-called Russian style of bowing, in which the index finger exerts pressure on the bow. This grip allows for great energy and speed but often at the expense of flexibility. There is certainly nothing wrong with this style; it is the hold Leopold Auer taught his students—whether Ono or greats like Heifetz, Elman, and Milstein. But Mogilevsky wanted Suwa to move toward a more flexible type of bow hold, broadly known as the Franco-Belgian style. According to this school, the curved fingers of the right hand balance the whole bow; there is no concentrated pressure from the index finger. Mogilevsky is thought to have picked up this style when he studied in Paris with Lucien Capet, who wrote the influential method book *La Technique Supérieure de l'Archet pour Violon* (The Superior Bowing Technique for the Violin) in 1916. Capet was a teacher to a generation of pedagogues even more influential than himself, such as Jascha Brodsky of the Curtis Institute of Music and Ivan Galamian of the Juilliard School.

Suzuki himself researched and adopted the Franco-Belgian bow hold, likely having been introduced to the style's advantages while "study[ing] together" with Mogilevsky. Suzuki wasn't focused on bow holds per se; what primarily interested him was tone, and while repeatedly listening to recordings of the world's greatest violinists, he was coming to suspect that beautiful tone was not a miracle but rather a matter of technique, and moreover teachable technique closely connected to bowing. This realization was years in development. Certainly Suzuki had learned many techniques in Berlin, had multiple teachers, and had taken up teaching himself; he was hardly blind to the possibility of instruction. But he conceded that, for a long time, he was not sure if tone itself was teachable. The beauty of Kreisler's playing, or that of Pablo Casals, seemed to emerge from "the tone made by a God-given talent."[17]

As Suzuki began to think more carefully about how to impart technical knowledge to his students, his opinion concerning the origins of tone changed drastically. More and more, he believed that even God could not explain the utterly wonderous properties of certain sounds. Rather, beautiful tone was a product of the universal "scientific condition" in which sound is produced by the friction between the bow and the strings. The seemingly otherworldly tone of the finest violinists, Suzuki conjectured, was a result of their ability to optimize that friction. Very few people manage this feat intuitively, but Suzuki believed that, with effective bowing instruction, any violinist could create more beautiful sounds.[18]

To be clear, Suzuki was not concluding that nothing is inborn. It is hard, for example, to otherwise explain why some children achieve better physical coordination than their peers or gain coordination at an earlier age. But as he analyzed bowing technique, and derived clues from Nejiko Suwa's education, he grew more convinced about the relative importance of effective instruction from an early age, conducted in a music-rich environment. It seemed impossible to truly develop one's talent otherwise. To be sure, the levels that each of us could hope to achieve would naturally differ, but anyone could be guided to their highest level of talent if properly nurtured.

This belief would guide Suzuki as he began to take on very young students. The first, a four-year-old boy named Toshiya Eto, came to him in June 1932. This student confirmed Suzuki's emerging conviction, for he was not only young but also surrounded by Western classical music. The name Toshiya is a Japanese rendition of Toscha, after the violinist Toscha Seidel, whom Eto's father, a violin enthusiast, very much admired. The boy was referred to Suzuki by Mogilevsky, who felt at a loss as to how to teach such a young child.[19]

As Suzuki took on more students, including very young ones, he began to develop novel techniques for teaching them effectively. For instance, he developed an unorthodox visual method to clarify the connection

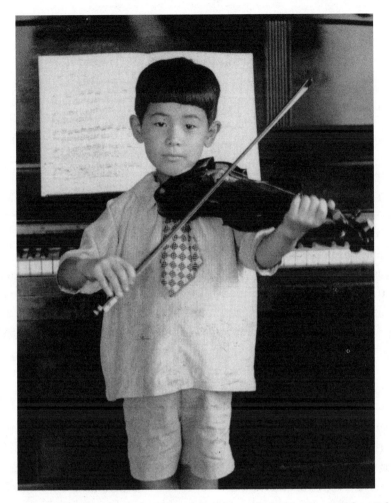

Toshiya Eto, the first child Suzuki ever taught, photographed in 1937. *Talent Education Research Institute*

between tone and bowing technique. Suzuki would urge students to imagine a triangular relationship between the bow's tip, the bow hair's point of contact with the strings, and the bow's frog (the lower end). This takes some imagination; one tends to think of the bow hair as a straight line, but of course the pressure at the point of contact with the strings presses the hair upward toward the bow stick and away from the two ends of the bow. In order to create a smooth, balanced tone, the same amount of pressure must be exerted at both ends of the bow, no matter where the bow makes contact with the strings. Achieving this result requires care and control. It is all too easy to exert far greater pressure at the frog, where the hand is located, than at the tip. Such variation in bowing pressure is essential to many folk styles, as it enables tonal distortions that add color and character. But in the classical context, one must first attain the norm of an even, pleasing tone before learning how to deviate from it artfully. And Suzuki, by employing the simplest geometry, had devised a clever way to teach tone production to anyone.

No one else in Japan was incorporating such a broadly intelligible approach, let alone making the attainment of beautiful tone the overwhelming focus of their teaching. Former Teion student Shinjiro Baba, recalling his lessons with Suzuki from those prewar years, was most impressed by his instructor's passion for tone. All of Baba's previous teachers, including those at Ueno, obsessed over scale and intonation exercises but paid no attention to either bowing technique or the qualitative differences in tone that emerged. Suzuki showed him how to approach music from a completely different angle. For the time being at least, optimal tone production became Suzuki's quest, and he researched the subject with the meticulousness and empirical rigor of a scientist. An early result of these studies came in 1937, with the publication of his fifty-page booklet *A Tone-Correction Method for Any Violinist*.[20]

If the encounter with Nejiko Suwa helped inspire Suzuki's teaching approach in its formative years, that would certainly have been enough. But her example imparted yet another powerful lesson on Suzuki, for Suwa's precocious expertise did not make her life easier. To the contrary, her adolescence was extremely difficult, thanks in great measure to her musical ability, the expectations it fostered, and the immaturity of adults confronting so-called genius. Suzuki would later assert that no one should be called a genius or prodigy before having had the chance to develop as a person and prove themselves through a lifetime of work, and there can be little doubt that Suwa was on his mind when he claimed as much.

The financial success and media attention that followed Suwa's public debut took a toll on her parents and on her. Her father Junjiro, like Suzuki, was born to wealth and resulting impracticality. But unlike Suzuki, Junjiro had no obvious enthusiasms to draw on, no skills he could put to good use to support himself, let alone his wife and children, once his family money ran out. Now that his oldest daughter was declared a genius and was being engaged to record and concertize, he was becoming dependent on her, provoking resentment. He also felt sidelined by his wife, Taki, who was rightly receiving credit for standing by her daughter through the thick and thin of violin practice. Marital discord followed— quarrels, physical abuse, and at least one extramarital affair.[21]

The deterioration of Suwa's family life was an object lesson for Suzuki and might have been for Japan at large, as none of Suwa's compatriots had been declared a genius of the violin before. But Europeans had ample experience of classical music wunderkinds run into the ground by adults intent on taking advantage of the sudden opportunities that young ones afforded them. Jascha Heifetz counted himself "among the few who had the good fortune to survive" identification as a child prodigy because he had a great teacher in Auer and a family that possessed a genuine regard for music. Heifetz believed that what he called "child prodigism" was a lethal disease brought on by parents of precocious children. Those parents, he maintained, are "so overawed by their good fortune that they lose their balance and take whatever short cuts are offered them to fame and fortune. So they send their poor little tots out into the competitive world at a time when they should be working hard at home, shielded from flattery and exploitation."[22]

Eventually the Suwa family was under such duress that it broke apart. In late 1933, Taki left Junjiro, vanishing into thin air with all four of their children. This disappearance, coming shortly after Suwa's successful performance as a soloist with the New Symphony Orchestra, had newspapers speculating feverishly on the whereabouts of the young violinist. Though only thirteen, she already had an air of world-weariness about her. What had made her so melancholy, and where had she been taken?

The newspapers did not know where to find her, but Suzuki did, for he was instrumental in her dramatic escape. During the year preceding it, Suzuki had taken over Suwa's violin studies and become intimately aware of her family life. This came about because Mogilevsky refused to see her until things were sorted out at home. (There is also speculation that Mogilevsky fell out with her parents over money matters, as they disagreed on how much of a cut he, as Suwa's teacher, and his wife, as her accompanist, should be getting from Suwa's professional engagements.) Suzuki did not see an opportunity in teaching the rising star; he wanted to help her family and ensure that she could return to Mogilevsky. So Suzuki went to the person he could count on in any emergency: Marquis Tokugawa. With Tokugawa's help, Suzuki was able to prepare for Taki and her children a seaside retreat in Kanagawa, 40 miles southwest of central Tokyo. They spent four months in hiding there, and, through intermediaries, Taki persuaded her husband to agree to a separation. She would take Nejiko and their third daughter, while their second daughter and their son would live with Junjiro. On May 3, 1934, when Mogilevsky resumed Suwa's lessons, the *Asahi* newspaper reported on their reunion with a photo of the two together under the sentimental headline, "Joy Wells Up in a Weary Heart." The article explained that "Mr. M will continue teaching Nejiko until the day her dream of studying abroad comes true."[23]

There was already an understanding between master and pupil that Suwa could achieve her highest potential as a musician only if she left Japan for the West, wherever exactly that might be. No matter Mogilevsky's caliber as an instructor, Suwa had to face the bigger world in order to grow. Suzuki and Tokugawa again came to her aid by gathering support for her overseas studies. Given his developing views on the overarching importance of environment in the maturation of a musician, it is clear why Suzuki felt so strongly about Suwa making her way elsewhere. Going abroad would not only enable her to leave behind her unhappy family life and grow into her own person, it would also expose her to a wealth of listening opportunities, beyond the records and the occasional recitals to which she was accustomed.

What is more, Suzuki understood personally how critical it was to nurture one's ear in different milieus, having done so himself. For instance, when he temporarily returned to Japan after four years of learning and listening in Berlin, he was astonished by how bad Japan's symphony orchestra sounded. "Its awful tone was so unpleasant" that he felt "soiled" afterward. But after attending a few of those concerts, he was again astonished—this time at himself for feeling less troubled by what he heard. By the time he was due to return to Germany, his ears were growing "so accustomed" to local classical musicians "that sometimes, I even thought they sounded very pleasant." Then, back in Berlin, the beauty of the Klingler Quartet struck him as though he were hearing its music for the first time. These experiences convinced him that human ears were able to adjust to a huge range of sounds and that musicians could therefore learn from varied exposure. This did not imply an equality of sounds; there undoubtedly existed, in his mind, music attaining different levels of "beauty," "nobility," and "warmth." But one could cultivate one's sensitivity only by listening intently and broadly.[24]

Suwa's childhood playmate—one of very few—and biggest rival was in a similar position. Shuntaro Ono had exhausted his opportunities in Japan when he successfully auditioned for the first violin section of the New Symphony at the age of twelve. So his mother, Anna Ono, drew up a plan for him to go abroad. He would study with Zimbalist, an old friend of his mother's from St. Petersburg and a fellow Auer disciple, now teaching at the Curtis Institute of Music in Philadelphia. Ono intended to accompany her son. But just as they were readying themselves to set sail for the United States, in late 1933, Shuntaro became ill. A doctor failed to identify his appendicitis, which quickly developed into peritonitis. He died within a day of falling ill. Ono was inconsolable over the death of her only child at fourteen. Had he lived and flourished under Zimbalist's guidance, Shuntaro might have become world famous long before his younger cousin Yoko Ono, his paternal uncle's daughter, became one of Japan's most recognizable twentieth-century artists.

Suwa did manage to get out of Japan—with the help not only of Suzuki and Tokugawa but also the Belgian ambassador Baron Albert de Bassompierre. Bassompierre felt that his country, known for its world-class violinists and the royal family's involvement in violin playing, was a perfect place for Suwa to study; Queen Elisabeth, wife of King Albert I and mother of King Leopold III, was a student and a friend of the legendary violinist Eugène Ysaÿe, ensuring that the instrument was a cultural focal point among the country's elite. Encouraged by Bassompierre's backing, the Japanese Foreign Ministry eventually put its financial support behind Suwa's studies, making her an official, state-sponsored scholar. On January 23, 1936, her sixteenth birthday, Suwa set sail for Belgium, traveling alone on the *Kashima-maru,* tracing the route Suzuki had taken to Europe a decade and a half earlier. She was to study with Émile Chaumont, something of a former prodigy himself, at the Conservatoire de Bruxelles.[25]

Autographed photo of Nejiko Suwa, signed "Dear Suzuki Sensei," presumably a parting gift before she set sail for Europe in 1936. *Talent Education Research Institute*

Suzuki's wish was for Suwa to develop as a person and a musician; Japan's wish was for her to represent the nation. As a state-supported artist with a significant media profile, she bore the expectations of her people. By becoming a world-class concert violinist, she would prove that Japan still cared about high culture and civilization, in spite of its declining international reputation and its increasing political radicalism.

Time was running out for Japan. While the liner bearing the young violinist was at sea, the country faced a bloody military insurrection. The February 26 coup attempt, known as the 2-26 Incident or the Young Officers' Rebellion, nearly succeeded. A group of army officers, frustrated with Japan's economic and social stagnation, tried to topple the government and claimed to be the righteous leaders of the new imperial Japan. They managed to tap into the grievances of lower-ranking soldiers, about 1,500 of them, who were mobilized to assassinate several key politicians. The soldiers who did the actual dirty work were not necessarily motivated by radical ideology. Many came from the rural, impoverished northeast, which had been hit especially hard by the slump and crop failures of recent years. Quite a few of the region's young peasant daughters—sisters, friends, and girlfriends of these men—were sold into city brothels and factories. Having lived through such extreme poverty, the soldiers agreed that something drastic had to be done to put things right, and they believed that the emperor approved of their actions. But about this they were wrong. Despite four assassinations, including that of a finance minister, the coup failed. That was because the emperor Hirohito put a decisive stop to the revolt by publicly denouncing the rebels. Making his political view known was something he rarely did in his role as a largely symbolic leader, who reigned but did not rule. The extent of his rage must have been great indeed.

Japan might have narrowly averted a coup, but its prospects remained grim, and a climate of fear prevailed. The military—both navy and army—made the loudest claims to power, along with the so-called New Bureaucrats, who held marked preferences for totalitarian state-planning. These self-proclaimed reformers were more often than not products of an extremely constrained type of meritocratic education in which obedience and high test scores were valued disproportionately over originality, creativity, and imagination. The New Bureaucrats almost always worked in cahoots with the military, which was an integral part of Japan's central bureaucracy to begin with.

As it turns out, Europe was nowhere for Suwa to avoid political disaster. While Japan descended into its Dark Valley, fascism rose in Germany and Italy, and Europe was increasingly divided by conflicting allegiances and ideologies. Within months of Suwa's arrival in Brussels, a civil war broke out in Spain between leftists and right-wing nationalists led by General Francisco Franco. That conflict would be another wedge sundering an already-divided Europe. Soon, for Suzuki in Japan and for Suwa abroad, the pursuit of beautiful tone would have to be a secondary consideration in the struggle for survival.

Suwa later said of her adventure, "It was as if I went [to Europe] to meet wars." Despite that, she thought it was her "greatest good fortune" to have had the opportunity to encounter all the great music Suzuki had intended her to hear.[26]

6

"NO SUCH THING AS A BORN GENIUS"

A YEAR AFTER SUZUKI SENT "GIRL GENIUS" Nejiko Suwa off to Europe, a "boy genius" emerged as if to fill the vacuum she left behind. It was early spring 1937 when Yoshimichi Toyoda, a multi-instrumentalist and a student of Suzuki's, asked his teacher to accept another pupil: his three-year-old son Koji.

At this point, such requests were not unusual. Since taking on four-year-old Toshiya Eto in 1932, Suzuki had unintentionally been acquiring a reputation for effectively teaching young children. Suzuki and Koji Toyoda had their first meeting in Tokyo's Nippon Seinenkan Hall, at Suzuki's studio recital. What Toyoda remembers of the day are fragments—he was, after all, just a toddler. But he recalls going up on stage to play Antonín Dvořák's "Humoresque," to his father's guitar accompaniment. They had been practicing the piece together at home. When they finished, the child received a huge round of applause; the public recognition left him buzzing with happiness. Then Suzuki approached him, patted him on the head, and said, "Ko-chan, you played very well." It was the beginning of a lifelong association.

Immediately after Toyoda's "debut," a newspaper gave him the boy genius title.[1] But Suzuki was not interested in such talk. What sparked his interest was little Ko-chan's home environment. (The term of endearment "-chan" is commonly applied to children's names or nicknames.) Music was abundant in the Toyoda household, even more so than it had been in Suwa's. Suwa had had only records to listen to, but Toyoda's father Yoshimichi played and taught various instruments, and the boy's mother, Mitsu, played piano and mandolin. The three-year-old had learned violin

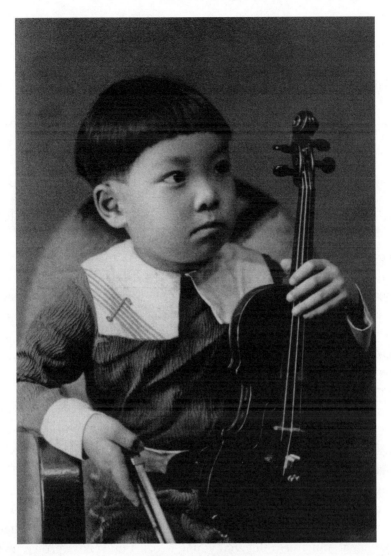

Koji Toyoda as a toddler in 1937. Toyoda would become one of Suzuki's cherished students, an esteemed performer, and, after Suzuki's death, leader of the talent education movement. *Talent Education Research Institute*

fundamentals at practically the same time he learned to speak. To Suzuki, this was a resounding affirmation that nurture was decisive in developing a child's musical ear. An ear for music was like an ear for language, and just as primary language acquisition was the opposite of exceptional, so too was musical ability. Thus, where others saw in young Toyoda a genius,

Suzuki saw the opposite. The toddler was evidence that anyone could be musically able if provided the right early exposure, under the encouragement of a caring adult.

The meeting with Toyoda brought about less an epiphany for Suzuki than affirmation of a belief based on observation. Upon hearing Walter Kaufmann effortlessly improvise various compositional styles on Einstein's piano, Suzuki had suspected that the secret lay in the man's early upbringing. And Kaufmann had indeed been brought up in an environment where he was allowed to "speak" music as his native language. Music was ever present in Kaufmann's childhood. He received his first music instruction from his uncle Moritz Kaufmann, a violinist and music historian who ran a music school in their hometown. Early on, he started lessons from distinguished teachers in Prague, including the composer Fidelio F. Finke and the violinist Willy Schweyda. To be sure, not everyone raised in a similar environment would reach Kaufmann's level of musical command; in fact, very few would. But for Suzuki, the bigger and lasting point was that all children could be guided toward a high degree of musical fluency, just as they mastered their mother tongues as a matter of course. Musical learning that earned the genius label could in fact be a standard part of growing up.[2]

Later in life, Suzuki said he first consciously connected musical ability with the process of native language acquisition in the early 1930s, after a rehearsal with his brothers. The group had been working on a Mozart quartet, which led to a discussion of the composer's music-filled childhood, including his early introduction to the works of J. S. Bach and Handel and the influence of Mozart's father Leopold, putatively the first person to have written a violin method book. The conversation had everyone imagining the home that young Mozart must have grown up in. It was at this point that Suzuki had his revelation. He was so moved that he rose to his feet exclaiming, "Children throughout Japan all speak Japanese!" Puzzled by this statement of the obvious, the others urged him to explain. What just dawned on Suzuki, he said, was that all children must have been endowed with "great brains." How else could they learn the intricate grammar, difficult nuances, and vast vocabulary of their native language? Children accomplish this tremendous task without even thinking about it. Suzuki posited that adults everywhere must be doing something right if they were able to nurture children's linguistic ability. Why could a similar approach not be applied to any other formidable undertaking, like learning to play the violin?[3]

Children mimic the speech they hear around them until they get it right. Even though they make mistakes along the way, they never give up until they become fluent, because they naturally intuit the joy of being able to express and communicate through language. At the same time, adults guide and nurture them, either consciously or unconsciously, by infusing the environment with "correct" speech. Learning music, for most of us, does not come as naturally as acquiring a mother tongue. But, Suzuki thought, one could make this process as natural as possible. The trick was to ensure that music was part of the child's everyday environment, such as by routinely playing recordings of great musical performances at home, while turning all the seemingly daunting, technical motions of playing music into fun activities.

In order to replicate a natural process of language acquisition and entice any and all children to become fluent in music, Suzuki needed a gripping approach that would keep youngsters—famous for their short attention spans—engaged. Specifically, he set out to create an appealing, incremental repertoire that could be used to tackle technical aspects of violin playing without making them seem like chores. The brilliance of his strategy is evident in his adaptations of "Twinkle, Twinkle, Little Star." Already in the 1930s, Suzuki was using the popular lullaby to introduce his younger students to their instrument. This was his game-changing answer to the traditional model of etude books, which, to Suzuki's puzzlement, often required that beginners use the entire bow to play long notes, which are difficult to sustain.

Instead of demanding the almost-impossible, Suzuki developed several rhythmic variations on "Twinkle" that would ask far less of children, so that they could from early on produce tones that sounded like, and indeed were, the stuff of music. Suzuki's insight was that long pulls and pushes of the bow made it more difficult to exert even and consistent pressure across the bowing motion, maintain steady speed, and keep an optimal point of contact between the bow and the strings. Such control was attainable, in most cases, only with considerable practice. Thus beginners had to be taught using a small amount of the bow—the short bowing required for, say, the *taka taka ta ta* rhythm of the first "Twinkle" variation. Suzuki observed that, in this way, even three- and four-year-olds could produce pleasant, ringing notes without making the infamously squeaky beginner's sound. The amount of the bow used could then be gradually increased as the repertoire unfolded, without compromising basic tonal quality.[4]

The 1930s were a gestation period for the Suzuki repertoire, which would be compiled into ten books after the war. Aside from the "Twinkle" variations, his students played François-Joseph Gossec's Gavotte, Friedrich Seitz's student concertos, Handel's sonatas, and Arcangelo Corelli's *La Folia,* all of which would appear in the method books. Karl Böhm's "Perpetual Motion" was a fun, lively staple of young violinists in Suzuki's prewar studio but was not included in the original method books for copyright reasons. (In the 1990s, after the copyright expired, this "unofficial" Suzuki piece would finally be included in the revised edition of Book 4 of the Suzuki Method.) Takeshi Kobayashi, one of the first generation of children Suzuki taught, confirmed that they played most of the current Suzuki repertoire pieces. "We were all guinea pigs," he told me. Suzuki also continued to use certain etude books for technical development, referring most frequently to Heinrich Ernst Kayser's *Thirty-Six Elementary and Progressive Studies.*[5]

In lessons, Suzuki was already exhibiting a flair for conveying complicated points playfully, thereby communicating the essentials without intimidating or boring his students. Recognizing that children often needed to learn by doing rather than through dry recitations of technical matters, he came up with clever demonstration techniques. For instance, to teach the muscular control necessary for even and smooth bowing, he would ask the student to hold the bow at the tip rather than the frog. The frog, usually a piece of ebony with metal fittings, is considerably heavier than the tip. By reversing standard expectations and placing the weight of the frog at the tip, Suzuki taught his students to be more thoughtful about how they distributed pressure across the length of a bow. By hearing the difference in sound, the student could experience firsthand—not just through explanation—the importance of weight distribution and could conclude, empirically, that in order to produce a smooth tone, they had to apply the same amount of pressure to the strings no matter which part of the bow was making contact. This "reversed bow" (*sakasayumi*) trick is still being used in many Suzuki studios, nearly a century later.[6]

By 1939, Suzuki's painstaking work with young children was showing conspicuous results. The eleven-year-old Toshiya Eto, who had been taking lessons with Suzuki since he was four, won a top prize in the violin section of the Eighth Annual Music Competition (today called the Music Competition of Japan). The establishment of this competition reflected a worldwide trend. Like the modern Olympic Games held in the spirit of cultural revival harking back to ancient Greece, music competitions had long historical roots. But unlike the modern Olympics with their ostensible insistence on amateurism, many music competitions were intended to discover future professionals, who would also generate business opportunities for those around them. It was no coincidence that the Naumburg Competition, one of the first modern-era classical music competitions, was held in New York in 1925. The city was the center of the American concert-management industry. Winning there improved one's chances of signing with a New York agent, which might lead to concert engagements, recording contracts, and, more and more, radio and other media exposure. True, such commercial interests were less overtly felt in European competitions. The International Chopin Competition in Warsaw, founded in 1927, and the Eugène Ysaÿe Competition (later renamed the Queen Elisabeth Competition), founded in Brussels in 1937, were both celebrations of national cultural legacies. At the same time, however, many an international career was propelled by those competitions, too. Nejiko Suwa heard David Oistrakh, the inaugural winner in Brussels, during the competition rounds and was in awe of his performance.[7]

The Annual Music Competition that Eto won in 1939 came to serve a particular function: identifying very young talents emerging outside formal conservatory structures. As such, prizewinners usually had received some sort of early childhood music education, and while Eto was young when he won the competition, he was not exceptionally so. In 1936, 1937, and 1938, the top prizes in violin went respectively to Hiroshi Hatoyama, Mary Esther Iwamoto, and Hisako Tsuji, all of whom were born in 1926, putting their older competitors to shame. Hatoyama was the son of a legendary Okinawan karate master and a preschool teacher, both avid amateur musicians; thanks in part to the patronage of an influential Christian educator, he was able to work with top instructors. Iwamoto, born to an American mother and a Japanese father, started playing violin early under Anna Ono. Bullied for being "mixed-blooded," she left school early to devote most of her time to the violin. Tsuji was the daughter of a professional orchestra violinist and dreamt of becoming the next Nejiko Suwa.[8]

Suzuki used the occasion of the competition to promote the theory that effective teaching and a nurturing environment were the bedrock of talent. To prove his point, he asked the competition jury to indulge him and allow Koji Toyoda, now six years old, to play the required preliminary-round piece for them: J. S. Bach's Violin Concerto in A Minor. As soon as the boy played it, it was clear that he could have easily proceeded to the final round. But Suzuki asked the judges not to score the performance. He merely wanted them to understand that, although they were marveling at the ability of eleven-year-olds, by the age of six any child could attain the level of playing ability that little Ko-chan had just demonstrated. It was not that Toyoda was a genius; as far as Suzuki was concerned, there was "no such thing as a born genius." The secret was that the boy learned the violin as his mother tongue. Suzuki bolstered his claim by announcing that he took on all of his young students indiscriminately, without auditions, and was recognizing remarkable progress in every one of them.[9]

It was not easy to convince the jury or, for that matter, the wider public. Toyoda was already three years into his status as a boy genius, and, with his competition win, Eto was also receiving the prodigy treatment. What is more, the research of the time seemed to show that musical talents—perhaps more than any other talents—were inborn. In 1919 the American psychologist Carl Seashore had introduced what came to be called the Seashore Tests of Musical Ability, which constituted the first known attempt to produce a scientifically calibrated measurement of musical expression, understanding, and appreciation. Based on the test results, Seashore believed that musical aptitude was inherited. His tests, however, were unable to show what he claimed they did, owing to a serious theoretical oversight. The battery was administered to fifth-graders, who would take the test again in eighth grade; as a result, Seashore was unable to address the fundamental question of whether a fifth- or eighth-grader deemed nonmusical could have achieved higher level of musical aptitude had they been instructed with an effective methodology from an earlier age. As administered, the tests were also subject to numerous flaws. For instance, one of the tests asks subjects to distinguish various pitches from each other, but doing so requires excellent pitch reproduction, which has not been easy with historical technology. In any case, Suzuki had been teaching a much younger group of children than those whom Seashore tested.[10]

Yet Suzuki's demonstration was hardly scientific, either. Toshiya Eto and Koji Toyoda were not the everyday kids that Suzuki presented them as. Both were exceptional, as evidenced by the distinguished careers each would later enjoy. True, they probably would not have risen quite so high without Suzuki's instruction beginning in early childhood. But one cannot reverse that argument and conclude that all children would be able to play like those two remarkable violinists, if only all children were brought up with similar nurturing. And Suzuki's dedication to unconditional acceptance of students was less than met the eye. His students may not have auditioned, but they were pre-screened in the sense that they would almost always have had unusually involved and dedicated parents. Their family backgrounds and financial resources might have varied, but those students all had the advantage of abundant parental commitment, which was an absolute precondition for their successful musical development. Neither Eto nor Toyoda, nor any other first-generation Suzuki violinists, was a typical Japanese child of the 1930s.

One measure of Toyoda's parental commitment is that his mother and father picked up their lives—and that of Koji's younger brother, who would also begin his violin studies—and moved so that their son could study with Suzuki. The Toyodas had lived in Hamamatsu, but the light-footed Suzuki frequently gave lessons in Nagoya, so the family first followed him there. After two years, they resettled again in Tokyo to be closer to Suzuki's main base. The family made it their utmost priority that the children be taught by Suzuki.

Between repeated moves and his dedication to the violin, Toyoda had a lonely childhood, with only his brother to play with. When he was not playing with his brother, he was practicing. Then his mother became ill and had to recuperate at her parents' home. Toyoda adored his father, but the man was uncompromising when it came to his son's violin practice. Toyoda has a very early memory of being locked in the closet alongside the family's futon beddings. It was punishment for his unruliness during practice.

The little boy's social life improved when he started elementary school, but during his first year, his mother died. At this point, the unceasing routine of violin lessons, at home and at Suzuki's house, with his father always chaperoning, became a kind of glue for the family, helping them adjust to life without their wife and mother. From time to time, that routine was interrupted by trips to the NHK radio studio, where Toyoda's performances were broadcast live.[11]

As time passed, Toyoda saw more and more children at Suzuki's studio. The number of young violinists under Suzuki's tutelage was fast multiplying, so much so that in his first decade of teaching, he taught about a hundred children.[12] The other children provided a sense of community that Toyoda otherwise lacked. When he was seven years old, another boy his age turned up for lessons. His name was Kenji Kobayashi, and his older brother Takeshi would soon join the studio as well. Accompanying the brothers was their father, Yonesaku Kobayashi, an eccentric and creative filmmaker who captured the first footage of living leprosy pathogens and made a host of scientific documentaries. Like so many parents who sent their children Suzuki's way, Yonesaku Kobayashi dreamt of becoming a violinist himself. The father's apparent projection onto his sons of his own unrealized yearning made life extremely difficult for them. Yet the Kobayashi brothers probably could not have become the professional violinists that they did without their father's near-maniacal drive and their mother's practical support, which included copying their music scores by hand. Yonesaku saw Toyoda as a rival to his sons and even resorted to spying on Toyoda's home practice. Despite their intense surroundings, however, camaraderie grew between Koji Toyoda and Kenji Kobayashi.[13]

Suzuki was wary of such competitiveness arising among his students and their parents. Yet his approach tended to stoke rivalries, and still does to this day. The Suzuki Method aims to nurture every child's potential, but every child does not have the same potential. And since all of the children use the same method books, it is easy to compare one child's progress with another's. Human nature being what it is, slow learners—and their parents—are sometimes looked down upon by those working through the books at a faster pace, creating a kind of "talent hierarchy" within a Suzuki Method studio.[14]

Suzuki's answer was, in effect, to ask students and parents to set aside their baser instincts. He did not admonish them outright but rather reminded them of what should be a higher purpose of learning. To this end, he urged students to judge themselves in terms of their own progress, not in comparison to others. Because of the Suzuki Method's emphasis on group-playing—a system that would emerge after the war—its underlying philosophy is often seen as collectivist rather than individualistic. But Suzuki was in his own way a strident individualist, who believed that students, teachers, parents, and adults generally could all become better people through self-reflection. The results of such an enlightened perspective would, he thought, be twofold. First, if every one of us tried to be the best we could possibly be, and if adults guided every child in the most nurturing way possible, society would be home to more wholesome individuals. Second, the average skill level would rise. "Great geniuses," he noted, "do not get born where the existing standards are low to begin with." In Suzuki's view, genius was attainable only with a lifetime of work and only by standing apart from a larger field of capable individuals. Already in the prewar period, Suzuki was thinking along these lines, and he was not just thinking about violin, but about a much bigger picture. He could see that his approach to early childhood education might revolutionize teaching and learning more broadly and reorient Japan's increasingly competitive society.[15]

Competitiveness was inevitable in a growing country. In the 1920s and the 1930s, Japan was feeling the impact of a population explosion brought on by the previous half century's rapid industrialization and urbanization. Further encouraging population growth was a kind of imperialist ethos, encapsulated in popular slogans such as "Rich Country, Strong Army" (*Fukoku Kyohei*) and "Good Wife, Wise Mother" (*Ryosai Kenbo*), which asserted that virtuous women produced as many children as possible, the better to ensure that the empire would have all the soldiers it needed. The crude birth rate, calculated as the number of live births per 1,000 population, hit a historic high of 36 in 1920. (By comparison, recent data put the US crude birth rate under 12 and the rate in Japan at 7—about a third of the world average and one of the lowest rates anywhere.) There were over 2 million births in Japan in 1920, 1.2 million more than the number of births in 1870. All the while, advancements in medicine continued to reduce infant mortality. As a result, the total population increased from 21 million to 56 million in the same period. Over the next two decades, until the late 1930s when material restrictions related to the war in China began taking a toll, the birth rate declined only moderately from this peak.[16]

One conspicuous social change precipitated by this runaway population growth was the intensification of competition for school placement. In 1927 alone, almost 70,000 young people were denied admission to middle or high school, neither of which was compulsory—or guaranteed. The chilling phrase "entrance exam hell" (*jyuken jigoku*) entered the lexicon around this time; admission to state and publicly funded schools was decided on the basis of an applicant's performance on a single entrance exam administered on specific days. Students, naturally, were placed under enormous pressure to perform.[17]

To its credit, the Ministry of Education acknowledged the need for reform, as it was clear that exam preparations were leading to "multiple adverse effects on the future of [Japanese] youths." The ministry drew up reforms to take effect in 1928. Most importantly, entrance exams were abolished, and middle and high schools were to instead base admissions on report cards and interviews. Yet this new arrangement, well-meaning though it was, gave rise to new problems. Now school administrators had discretion, which created space for corruption, as schools were tempted to pad or even falsify student records to help their graduating students gain admission to later grades. Within two years, the ministry was forced to concede defeat and reinstate the old exam system—a system that remains largely intact to this day, along with the phrase, and reality of, "entrance exam hell."

The shortage of spots in desirable public schools was a product not only of population growth but also changing attitudes toward education. Especially in urban centers, parents were increasingly interested in ensuring that their children would grow up to be eligible for white collar jobs, which portended the best possible economic future in a modernizing country. In addition, the tradition of the multigenerational family under a single roof was quickly dissolving in favor of nuclear-family households. With fewer adults around to guide and nurture, the advice that "it takes a village to raise a child" was less and less viable for urban Japanese families. In the absence of the proverbial village, more families desperately sought schools that would aid in their children's intellectual, moral, and social development.

Responding to such urgent needs, the Taisho Era, in much the same way that it fostered the growth of political liberalism, gave rise to social experiments in the field of education. As adults looked for new opportunities for their children, many Japanese became enamored with the same progressive education movements that were taking off in Europe and North America. In another example of modernization-by-Westernization, the Taisho Free Education Movement (*Taisho Jiyu Kyoiku Undo*) drew enthusiastically on the pedagogical writings of John Dewey, Maria Montessori, and Rudolf Steiner, all of which were contemporaneously introduced to Japanese readers.

A more distant, and surprisingly overlooked, philosophical precedent for Japan's changing education landscape was provided by Robert Owen, the early nineteenth-century Welsh entrepreneur, social reformer, and educator. Owen famously started experimental schools in New Lanark, Scotland, and New Harmony, Indiana, a town he purchased in hopes of installing a utopian community. Those experiments had emerged in response to a constellation of problems brought on by the Industrial Revolution in Europe: problems caused by overpopulation, rapid urbanization, and absence of effective public education—the very kinds of problems that Japan was now confronting. Like the operators of Owen's schools, Taisho educators focused on self-directed, child-centered education, often incorporating music and arts-related subjects. New private schools founded on such principles included the Seikei Elementary School (1912), Seijo Elementary School (1917), Jiyu Gakuen (1921), and Tamagawa Gakuen (1929), which branched out of Seijo.

At the same time, Japanese writers were beginning to preach the importance of early education in the home. Examples of this genre were Shozo Aso's *Principles and Practice of Home Education* (1915), Kichisaburo Sasaki's *Home Improvements and Home Education* (1917), Genzo Ichikawa's *Home Education* (1924), and Kuniyoshi Obara's *Pedagogy for Mothers*, published in two volumes (1925 and 1926). Many of these authors were teachers, and quite a few were inspired by Christian egalitarian principles. Obara, a devout Christian, was founder of Tamagawa Gakuen.[18]

Another leading figure in early childhood education was Haruko Hatoyama. A cofounder of Kyoritsu Women's Academy and the progenitor of a prominent political and academic dynasty, Hatoyama wrote the influential 1923 book *Education of One's Child,* which discusses approaches to homeschooling before children enter elementary school. "The goal of home education," she writes, "is the formation of the child's body, intellect, and character," acquired through good habits passed on by the parents. Hatoyama, like some education reformers in the West, argued that children possessed a right to education. Indeed, and even more so, "children have the uncontested right to be raised properly," she writes, suggesting that parental carelessness is a kind of crime. Her book sounded a prenatal warning of sorts, calling on adults to better understand the challenges of parenting before having children. And once a child was born, it was up to the parents—in particular the mother, who was expected to stay home with child until school age—to stimulate the baby's senses. This was done, Hatoyama said, by constantly exposing the baby to music, including singing lullabies and playing simple instruments.[19]

The child-centered, holistic approaches recommended by Japanese early education literature resonated with Suzuki. As he continued to see progress in his students, he became more convinced that a conducive home environment was essential to all learning, whether musical, academic, moral, or otherwise. At-home learning was continuous with formal education, he believed, as children needed to build basic social habits and intellectual skills in order to perform their best once in school. In this way, home education could have enormous impact on later life, overdetermining who succeeds and who does not in school and therefore what opportunities are available to children once they grow up.

Of course, not every home was in fact conducive to learning. Such differences might be overcome with individually catered, needs-specific guidance, but few families could afford the private schools that provided it. And while there were publicly funded experimental schools in Tokyo and Yokohama that embraced progressive education agendas, these were too few to meet demand. So parents stretched their funds.

Takeshi Kobayashi, for instance, received an expensive private education at the liberal Tamagawa Gakuen middle school. Alas, he was expelled when he was caught dodging a train fare. Many years later Kobayashi surmised that his expulsion probably came as a relief to his father, the freelance documentary filmmaker. The family could ill afford the school tuition on top of violin lessons, even though they were paying only for his younger brother Kenji. Suzuki, in his typical openhanded manner, waived Takeshi's fee.[20]

Financial hardship was one obstacle to holistic education. Another was the rise of ultranationalism. Even as Westernization and attendant educational experiments continued throughout the 1930s, public schools were turning into organs of right-wing indoctrination, as detailed below. This alarming trend, accompanied by militarization of all aspects of society, did not set in overnight, nor was it so total that Western-style education and music disappeared. Even during times of the most intense, xenophobic ultranationalism, classical music had its place in Japan—unlike jazz, which was deemed egregiously decadent and was banned in the middle of the war with the United States. The Suzuki Quartet was actively recording at least until the late 1930s. And Suzuki was able to immerse himself in research and teaching. As late as six weeks before Japan's attack on Pearl Harbor, his studio held a recital before a packed audience at the 2,000-seat venue Hibiya Kokaido. And his household in Yoga, a plush Tokyo suburb less than three miles south of the Teion music school, remained a window on the Western world. Both Koji Toyoda and Takeshi Kobayashi, in their eighties, remembered the Suzuki version of the West. Toyoda recalled a lesson in Suzuki's home, after which Waltraud made him lunch. It was just a slice of bread with butter and jam, but it was like nothing he had ever tasted. Kobayashi's memory is more bittersweet. One day at a lesson, he had to use the bathroom, but he did not excuse himself because he was intimidated by the prospect of using the Suzukis' Western-style flush toilet. Panicked, the boy had an unfortunate accident.[21]

Unbeknownst to Suzuki's young violinists, a combination of ideological and strategic factors was driving Japan onto a hazardous policy course. The ongoing economic slump reduced confidence in the liberal, democratic governance of the Taisho period, buttressing the position of the ultranationalists who loudly called out the West's sudden, hypocritical about-face with respect to imperialism. Britain, France, and the United States were all espousing internationalism and self-determination, even as they continued to hold on to their colonial possessions. Large segments of the Japanese public still expected their country to compete for imperial prestige; to do otherwise would be to squander all the human and material sacrifices that the Japanese nation had been making since Meiji times.

But this imperialist premise came back to haunt Japan both strategically and diplomatically, especially after an ill-planned, full-scale war with China broke out in the second half of 1937. Japan both expected and needed a quick victory, as domination in China was supposed to help Japan out of its economic doldrums by ensuring access to resources and new markets, while containing a Soviet advance from the north. But the situation spiraled out of control. In response to Chinese resistance, Japanese troops inflicted atrocities on their enemies; when news of war crimes spread, Japan was dealt punitive sanctions by the United States and its partners. As it became isolated economically and politically, Japan drew closer to the fascist powers of Italy and Germany, fellow rogue states.

Military and diplomatic missteps made for an increasingly restive domestic situation, leading to fears within the government of an uprising from below—the kind foreshadowed by the nearly successful military rebellion, the 2-26 Incident of 1936. So Japan's diffident and irresponsible leaders did what they could to project strength: they effectively turned over policymaking to midranking military strategists who had no long-term vision for solving the country's problems but who did have a fanatical faith in their own bellicosity and in Japan's destiny as leader of Asia. It was madness to think that Japan could fight the United States while still engaging in the quagmire in China. But those strategists, now put in the driver's seat of Japan's future, loudly trumpeted a now-or-never approach: the longer Japan waited to free itself from the oppression of the United States and its allies, they contended, the less opportunity Japan would have to exploit natural resources in Southeast Asia to keep fighting in China. The humiliation of never putting up a fight, so the argument ran, was worse than a real defeat. War with the United States was a suicidal gamble, but no leaders, military or civilian, were brave enough to say so given the high emotion of the appeal. By late autumn

1941, those at the top, who could and should have stopped the momentum toward an unwinnable war, had talked themselves into believing that they were in the midst of an existential emergency—that a confrontation with the West was inevitable, so they might as well start the war themselves. A secret timetable for mobilization was set—even before diplomacy failed—and within a couple of months the die was cast with the attack on Pearl Harbor.

Children's education had already started suffering as Japan contemplated a suicidal clash. The intensification of the war in China compelled the government to announce national emergencies and reorganize society for mobilization on the home front. The National Education Order issued in March 1941 declared all public elementary schools would be renamed National Schools (*kokumin gakko*) and "carry out elementary general education in accordance with the Imperial Way" in order "to provide our people with the basic training required of Imperial Subjects." In plain language, this meant that the point of public education was now to cultivate and celebrate the virtues of self-sacrifice and loyalty to the emperor, with the utmost emphasis placed on obedience. Challenging authorities was out of the question.

One concrete manifestation of indoctrination was the *hoanden*. A hoanden is a kind of shrine that houses imperial portraits and a copy of the Imperial Rescript on Education, a government guideline filled with paternalistic, Neo-Confucian vocabulary that had been promulgated by the Meiji emperor in 1890. While these structures existed before, at the National Schools, the hoanden became a sacred object. The children were taught to bow deeply when they passed by the hoanden; during the war, teachers would lose their lives trying to protect the shrines from air raids. In classrooms too, changes were palpable. Textbooks overflowed with military slogans and music classes with martial tunes.[22]

Many Japanese supported these measures—economic, strategic, educational—but most just kept their heads down. Suzuki was in neither camp. In his own way, he acted bravely and independently, sounding a voice of protest. As the country's education system crumbled around him, he felt that the need for comprehensive reform was urgent. Not everyone agreed, of course, that the system was failing, but Suzuki was appalled by what he witnessed: the undermining of humanistic values. In their place, schools were inculcating their students in xenophobia and the sort of steroidal national self-regard that can only betray a deep-seated sense of inferiority and grievance. Suzuki, in contrast, shared Einstein's conviction that all people are the same, that no one is superior or inferior. That perspective undergirded his educational mission and his views concerning human development, and it was absolutely incompatible with the new official line.

In September 1941, Suzuki responded with a treatise called *Powerful Education* (*Chikarazuyoki Kyoiku*), in which he laid out the twin pillars of his philosophy, namely, the concepts of talent education and the mother-tongue approach. These ideas constituted frontal rebukes of the government, but Suzuki did pay lip service to the powers that be. Throughout the document, he takes pains to suggest that his proposed reforms are the right choice for Japan. He even lauds the National Education Order, meant to create "a genuinely Japanese, strong, industrious nation possessed of superior intellect," which was especially necessary "in light of the present world situation." Yet, without blatantly appearing subversive, *Powerful Education* conveys Suzuki's dissenting spirit, alongside the substantive ideas that would animate his postwar work. Liberally sprinkling his words with typographical emphases, he writes:

The new system, as I understand it, is meant to be an innovative and meritocratic system. It reexamines our past educational policy that had been a grab-bag of foreign educational approaches . . . But [the new reform plan] strikes me as impossible if *things remain the way they are now* . . . If we were to try to achieve our innovative goals, it would not be enough to merely have educators make up their minds to achieve them. For that, I think we need a clear and unwavering approach to direct us so that we can carry out *powerful education* effectively. The aim of the National School system is to *bring up all children, with not one left behind, as fine Japanese* . . . But do all our educators really have the knowhow to make all of them into fine Japanese? In reality, most Japanese educators approach their tasks with a sense of resignation, along the lines of, "One cannot alter what one is born with." For example, imagine a child having a hard time with math. Seeing this child, his teacher would be inclined to conclude: "This child is *born being not very smart, therefore he cannot be able"* or: "A genius or an ordinary person, either way, *one is born with what one has got* and one cannot do anything about it." As long as we keep on thinking in such a passive manner, educators cannot educate . . . The goal of "turning all children into fine Japanese" remains an empty declaration of intent if it lacks practical ways of achieving it . . . *There exists a way to ensure that not one child will be left behind.*

Despite the many formulaic references to the official goal of raising "fine Japanese," Suzuki was urging that Japan adopt a universally applicable methodology, an approach to education that could work anywhere and therefore stood at odds with the National Education Order's chauvinistic claims. Much of the book is devoted to Suzuki's research into what he considers a universal developmental pattern and, by extension, serves as a critique of the existing system, which, he suggests, discouraged such development.

The argument is far-reaching, indicting decades of stifling education practices, which were made that much worse by the rise of ultra-nationalism. It is only when he introduces his mother-tongue approach that he falls back on his experience teaching violin. He knows that it works, he explains, because his young students have developed extraordinary playing abilities that invariably amaze adults. Given this experience, he argues that his methods can be applied to other subjects and in public school settings. True, most teachers did not have the luxury, as he did, of teaching students one-on-one. Striking a sympathetic tone, he notes that public school teachers are burdened by an overloaded curriculum and have neither the time nor the means to help all children, even if they notice that some are falling behind. He is aware of the vicious circle in which most teachers are trapped. The more that teachers try to keep up with the official curriculum, the more children get left behind.

But there are ways for everyone to get out of this rut, Suzuki insists. He offers three principles whose success he has observed firsthand. First, the teacher must not let the task at hand look difficult to children; the student must be able to feel that the challenge can be overcome. Second, the teacher must not expect great leaps in progress but should instead proceed in incremental steps. Finally, the teacher must not obsess over tangible results. Rather, teachers should always have foremost in mind the larger goal of education, which is not merely to pass on knowledge but to "empower" students, so that they will eventually be motivated enough to want to aim for higher goals. He uses a metaphor of playing catch, in which the teacher does not simply throw a ball at the student but expects the student to catch it and then throw it back—faster, stronger, each time with more control than before.[23]

His words carry a certain weight, as Suzuki draws on his decade of successfully working with young children facing a variety of challenges and possessing a range of temperaments. Despite their differences, he says, the same formula of goal-setting, encouragement, repetition, and memorization has proven effective with all of them. He is certain that the manner and method of teaching matter more than students' innate potential, so he proposes that his formula be applied to all school subjects. For, given the great variations in children's home environments, it is only at schools that such an education can be universally realized.

He concedes that, even though his principles are simple and have worked in his own studio, implementing them in schools will not be easy. Many forces are arrayed against reform. Most basically, teachers have a hard time *not* treating students differently, according to their perceived ability. After all, variation in learning capacities does accrue before children start school. So when a teacher encounters a "good" student, he or she usually makes the hasty error of presuming the student is blessed with a special talent. Teachers, Suzuki suggests, should be encouraged to investigate the reasons for such variations in students, and they will likely find answers in the home environment. And teachers must resist the desire to treat better-performing students differently, which will make the "good" student arrogant while feeding resentment in the rest of the class. Suzuki opposes placing high-achievers in accelerated courses, for he thinks they could still benefit from repeating and refining what they already know how to do.

Although Suzuki speaks forcefully on these points, in his private teaching practice, he was not so categorical. As a working educator, he well knew that students learn at different rates and that quick studies lose interest when they are not challenged. In his studio, he was always accommodating fast learners by teaching them more difficult repertoire, while still making sure that they repeated and improved the pieces they had already learned. This option has never been available to public school teachers, or even to many in private schools. Concerning public schools, he would, in time, become more amenable to the idea of separate courses for advanced students and those with specialized interests.

While Suzuki never wavered on the priority of nurture over nature, he also never denied the existence of variance in demonstrated abilities. And he knew that such variance gave rise to social comparisons, making it yet more difficult to convince people that every child really could develop a high degree of ability in any subject or endeavor, whether music, athletics, painting, or mathematics. Suzuki believed that the true value of education lay in doing and being better today than one did yesterday, but few people actually think and live this way, suffering comparison only to their own latent potential. The kind of humility Suzuki proselytized is as admirable as it is hard to find in real life. Even those who share his high ideals on this score can only do so much to protect their children from competition and assessment. Suzuki never gave up the struggle, however, and took his convictions to his grave. The principles he developed across the 1930s, and put to paper in 1941, remained with him forever.

It is important, though, to keep in mind exactly what Suzuki was arguing and why. He was not of the view that people should never compete or were inevitably hurt by engaging in competition. For example, those of his students who grew focused on becoming professional musicians would be at a great disadvantage if they eschewed competitions, so Suzuki did not prevent them taking part. At times, he even acted as a competition judge himself. But Suzuki did feel that competition, especially at a very young age, was damaging to character formation. He therefore rejected prize-giving culture in elementary schools, or any other attempts to put a small number of students on a pedestal.

Suzuki's holistic vision also led him to reject homework and exams. In *Powerful Education*, he describes both as feeding a misguided notion that children need to experience "hard work." Instead, he argues that these demands merely create busywork that keeps children up at night when they should be in bed. Sounding remarkably ahead of his time, he suggests that the stress of homework and exams makes young people sick, an argument one is far more likely to hear today, when biological research has shown that chronically elevated levels of stress hormones contribute to all manner of physical and mental health problems in children and adults.[24]

At the end of *Powerful Education*, Suzuki outlines two policy proposals whose ambition is nothing less than a complete overhaul of Japan's education system. One is the establishment of a national research institute to explore how best to nurture and instruct preschool-aged children and to guide families in developing "the health, character, and talent" of children before they enter elementary schools. Occasional lectures on early childhood education were not enough, he believed, because the parents and guardians who bothered to attend were probably already doing what was necessary in the way of education at home. To universalize the benefits of early education, the government would have to take the lead. Suzuki thought the proposed national institute should have an outpost in every neighborhood, much like the small police boxes (*koban*) one finds all over Japan. These outposts would offer free health checks and parenting consultations to even the poorest families.

The second proposal is for the establishment of yet another research institute, this one geared toward elementary education. This outfit would unify and oversee the school curriculum. And more importantly in Suzuki's eyes, it would carry out the reeducation of schoolteachers. He suggests selecting exemplary teachers from all over Japan and allowing them to run an independent school in each city. He believed that such schools, run by people with a high awareness of what education should achieve, would naturally produce great results, with not one child left behind, and would provide a model for other schools to emulate. This, in turn, would produce desirable spillover effects throughout Japan and in short order.[25]

These proposals bear an uncanny resemblance to the ideas of Robert Owen, the utopian Welshman. His Institute for the Formation of Character, established in 1816 in the Scottish mill town of New Lanark, was intended to "form the new character of the rising population." Owen, like Suzuki, was a believer in the power of the early childhood environment; Owen advocated that moral character formation had to begin from the

Illustration (1823) of a dance class at Robert Owen's Institute for the Formation of Character, with live string music and observers looking on. Some of Suzuki's teaching practices bore strong, if coincidental, resemblance to Owen's. *The JR James Archive/flickr/CC BY-NC 2.0*

moment a child "can walk alone." His school, attended by children ranging from one to six years of age, was famously effective in its lessons, which included music and dance drills. Learning was accomplished primarily through observation, reflection, and experimentation. This empiricist approach was also much like that promoted by the Swiss educator Johann Heinrich Pestalozzi, Owen's contemporary. Pestalozzi was in turn inspired by Enlightenment thinkers of the previous era, especially Jean-Jacques Rousseau. These famous advocates were Suzuki's kindred spirits not just in their awareness of the necessity of an early start and a nurturing environment but also in their belief that love, patience, and benevolence were educational principles. (Though in Rousseau's case, his actual practice of abandoning his illegitimate children makes his commitment to these principles highly questionable.) Suzuki, living in a militarized, chauvinistic society where coerced discipline was becoming the norm, would have found the Owenite approach of sticking to "a kind voice and a pleasant manner" appealing indeed.[26]

Suzuki also had international contemporaries. Among them was the Hungarian composer Zoltán Kodály. The two men never met, and it is doubtful that they knew each other's work in this period, but Kodály would have agreed enthusiastically with Suzuki on the importance of early childhood education. Kodály's efforts to reform Hungary's elementary and middle school music curricula originated in the mid-1920s. A decade later, he and his colleague and former student Jenő Ádám launched a full-scale reform effort. Like Suzuki, Kodály pushed for a sequential learning program; acolytes eventually built it and called it the Kodály Method. Kodály's pedagogical and philosophical principles matched Suzuki's at the most basic level. Both men believed that every child had the right to develop fully and that regular schools should guide them effectively in that endeavor, beginning at the earliest age possible.

One stark difference, though, is that the Hungarian government adopted Kodály's project, while the Japanese government ignored Suzuki's. Indeed, it is rather astonishing that Suzuki did not face a worse fate given his daredevil writing. Still more remarkable is that he was allowed to publish it on the eve of Pearl Harbor. There are several possible reasons why *Powerful Education* eluded Japan's increasingly tight censorship. For one thing, censorship is always hard to enforce comprehensively; inevitably, something breaks through. Censorship was particularly challenging in Japan, where, before the ultranationalists began to dominate the climate of opinion in the late 1930s, the world of publishing had been lively, versatile, and growing, and a place where dissenting views were expressed. Banning therefore tended to be haphazard, and *Powerful Education* could have eluded the censors by sheer chance. Another possibility is that the book simply did not register as dangerous because it was seen as announcing a pipedream. One devious strategy of authoritarians is to selectively allow the publication of nonconformists, so as to disarm opponents who decry their illiberalism. Or perhaps there were just bigger fish to fry, what with the war in China and another approaching with the United States. Yet another possibility is that Suzuki had successfully cloaked his argument in patriotic language. Besides, Suzuki had powerful friends with links to the government. The book does not fail to mention the name of Marquis Tokugawa, noting his endorsement of Suzuki's educational approach. Despite his core belief in democratic socialism, Tokugawa did draw close to a group of military officers in the 1930s. The marquis was, as always, well-connected, and Suzuki's intimate association with the celebrated nobleman would likely have ensured publication even if all else failed.[27]

Whatever the actual circumstances surrounding the publication of *Powerful Education,* few were able to appreciate the revolutionary nature of Suzuki's proposals. Given his public profile, he was not immediately legible as a firebrand. He was not known for making waves, and he seemed himself to be a beneficiary of the society he was critiquing. Suzuki was the son of a famous and successful businessman, the leader of a noted quartet, and husband to a German woman he met while studying in Berlin. He was also the teacher of little geniuses. Multiple layers of exclusiveness and privilege surrounded Suzuki. That such a person could level a deep and thorough condemnation of Japanese education was hard to fathom.

That said, *Powerful Education* would likely have been a tough sell no matter its author. Suzuki's case in these pages is enormously ambitious, addressing not just music education, or even public education, but also the loaded and cherished concept of talent—and, to my mind, not very effectively. The discussion of talent leads to more questions than answers. A basic source of confusion is Suzuki's investment in the idea of talent; the term *saino kyoiku* or "talent education" is conspicuous throughout the book. But why focus on talent, instead of something more neutral, like ability? Why try to democratize a concept universally understood as exclusionary, even as less value-laden concepts also exist? Saino, in Japanese, implies the same generous dose of exceptionalism that talent does in English. The two characters comprising the term are *sai* (才) meaning exceptional, inborn ability, and *no* (能) meaning ability to get things done. Saino could, depending on context, be interpreted as referring simply to the potential to achieve certain tasks. Yet, in practice, saino connotes a rare possession that cannot be acquired through even hard work. What is more, in Japanese, talent is etymologically related to genius—*tensai* (天才), which combines the character *sai* with the character *ten* (天), meaning heaven. Genius is literally heaven-sent talent.

Suzuki's insistence that all children possess talent is especially striking given that others who share his educational vision see no need to redefine talent in this way. For instance, in *Jane Eyre* (1847), Charlotte Brontë presumes the canonical definition of talent while suggesting, through her fictional characters, that education can overcome the lack of it. The novel's namesake heroine, one of the most famous governesses in English literature, observes that her young pupil Adèle "had no great talents, no marked traits of character, no peculiar development of feeling or taste which raised her one inch above the ordinary level of childhood; but neither had she any deficiency or vice which sunk her below it." And so Jane Eyre will teach her, believing that, with proper guidance, the girl can be much improved. The role of an educator, then, is to ensure the welfare and progress even of those in whom "no great talents" can be discerned. In substance, this belief is not far removed from Suzuki's. What differs is mainly terminology.[28]

Yet there was a method to Suzuki's madness for talent. Yes, had he focused on ability or capacity rather than talent, his reform program might have been better understood by a greater number of people. But this would not have been enough for him. Suzuki was aiming for something more when he redefined talent as the manifestation, via learning and practice, of *noryoku soshitsu*, "innate potential" or "raw aptitude." These were inborn, while talent came to those who stretched their latent potential through nurture and effort. And the reason it was so important that talent be thus redefined was that Suzuki believed existing notions of talent were harmful to children and society at large.[29]

Experience taught Suzuki that children were oppressed by talent. He spent the 1930s developing a studio famed for teaching very young violinists, and in the process witnessed what labels like talented, genius, and prodigy did to his students and their families. Nejiko Suwa's identification as a genius ruined her family life and derailed her musical studies at a critical period in her development. Students who believed in their own talent were at risk of becoming egotists, and parents who believed in their children's talent became obsessed and hypercompetitive, provoking destructive rivalries and damaging their children emotionally and morally. Suzuki the empiricist trusted his own eyes, and what he saw was that no child should ever be called a genius in music or in any other pursuit.[30]

Suzuki's heterodox sense of talent was therefore central to his mission. He deliberately used this language in a new way, in order to protect children from the mistakes of adults. And he added the language of talent to almost everything he touched. One of the government organs he proposes in *Powerful Education* is called Saino Kyoiku Kenkyukai: the Talent Education Research Institute. When the Japanese government did not follow his advice—before or after the war—Suzuki built the institute himself. Today he is known as the founder of the Suzuki Method, a system for teaching and learning the violin and other instruments. But what he introduced in 1941 was more than that: talent education aimed at nothing less than a social revolution, and it was this idea that drove the work he would do for the rest of his life.

Only two months after the publication of *Powerful Education*, Japan went to war with the United States and its allies in a most spectacular fashion, with a set of successful stealth attacks carried out in the Pacific and Southeast Asia, including at the US naval base at Pearl Harbor. At least on the surface, the Japanese people embraced their country's new military adventure with something resembling euphoria, for at last they were fighting their true enemies. Over the previous four years, Japan had been fighting a war in China ostensibly to free Asia from corrupt Western influences—to restore Asia to Asian rule, specifically the enlightened rule of Japan. This official pan-Asianist war aim was adopted well after the conflict in China spiraled out of control, and many thoughtful Japanese, especially young intellectuals, were suspicious of the government's claim that Japan was fighting fellow Asians in order to free them. But now that the new phase of the war included actual Western, colonial powers, those suspicious minds were being allayed, if only for the time being.

Still, even at the height of anti-Westernism fueled by Pearl Harbor, the Japanese love of things Western, cultivated with gusto and at full speed over several generations since the Meiji Restoration, died hard. Certain expressions of Western culture remained unchecked or were even encouraged under the thin veneer of promoting Japanese patriotism and the war cause. The movie industry was the most salient example, using Western-style music in propaganda films like *The Naval Battle from Hawaii to Malaya* (1942), commissioned by the Navy Ministry for the one-year anniversary of Japan's victories at sea. The film's score was composed by Seiichi Suzuki (unrelated to Shinichi Suzuki), who had trained on Western instruments—organ, mandolin—and in European vocal styles. Despite the film's celebration of Japan's triumph over the West, the music is heavily Western, including tunes borrowed from Wagner's *Lohengrin* and *Die Walküre*. Perhaps that is not so incongruous, since the Germans were Japanese allies, but clearly some official contradictions were being overlooked. (Incidentally, the film's special effects were provided by Eiji Tsuburaya, whose brilliant postwar career included creating *Godzilla* and *Ultraman*.)

Even more than before, songs sung at schools were colored by military themes. The most famous was the plaintive "Umi Yukaba" ("If I Go to the Sea"), which idealizes honorable deaths in battle. The song is a chilling manifestation of the cult of self-sacrifice that reached extraordinary heights in wartime Japan, drawing on verses from an eighth-century Japanese poem. But despite its professed nativism, the song is set in the Western compositional form of a military march. Its composer, Kiyoshi Nobutoki, was the son of a Protestant pastor and had trained in Berlin with Georg Schumann, the longtime director of Singakademie, where Suzuki attended so many intoxicating chamber music recitals.

Suzuki carried on after the outbreak of the Pacific War as best he could, teaching and playing the violin. He also gave public talks on his educational philosophy, which were allowed presumably for the same reasons that *Powerful Education* had escaped censorship. His proselytizing efforts touched at least one young woman, who was expecting a baby. That baby, Nobuko Imai, went on to become one of the world's foremost violists. Likely sometime in 1942, her mother heard Suzuki's lecture on early childhood education while evacuating to Kamakura, about thirty miles south of Tokyo. After the war, recalling this lecture, she had her daughter study with Anna Ono.[31]

Suzuki kept up with his writing as well. Two years into the Pacific War, he had another manuscript ready for publication, but this one was banned: *Reform of Elementary School Education through the Mother Tongue Pedagogical Method*. Even Suzuki's Tokugawa connection could not help this time. Besides, it was no longer a time for publishing and reading books. Because of the increasingly dire war situation, Japanese were short of pretty much everything, including food, fuel, and paper. Day-to-day survival was a national priority.

Teion, the music school where Suzuki had been teaching since 1931, was also in deep trouble. Owing to political infighting and financial difficulties, the school operated from 1935 until 1939 without an official Ministry of Education certification, which meant that it was unable to confer a standardized degree. Suzuki did a great deal to backstop the flailing institution, acting as its president at one point and helping students by dipping into his own pocket. After regaining its officially certified status, Teion rebounded for a time; its strings department enjoyed a high reputation and its chamber groups were heard frequently on NHK radio. But the outbreak of the Pacific War checked that upward momentum. A couple of years into the war, there was no escaping total mobilization, and the school was nationalized and turned into a garment factory in 1944.[32]

Total mobilization meant that Suzuki Violin in Nagoya would also have to set its business aside. Already in 1943, it was ordered to manufacture seaplane floats. At this point, Suzuki decided to evacuate Tokyo and head to the mountains of Kiso Fukushima in Nagano Prefecture, 140 miles to the west. (Fukushima, another city, lies to the northeast.) Suzuki left Tokyo in part to encourage his coterie of loyal pupils— about fifty of them at the time—to do the same. The city would not be safe, he rightly figured, once US air raids started. Another reason was a sense of family obligation. His new mission in the Kiso Valley was to procure lumber for the factory's seaplane floats. Waltraud, meanwhile, joined a German expatriate community in Hakone, at the foot of Mount Fuji. The couple had spent more than a decade together in Tokyo. Their abrupt departure probably saved their lives.[33]

7

PICKING UP THE PIECES

FOR MOST JAPANESE, the war ended at noon on August 15, 1945, when NHK aired Emperor Hirohito's speech. The radio broadcast began with an announcer urging listeners to stand for the national anthem, "Reign of His Imperial Majesty." Then, for the first time ever, the nation heard the voice of an emperor. Many found Hirohito difficult to understand. His manner of speaking was labored and his voice high in pitch. The speech was filled with lofty, formal vocabulary rarely used in modern Japanese. Yet the emperor did not fail to communicate the gravity of the occasion: Japan was surrendering unconditionally to the Allied powers.

Some 3 million Japanese soldiers and civilians had died—and Japanese soldiers had killed or otherwise caused the deaths of many more in the parts of Asia they had occupied or destroyed. The exact number lost in China alone is hard to establish, but numerous researchers put the figure above 10 million after Japanese expansion began there in 1931. This was the war the emperor officially described as necessary for "Japan's self-preservation and the establishment of peace and stability in East Asia." No matter, the war had been a failure. Japan was vanquished and stripped of international legitimacy. For the sake of a better future, the country would first have to "endure the unendurable" and "suffer the unsufferable."

Beginning in late 1944 and ending with the nuclear attacks on Hiroshima and Nagasaki in August 1945, about 200 Japanese cities were bombed to ashes. Everyone lost something, or someone. Suzuki was no exception. There was no longer a life to return to in Tokyo. There was no Teion to teach at; the school-building-turned-garment-factory was wiped out in an air raid. There was no Suzuki Quartet to play in. Fumio, the group's cellist, composer, and arranger, was killed in the bombing of Nagoya. He had returned in order to help supervise the seaplane float operation after Masakichi died in 1944, at the age of eighty-five. Nagoya was raided several times; Fumio likely died during the bombing run of March 24, 1945, when 130 US B-29s obliterated an expansive area that included the violin factory, killing 1,617 civilians. According to a former student's recollection, Fumio had become skilled at extinguishing incendiary bombs, but when he tried that night, the bomb exploded and so did he.[1]

Suzuki was spared direct experience of the horrific air raids, but the circumstances of the war left him feeble and emaciated. Food was scarce, yet even by the standard of the time, Suzuki lived like an ascetic. He foraged in the mountains for barely edible plants and ate as little as he could, so that more would be left for others. There were many to feed: by the end of the war, Suzuki's household had grown with the arrival of siblings and their young children evacuating urban areas. Suzuki's niece Hiroko, who was born in 1940, had her first violin lessons from him during the war. The family lived in a simple, rented Japanese-style house—a far cry from Suzuki's Westernized home in Tokyo. His chief partner in the daily struggle to survive was his devoted younger sister Hina, a widow with two young sons, who managed Suzuki's household affairs in Waltraud's absence.[2]

After the war, it was not at all clear whether Suzuki's marriage would continue. Waltraud was intent on establishing her life as a working woman. Reinventing herself as Miss Joan Prange in a country now under US-led occupation, she worked at the information desk of the American Red Cross in Yokohama. Then she took clerical jobs in Tokyo, first at a Hong Kong–based shipping company and later at a British bank. Japan's defeat was a liberation for her. During and after the occupation, there were many opportunities to work for foreign organizations, and she could use her language skills to earn a decent living. There were fewer social obstacles, too. Waltraud could hold her head high working and being paid, something respectable housewives in prewar Japan were not inclined to do. From then on, the Suzukis lived separately, except during her occasional weekend visits.

Suzuki stayed in the Kiso Valley area, where he oversaw the family's lumber operation. Now, instead of producing materials for seaplane floats to be sent to Nagoya, the factory in Kiso would make traditional clogs. But Suzuki was more preoccupied than ever with the question of early childhood education. The trees he saw in the surrounding forest became a metaphor for the importance of the childhood environment. He noted that no two trees, even of the same kind, were ever the same; soil, light, and other environmental factors lent different characteristics to each tree. The differences were all the more apparent when logs were cut into lumber, revealing a huge range in color, texture, and grain. And yet another powerful example of the reverberation between the environment and children's learning was happening in front of his eyes. After two years in Kiso, he still could not speak in the local accent while his toddler niece could prattle away like a native.[3]

Clearly Suzuki was ready to set aside lumber and return to the work that had been interrupted. But where, and how? The answer turned out to be a school he would establish with the citizens of Matsumoto, a city 40 miles northeast of Kiso. Matsumoto had a certain allure that set it apart from other provincial Japanese cities. It had long been known for its natural beauty, culture, and scholarship. In 1945 its claims to fame were its sixteenth-century castle and Matsumoto Higher School (Matsumoto Kotogakko). Founded in the Taisho mold in 1919, "Matsuko" became legendary for its humanistic training of future elites heading for university and postgraduate degrees. My own paternal grandfather spent his formative years there. I inherited some of the books from his school-days, and they still impress me with their variety. Goethe, John Maynard Keynes, and Thomas Carlyle feature prominently in his library, and all in the original language.

Matsumoto entirely escaped US bombings, making it one of Japan's few intact cultural and education centers. The city became a regional hub of artists, intellectuals, and music lovers yearning for the kind of life they had before the war. One of them visited Suzuki in Kiso Fukushima: Tsuneo Maruyama, a postmaster and amateur violinist. He and his friend Heishiro Kanda had formed the Matsumoto Strings Society, which put on chamber music performances in the music shop that Kanda owned. The society was thriving, adding members. They even counted among their number a professional musician of some renown, the London-trained baritone Tamiki Mori, who had been Suzuki's colleague at Teion. When Maruyama learned from Mori that Shinichi Suzuki of the famous Suzuki Quartet was living only an hour away by train, he rushed to Kiso to beg him to coach his chamber group.[4]

Suzuki flatly declined the request, but something had sparked his interest. He and Hina paid a visit to the Strings Society in late 1945 or early 1946. Suzuki had not changed his mind; he reiterated to the organizers that he did not wish to teach the chamber group because, he explained, adults were guaranteed to be clumsy. "But, small children," he said, "I do want to teach them." And soon after this brief and enigmatic visit, he would return to Matsumoto to judge a music competition sponsored by the newspaper *Chunichi*. Suzuki had his eye on the city. It seemed like he could write his next chapter there, among the enthusiastic and culture-hungry locals.

One day in early May 1946, Suzuki arrived at Kanda's music shop armed with a thick bundle. It was both a proposal and a kind of manifesto, some 300 pages long, written on formal manuscript paper. The text outlines Suzuki's philosophy of early childhood education, focusing on the child's environment and making an impassioned case that effective guidance of the next generation would be vital to Japan's rebirth. With this in mind, he urges the people of Matsumoto to build a new music school, where he will demonstrate the effectiveness of his approach.[5]

It would be fair to say that Suzuki was high-minded, his head often stuck firmly in the clouds. But if he was attentive to anything on the ground, it was potential. He saw it in children. He saw it in Matsumoto and indeed in defeated Japan. The beginning of his Matsumoto endeavor coincided with a time of great uncertainty and equally great possibility. Japan's postwar constitution—called the Peace Constitution because of its clause renouncing war—would not be promulgated until November, leaving the country in a particularly liminal place. Children felt the weight of the moment. Only months earlier, the highest authorities were telling them that the ultimate honor was to die for their country in a holy war. Now, suddenly, the guns were no longer firing, and someone new was in charge. In March 1946, even before the constitution was in place, the first US Education Mission arrived, aiming to reconstruct Japan's schools.

Mineo Nakajima, a Matsumoto pharmacist's son, recalled in a 2006 newspaper series what it was like to be nine years old at the time of the surrender. He listened to the imperial broadcast with tears trickling down his little cheeks, his head buzzing with fears. He worried that everyone he knew would be imprisoned and tortured. Nothing of the sort happened, though, and he fell into a state of numbness. He did not know whether to be sad or happy. But when an officer from the US Education Mission drove up to his elementary school in a Jeep, the reality of the situation finally sank in. While chatting with students, the officer, named something like William Kerry, sat back in the teacher's chair and casually rested his dirty shoes on a student's writing desk—an unthinkable breach of etiquette in Japan, even for a senior military officer. Seeing this, Nakajima began to feel again. All at once, the awareness of national defeat hit him, as he understood that his education and his future were at the mercy of this GI and the victorious country he represented.[6]

But Suzuki was not content to let the Americans make all the decisions. The time to try new things was long overdue, he believed, and the art lovers of Matsumoto would be partners in his experiment. Excited by Suzuki's educational vision, a local citizen group took him up on his proposal and agreed to help found a music school. A preparatory committee formed in May, and the school was opened in October. It was named, simply, Matsumoto Ongakuin—the Matsumoto Music School.

At first the music school was less a place than a sort of club. It had no specific location, and finding venues fit for teaching was a challenge. Piano classes were held in a space rented from a kindergarten, while voice lessons were given at a nearby girls' school. The upstairs of Kanda's music shop became a violin classroom, but at first there were no violins. So Kanda, who had trained as a sculptor, got together with a local cabinetmaker to produce small instruments for preschoolers. The production of fractional-size violins would later be delegated to the Kiso Suzuki factory, as opposed to the Nagoya Suzuki factory. Eventually production was run by Suzuki's younger brother Shiro, who became a respected luthier in his own right.[7]

Suzuki was able to work only one day per week at the ongakuin in its early days. He had too many family and business obligations in Kiso Fukushima. And he was beset by a crisis: Koji Toyoda, the prized student who had wowed the judges of the Annual Music Competition at the age of six, had gone missing. Toyoda's father, who was so instrumental in bringing up his son according to the nascent Suzuki philosophy, had died during the previous year, hit by a bus while riding his bicycle. Unbeknownst to Suzuki, Toyoda and his younger brother were taken away from their stepmother and half-sister in Tokyo and sent to their uncle's home in Hamamatsu.

Hamamatsu was hardly a safe choice, as it lay on the coast between the major air-raid targets of Tokyo and Nagoya. It was easy for bombers approaching from the water to attack Hamamatsu while en route to one of the larger cities. And Hamamatsu itself was home to strategic targets, including a Yamaha factory that, during the war, had been ordered to set aside organs and pianos in favor of airplane propellers. Hamamatsu was raided six times; during the fourth raid, on June 18, 1945, Toyoda was nearly burned alive. That night, the eleven-year-old carried his grandmother on his back to a bunker, zigzagging his way through fireballs falling from the sky. When he crawled out of the bunker the following morning, charred bodies lay along the road he had taken the previous night. The place was pervaded by silence and the smell of death. About 1,800 people were killed on that night alone. The sound of the violin had no place in this sorrowful landscape.

Now homeless, Toyoda and his extended family moved forty miles north, deep into the mountains, to live with distant relatives. There he found some peace of mind and was able to attend school. But he was put off by the repeated requests he received from his teachers and classmates to play the violin. Even in that remote part of the country, he could not escape the label of boy genius. He had not touched the instrument for a long time and felt no desire to perform, so it was with uneasiness and a sense of resignation that he obliged.

Toyoda stayed in the mountains for less than two months. After the August 15 surrender announcement, he was able to return safely to Hamamatsu, where he would stay with another uncle. Though an engraver by profession, the uncle was making ends meet by running a food cart near the train station where he served *oden*, a hotpot containing vegetables and fishcakes. Toyoda was expected to help out. Since food carts were unofficially protected by mobsters marking their turfs, the clientele included rough types. Only two years before, Toyoda's hands had produced music that gave much joy to the guests in Marquis Tokugawa's salon. Now they were pouring cheap sake into a gangster's cup. Life as he had known it was fast slipping away.

On the cusp of adolescence, Toyoda would have to choose a middle school and by implication his eventual career. He decided on a technical school, with a view to becoming an architect. Surrounded by ruins, he knew that the future would include a great deal of construction. Everything had to be built from scratch. He was accepted at a competitive technical school and began his studies in the spring of 1946. The original school building had been obliterated, so Toyoda took classes at a makeshift campus an hour's walk from home. He loved classes and found the teachers inspiring. He even relished the long commute. But his busy daily routine left little time for music.

Toyoda's road back to the violin began with a broadcast on the Hamamatsu NHK station. A pianist asked Toyoda if he would play with her and, though rusty, he agreed. This felt different than playing for badgering classmates and teachers. As Toyoda and the pianist played their first notes together, Toyoda was overwhelmed by a feeling that he could no longer live without music. Through the pianist's family, he was introduced to another family, the Matsuos, local notables who took him in so he would not have to earn his keep at the food stall. Instead he could come home from school and concentrate on the violin. Like many Japanese children of his era, Toyoda was still, in a sense, on the run. The war and its aftermath had driven him from countless homes. But finally he was getting his life back on track.

Toyoda was two months into his stay with the Matsuos when his uncle delivered an urgent message: the name of Koji Toyoda had been spoken on the radio program *Missing Person*. After the war, friends and family of the lost would call in, hoping for a reunion—or at least information about the dead. The caller in this case was Shinichi Suzuki, begging to hear from his pupil. In December 1946, Toyoda rushed to Kiso Fukushima. He dropped the idea of becoming an architect, transferred to a local school, recommenced his violin studies with Suzuki, and became a member of his teacher's household.

This Suzuki was not the same man Toyoda had known before the war. He was skeletal, and seemed much older. In 1947, he decided to relocate to Matsumoto to work full-time at the ongakuin, but no sooner had he arrived than he fell seriously ill. He was becoming, in his own words, "devoid of all senses, physically and emotionally, except for the feeling of acute pain in the stomach." The illness was thought to be gastric atony caused by prolonged wartime malnutrition. Doctors of modern medicine were unable to alleviate it. Instead, Suzuki, joined by Hina, rested at Asama Onsen, an ancient spa town just outside Matsumoto. (Toyoda, along with Hina's two sons, remained in the Kiso Valley with Suzuki's extended family.) It seemed that Suzuki would surely die. The ongakuin's organizers began to seek a successor in Ayako Yamamoto, who had been a devoted student in Suzuki's prewar studio. But after a regimen of ginger compresses and brown-rice gruel administered by a local medicine woman, Suzuki came back to life, a seeming miracle. Yamamoto, still in her mid-twenties, would die of typhus the following year.[8]

By the end of 1947, Suzuki had survived the war and a nearly fatal illness and was filled with a renewed sense of purpose. He channeled all his energy into the Matsumoto project. With Toyoda, Hina, and her two sons, he settled in the center of town, in a white-walled former samurai house. The respectable home was purchased by Kitaro Watanabe, the heir to a seafood wholesaler and a key supporter of Suzuki's movement in Matsumoto. In the decade to come, the building would welcome a constant stream of visitors, including students traveling from all over Japan, who would stay overnight while taking lessons from Suzuki. On the same property sat a warehouse that served as the ongakuin office and occasionally as a classroom.[9]

Much of the teaching could now be carried out in a permanent space. After a long and frustrating search, the ongakuin organizers had found their schoolhouse: a defunct training facility for apprentice geisha. In this drafty wooden structure lit by bare bulbs, girls of a bygone age took lessons in singing, dancing, and traditional musical instruments like the shamisen, before they were sent off as professional entertainers. The spartan facility's 800-square-foot upper floor provided an ideal space for the group-playing that would quickly become a central component of Suzuki's teaching. To secure the building, Watanabe's financial backing was again indispensable.

Almost everyone was poor in those days, but the ongakuin's chronic financial difficulty also stemmed from its founder's casual way with money. One of the ongakuin's first students, a son of the original organizers, recalled many years later that the more famous Suzuki's talent education project became, "the more money somehow drained from the movement into somewhere else." The ongakuin also had a policy of accepting every child who wished to study, regardless of their family's ability to pay. It fell to Watanabe and a few others—those with just enough money and good will—to save the day.[10]

Although hardly a route to financial stability, the open-door program had many benefits. People from different backgrounds whose paths would not normally have crossed were able to mingle at the music school. Single mothers—of whom there were many in those days, their husbands having either died in the war or been taken prisoner on the continent—lingered at the school after their children's lessons were over. The mothers would listen to older students perform with their children and copy music scores by hand. As a result, poor students were better able to keep up, even though their families could not afford record players. And with children and parents hanging around, the school took on a deeper spirit of community. Soon, there were Sunday group lessons, bringing all levels of students together to play. Suzuki did not consider group lessons or listening sessions adequate substitutes for the extensive at-home listening he prescribed, but they would do for the moment. Eventually he would ask all families to do whatever was necessary to invest in a record player.

Privation was an opportunity for learning, and Suzuki absorbed lessons he never would have as a sought-after instructor in Tokyo. For instance, during this time Suzuki came to recognize how valuable it was for prospective students to observe lessons underway. This auditing practice was a result of the shortage of fractional-size instruments at the ongakuin, which forced more than a dozen preschoolers onto a waiting list for lessons. But Suzuki had a sense that it might be useful for them to observe group classes even if they could not participate. Some stayed away, but others showed up religiously. Small children do not spend two hours silently watching and listening, and these were no exception; they often occupied themselves by playing with others. Yet, when the instruments arrived, the differences between those who had been observing and those who had stayed away were striking. The observers were able to stand in a proper position and hold their instruments correctly. They

A scene, mid-1950s, outside the ongakuin, the music school Suzuki established in Matsumoto after World War II. *Talent Education Research Institute*

even started bowing right away without instruction. They progressed markedly faster, too, as they had already internalized the rhythms and melodies of various pieces. Suzuki would thereafter make a point of recommending that prospective students sit in before commencing lessons.[11]

Following from this experience, Suzuki felt that parents of very young beginners, too, could smoothly transition to life with the violin. His idea was that parents who knew the rudiments of playing would have a better understanding of what their children were experiencing and therefore be equipped to support learning at home. So he asked parents to take some basic instruction before their children began lessons of their own. Reflecting his essentially undogmatic nature, however, neither class audits nor parental lessons were required. Today, it is left to the discretion of individual Suzuki instructors to incorporate any such preliminary steps for beginning students and their families.

Perhaps it was also in light of the poverty surrounding him that Suzuki made sure the ongakuin was not just a place of education but also a place in which to feel safe and loved. The children needed release, and so did their parents. Suzuki provided it and quickly found that an atmosphere of joy did wonders for his young learners. This was not a novel concept, exactly; Suzuki had spent the 1930s developing techniques for engaging children. But at the ongakuin, his commitment to play—in the sense of games and jokes rather than performance—intensified. The group lessons were a major factor in this respect, both a highlight in themselves and a way of bringing children together to have fun with each other and with their favorite teacher. When it was cold out, the children would gather around a potbelly stove with Suzuki and chat before the group session. There were tea parties, badminton tournaments, and softball matches to celebrate good lessons.[12] On the evenings of recitals, Suzuki made sure there were special rewards for the students. He would assemble the sweets on a table covered in white linen, creating what Junko Yasuda, a former student and later Suzuki Method instructor, recalled as an otherworldly aura in the simple, drafty building. Even more magical were the New Year's parties Suzuki and Hina hosted at their home. Treats and games abounded. Hiroko Masaoka, another former student who became a Suzuki Method instructor, marveled at how patiently and deftly Suzuki guided preschoolers and primary schoolers to learn through playing, with or without violins.[13]

It was at the ongakuin that Suzuki began pursuing another of his legacies: teacher instruction. The Suzuki Method is today a global phenomenon because its creator did not keep it to himself. This is one of the ways in which Suzuki differs so significantly from other great violin teachers of history. He not only developed novel pedagogy. He also linked that pedagogy to a widely applicable philosophy of and trained other teachers so that they could help him turn his ideas into a movement. The process started in 1949, when Suzuki began soliciting interest among professional musicians, who helped spread the word. Then the tryout came. About a dozen applicants, mostly students of the established musicians in Suzuki's network, gathered at a piano shop in Tokyo's

Suzuki chatting with students at the ongakuin. *Talent Education Research Institute*

Ginza district for an audition. Three assessors, including Suzuki's violist brother Akira, sat before them and listened to them play. Suzuki was nowhere to be seen, though. He was in the next room, intently listening to the sound that each violinist was making.[14]

Blind auditions are fairly common these days, designed to ensure that musicians are judged solely on their playing rather than the biases of assessors. Suzuki was also interested only in what he could hear, for he had come to believe that nothing mattered more than tone. He knew that tone could be taught; that achieving good tone was a matter of technique. Yet he also discerned in tone something beyond mastery of the physics of vibration. Tone, he believed, revealed the player's soul, her innermost self. *Oto ni inochi ari,* Suzuki would often say: "Life is distilled in a tone." From the next room over, nothing would distract him from life distilled. He picked his first four teacher trainees based solely on their tone. He was known to apply a similar approach in private lessons. He would turn the light off before a student began playing, so that he could concentrate on listening.[15]

The successful applicants were brought to Matsumoto, where they learned first and foremost by observing Suzuki's classes. Even after they completed their course of studies and started setting up their own studios in their respective communities, they would regularly return to Matsumoto in the spirit of continual learning. For Suzuki's disciples, education never stopped.

Besides bringing up a new generation of instructors, Suzuki relied on his former students—the ones he guided from an early age starting in the 1930s—to help with teaching. After Ayako Yamamoto's premature death in 1948, Koji Toyoda became Suzuki's de facto chief assistant. Students adored the fresh-faced, teenaged teacher. Like Suzuki, they addressed him as Ko-chan.

Toyoda had plenty of time to help because he had decided, on Suzuki's advice, to skip high school altogether. Suzuki believed that Toyoda's time would be better spent improving his art while being tutored in languages, literature, and other subjects by local university professors. In the years to come, Suzuki would give similar advice to other students with professional aspirations.[16]

Besides, Suzuki was no fan of formal education as it was developing in Japan after the war. He openly referred to public schools, still tightly controlled by the conservative Ministry of Education, as a "mass homogenization system." Instead of nurturing students' potential, schools were ensuring large-scale mediocrity. In Matsumoto, Suzuki's combative stance quickly earned him a reputation as not only anti-authoritarian but also and more specifically "anti–Education Ministry" (*Han-Monbusho*). As such, Suzuki was a serious iconoclast in a society that historically looked up to officialdom—bureaucrats selected because they were well-connected or performed well on civil-service exams—as the only rightful maker of public decisions. Yukichi Fukuzawa, a notable modernizer and educator of the Meiji period, had decried this mindset half a century earlier. The mantra of Japanese politics, he quipped, was *kanson minpi*: "Revere the officials, slight the people."[17]

Yet if there was ever a moment for iconoclasm, it was in the wake of defeat, when Japan's leaders had proven themselves very much worthy of second guessing. The Matsumoto Ongakuin community certainly thought so: Suzuki's proposal, which had moved them to action, was not complimentary toward the kind of education carried out at state-run schools. In fact, it is likely that the heavy bundle of papers Suzuki dropped on Heishiro Kanda's desk in May 1946 was a draft of an article published that year, which became a kind of manifesto for the talent education movement. The argument is incredibly bold and forthright, holding that Japan's predicament was a product of the failure of education and that the society would collapse unless it discarded old ways of schooling that left too many children behind. "If we now look at the state of our country, and at the hearts of its people," Suzuki writes, "one cannot help shedding tears."

In a radical gesture, Suzuki in this article puts his faith in women. "I believe the greatest power to salvage our national fortune lies in the hands of Japanese women, especially mothers," he writes.[18] It hardly need be said that Japan had long been a patriarchal society, like all its models and competitors on the world stage. Suzuki's life was no exception. He learned much from his mother, but he worked for his father. His father was the one whose permission mattered when it came to choosing a profession, going abroad, and marrying Waltraud. And Suzuki's most able students—Toyoda, Toshiya Eto, the Kobayashi brothers—had been pushed by strong-willed fathers. The most extreme case was Yonesaku Kobayashi, who was so obsessed with his sons' advancement that, even during the war, violin studies dominated his thoughts. As a military news photographer in Indonesia, he managed to visit Szymon Goldberg, a Polish-born virtuoso and former concertmaster of the Berlin Philharmonic, in a POW camp in Japanese-occupied Java. Kobayashi asked Goldberg to let him take photographs of him playing the violin so that his children could study them. Moved by a father's love and by the possibility of instructing even through photographs, Goldberg promptly agreed. But he was in for a surprise. What Kobayashi had in mind was not just a few images showing how Goldberg held his bow or his violin. Kobayashi wanted to record everything and kept asking Goldberg to demonstrate specific passages of one or another piece. Kobayashi took several hundred photographs, and his sons studied Goldberg's technique from the film negatives.[19]

Despite all his encounters with uncompromising fathers, Suzuki was, as late as 1948, suggesting that violin studies at home would be more effective with fathers in charge. But his perspective was also changing. For one thing, women had always been more present in Japanese family life. This is a socioeconomic reality of any population in which male breadwinners are presumed. And after the war, fathers were even more absent than before. But it was probably not just raw numbers that had Suzuki newly focused on the role of women in resuscitating the nation and transforming education. In a 2018 interview, Koji Toyoda told me that Suzuki had seen enough to know that mothers tended to be relatively restrained, evenhanded, and nurturing in their guidance, making them more suitable overseers of home practice and education generally. "I think fathers are scarier," Toyoda said, based not least on his own experience. "There is usually no room for negotiation." Toyoda saw more Tiger Fathers than Tiger Mothers during his violin-infused youth, and of course Suzuki witnessed the same dynamics.[20]

Suzuki decided to appeal directly to girls in middle and high school, as they were, by the conventions of the time, expected to become mothers in the not-so-distant future. So Toyoda, sometimes together with the Kobayashi brothers, would follow Suzuki around Japan performing at girls' schools. Suzuki's passionate ally in this effort was Kiyoshi Kato, a fellow Nagoyaite and old family friend as well as a former student of Mogilevsky, Suzuki's Teion colleague. Now based in Tokyo, Kato would support Suzuki's public relations effort in the capital, helping him target schools, including Christian missionary schools, where daughters of affluent, well-educated families attended. The events would begin with a lecture by Suzuki, who would introduce his mother-tongue approach and his understanding of talent. Then there would be a violin demonstration by his students. Many adolescent boys would have abhorred performing in front of girls their age, but Toyoda rather liked the attention. He remembers one appearance at a Catholic school, Sacred Heart, where Kato's daughter Koko was a pupil. Another student in the audience was Michiko Shoda, a dedicated pianist and future empress of Japan. She married into the imperial house in 1959, the first commoner to do so.[21]

This episode from Suzuki's Tokyo tour struck me personally because Sacred Heart was my own family's milieu. Women on my mother's side almost invariably attended the school, though my mother would have been just too young to have attended Suzuki's lecture and Toyoda's demonstration. Koko Kato, instructed by her father as well as by Suzuki during the formative years of the talent education movement, was a classmate of one of my aunts. Moreover, I only realize now that I knew Koko in Tokyo, albeit briefly. In my ill-conceived attempt to learn the violin in the summer after high school—I was in need of a diversion, and a friend conveniently had a violin I could borrow—I received several lessons from Koko through my aunt's introduction. Koko was then on an extended leave from Rome, where she was playing professionally. She was a warm, vivacious, and fun-loving soul. I got through the first few pieces of the first Suzuki Method book with her, but we ended up spending more time chatting about opera, Italian food, and life in general. She made it clear, in the gentlest manner possible, that I was "too old" to be any good at the violin anyway.

Suzuki does not seem to have lectured at my father's private, coeducational school, Gakushuin. But there, too, students were exposed to a fragment of cultural life as Japan struggled to reclaim what had been lost during the war years. My father remembers a visit to his school by none other than Nejiko Suwa—the original girl genius—presumably because Gakushuin was Marquis Tokugawa's alma mater. My father sat in the balcony looking down at a tall, slender figure in a long dress performing in the school auditorium. He was at once bored and impressed. She was so absorbed in her music that, even though he was not especially interested, he knew he was witnessing something he had to respect.

Suwa's wartime experience was singular. After her study with Émile Chaumont in Brussels, she moved to Paris, where she became a student of the Russian violinist Boris Kamensky, a former pupil of Ysaÿe, Auer, and Joachim. But soon Paris was under Nazi occupation. After declining several invitations to perform in Berlin, she finally gave in—and became a tool of Axis information warfare, traveling with the German Red Cross and performing for German soldiers. While she was in Berlin, Reich Minister of Propaganda Joseph Goebbels presented her with what he claimed was a Stradivarius. She played this instrument as a soloist with the Berlin Philharmonic. Throughout the war, Suwa was attached to the Japanese diplomatic mission in Europe, making her understandably suspicious in the eyes of the Allies. Eventually Suwa was captured and detained by US forces and then returned to Japan in December 1945. By that time, she had lost nearly everything, but she still held tightly to her violin. She would not bend to any pressure—ethical or political—to part with her supposed Stradivarius. The true provenance of the instrument remains a mystery; after Suwa died in 2012, her surviving family members insisted it had been declared a forgery.

Sometime in 1947, Suwa went to Matsumoto. The only purpose of her visit was to see Suzuki and play for him. Koji Toyoda remembers eavesdropping on their meeting. He held his breath and furtively listened to her play Henryk Wieniawski's Etude-Caprice through the paper sliding door. We cannot know what Suzuki thought of this reunion, or of Suwa's playing a decade after he had last heard it—after all she had been through and all she had done. Did he feel the weight of broken dreams? Japan had taken such pride in Suwa, convinced that she would make a huge splash on the world stage. Now she had crawled back home in desperation and was emblematic of the country's descent.[22]

How many more dreams would be compromised if Japan failed to reject what it had become? Such questions motivated Suzuki powerfully, as evidenced by his constant, passionate arguments for reform. The need was truly fundamental. For the moment, Japan was in the midst of the postwar emergency. But once that abated, it would have to become a new nation, lest it ruin itself and so many others again. How could Japan be made to choose humanity? Suzuki put his faith, as ever, in art and in young people: the next generation could be made virtuous through thorough and thoughtful education. But reform would not come about simply by preaching peace or lecturing on talent education. For that matter, teaching music would not be enough. Suzuki had to show, with concrete examples, how his approach could transform Japanese education, Japanese youth, and the national future.

In spring 1948, Hongo Elementary School in Asama Onsen became the first public school to apply Suzuki's approach to subjects other than violin study. This bold experiment was made possible equally by the chaos and fluidity of the postwar period and by the courage of the school's principal, Shigeru Kamijo. After hearing Suzuki's little violinists play in a local recital, Kamijo became acquainted with the man and fascinated by his philosophy. Together, they conceived of a talent education program for Hongo Elementary and put it to the test.

In the first year, twenty girls and twenty boys were chosen from among the incoming first graders. These children had no class schedule and no homework. The traditional curriculum—covering mathematics, science, the Japanese language, and so on—was set aside. Instead, in a relaxed and playful atmosphere, the students took part in various projects intended to train memory, concentration, motor and computational skills, and creativity. Suzuki had a close hand in devising these projects: drawing lines, painting with vivid watercolors, memorizing through storytelling and music, observing nature, feeling music through rhythmic exercises. The hope was that, by joyfully developing basic cognitive faculties, the children would gain the foundation necessary for any other form of learning.[23]

Principal Kamijo was taking a major risk by adopting a pedagogy that defied the official guidelines set by the Ministry of Education. But he was fully committed. He put Shigeki Tanaka, a young teacher whose child was a violin student at the ongakuin, in charge of the program and reassured him that he, as a principal, would take full responsibility for any repercussions. Kamijo must have known that the plan would prove controversial—not just because it was rebellious but because novelty always provokes skepticism, and all the more so when the test subjects are people's children. And there were entrenched interests to consider. Most of the teachers at Hongo Elementary were averse to the program; they were not oblivious to—and took offense at—Suzuki's public assertion that teachers were doing a bad job and left too many students behind.[24]

Perhaps unsurprisingly, talent education proved more popular with parents than with teachers—another sign of the disconnect forming between the public and the authorities—and by its second year, more families applied than could be accommodated. Then, three years in, Principal Kamijo died unexpectedly. No one succeeded him as standard bearer for the maverick program, and the experiment came to an abrupt end. We will never know how much could have been achieved at Hongo, or if the school would have become a model for others.

Suzuki nonetheless cherished the two years of success for the rest of his life. In later writing, he would cite a potent example from the class: a girl who simply could not count to three when she arrived for first grade. In any other school, she would have been identified as "slow" or intellectually handicapped. The system would have branded her as hopeless. But in the talent education program, she was able to acquire effective learning habits through repetition. Not endless drilling, mind you. There is no better way to exceed the limits of a student's attention and concentration. Instead, by embedding skill-based learning in fun games, her teacher Tanaka ensured that she was able to stay focused. She would eventually go on to pass a competitive high school exam.

Cases like these were hugely exciting for Suzuki, seemingly confirming that his approach was both versatile and could be applied immediately and widely. After all, Hongo was not unique; it was a typical public school. But it was not Suzuki who needed convincing, it was Japan at large—policymakers, specifically. How could they be made aware of talent education's enormous potential? This question of course was tied to a much deeper one that Suzuki and many others were contemplating in the late 1940s: How to prevent Japan from reverting to its prewar ways?

After defeat, the country did not clean house. Despite unconditional surrender and the trial of selected war criminals, many of the prewar elites and much of the central bureaucracy survived in important roles well into the postwar years. The old order was allowed to persist, above all, by the US occupiers. Significantly, General Douglas MacArthur, the supreme Allied commander and head of the occupation government, spared the Imperial Household. Emperor Hirohito would remain on his throne, though now he was to be a symbol of peace rather than a divine patriarch of a Japanese family bent on war. This alone meant that discussion of war responsibility would be compromised, as any consideration of responsibility would necessarily implicate the emperor. Whatever he personally thought of the war, he did not oppose the deaths of millions in his name. And it followed that, if imperial responsibility was both unclear and a taboo subject, it would be that much harder to hold Japan's leaders accountable. They had been acting on behalf of an officially blameless emperor.

This is not to suggest that nothing changed after the war. At first the occupation imposed significant policy changes aimed at demilitarization and devolution of power. But the rapid intensification of the Cold

War dramatically altered US objectives in Japan, resulting in what historians have called the "reverse course." By 1947, the goal had shifted decisively from demilitarization and democratization to reconstruction, economic growth, and the preservation of self-defense capacity, as US strategists sought to establish Japan as a fortress against communism in East Asia. The matter being urgent, General MacArthur decided that Japan's old elites were now his allies. No one else could rebuild the country quickly, so he elected to support rather than punish them. Indeed, punishments were reversed. On Christmas Day 1949, MacArthur pardoned forty-six war criminals serving sentences of less than four years and reduced the sentences of many others.

To be sure, not everyone was happy with this arrangement. The discontented expressed themselves in films, literature, and scholarly and journalistic writing. To this day, critics of the postwar settlement continue to call for a searching examination of Japan's prewar and wartime past. But these promoters of accountability, often from the political left, are overwhelmed by conservatives, who have managed to stay in power for most of the postwar period. In any case, in the immediate aftermath of Japan's defeat, most people were just trying to survive, and if hardship was not enough to prevent the mobilization of popular protest, the reverse course prevented the blossoming of a truly broad-based, democratic culture strong enough to challenge the reinstatement of the old system. With the blessing of the United States, Japan's mighty central bureaucracy—which included the Ministry of Education—would be firmly back in control by the mid-1950s.

How much could one man, however energetic, achieve in the face of a bureaucracy resistant to change? Suzuki tried to find out. In October 1948, in the first democratic election of its kind in Japan, Suzuki ran for a seat on the Matsumoto board of education, established in keeping with US occupation guidelines. He lost the election, and so did most of the reformist candidates running for schoolboard positions nationwide. Voter turnout was relatively high across the country—57 percent, despite the enormous challenges confronting ordinary people. They came out to speak on behalf of the old order, electing former teachers and school inspectors steeped in the Ministry of Education's longstanding ways of doing things. By 1956, with the US occupation over, democratic elections were no longer being held for education boards, giving the local and central governments power to appoint their preferred board members. This ensured that only those willing to follow the ministry's guidelines would be chosen.[25]

Although Suzuki failed to win office, his campaign attracted significant national media attention, stimulating grassroots interest in his philosophy. As a result, a smattering of ambitious and inventive public school teachers throughout Japan began to incorporate aspects of Suzuki's approach in their classrooms, even under the increasingly watchful eyes of policymakers in Tokyo. Meanwhile, Suzuki continued to give lectures and publish articles. As his ideas spread, violin studios following his teaching method sprouted across the country. By late 1949, there were thirty-five such studios, with approximately 1,500 young children enrolled. The studios were housed under a new organization Suzuki established the previous year, the Talent Education Research Institute (TERI). This is all quite remarkable considering that most Japanese had not yet recovered, psychologically or materially, from the devastation of the war.[26]

Such growth is even more impressive in light of the talent education movement's continuing financial difficulty. TERI had an administrative office in Tokyo, headed by Suzuki's Teion colleague Kenko Aoki, but the branch was forced to close in 1950 for lack of money. Aoki tried to keep the office open by dipping into his own pocket. He even sold his house to support the project. Those funds lasted less than half a year, and TERI's key Tokyo branch remained closed for at least six years.

The organization muddled through, mostly on the strength of its violin-instructional component rather than the larger program for education reform. In October 1950, again thanks in part to Aoki's generous contributions, TERI began publishing the journal *Tarento*—its title a Japanese transliteration of the English "talent." The journal would go through many names—*Saino Kyoiku Kaiho* (*Talent Education Association Journal*), *Saino* (*Talent*), and then *Saino Kyoiku* (*Talent Education*). Publication frequencies also fluctuated. Whatever the journal was called and however often it was printed, Suzuki was its main contributor, and he used its pages to lay out the conceptual foundation of the Suzuki Method as it is known today.

Yet, ever the empiricist, Suzuki preferred to lead by example. Deeds were more convincing than words, and deeds were what Japan needed:

real change, in real lives. Moreover, Suzuki was at pains to show that his techniques were suitable for teaching all kinds of subjects, not just music. With all this in mind, in 1949 he opened Yoji Gakuen (Children's Academy), a preschool at the ongakuin. As a private entity, Yoji Gakuen was free of official restrictions and bureaucratic oversight and so was able to replicate many of the projects proven effective at Hongo Elementary—with even younger children. A unique and lasting element of the Yoji Gakuen experience was *Issa Karuta,* a card game Suzuki created for the students. Half of the 200 cards in the deck feature a haiku written by Issa, a preeminent late eighteenth and early nineteenth-century poet. The other half contain illustrations depicting the contents of the haikus. One player recites the haiku on a card, and the others must quickly determine which haiku it is and swipe the associated picture card from an assortment spread over the floor. Even preschoolers could easily recognize and memorize haikus this way, improving their facility with an important part of their literary heritage. (Although Issa is revered throughout Japan, he is a special favorite in his native Nagano Prefecture, where Matsumoto is located.) The cards, drawn by the painter and beloved children's book illustrator Yoshisuke Kurosaki, are sold by TERI to this day.

Very young, malleable children delighted Suzuki's heart, but he did not neglect those who had already been "dropped out" by mainstream society. In 1950, he recommended a routine he had taken up in Tokyo before the war: lecturing in juvenile prisons, with his young violinists in tow. Speaking with officials at Matsumoto's prison for boys, Suzuki was shocked and disappointed to learn that some of the young offenders were rejected by their parents even after they had served their time. Refusing to accept this attitude of endless punitiveness, he spoke to the inmates about the amazing abilities each of them possessed. He urged that they could discover and unleash their potential through self-reflection and encouraged them to focus on what they could do to find fulfillment now and tomorrow. Where others lingered over past mistakes, Suzuki was attentive to the future. He thought that violin lessons in prison would help facilitate this process of self-reflection and growth, but prison officials turned down his proposal. At the very least, the authorities were sympathetic to Suzuki's suggestion that they abolish the jarring chimes played each morning and night. Beginning in 1953, the boys woke up

Lessons—or, simply, fun times—were not confined to the classroom. *Talent Education Research Institute*

to the sound of Tchaikovsky's "Troika" from *The Seasons,* performed by Sergei Rachmaninoff, and fell asleep to the berceuse from Benjamin Godard's opera *Jocelyn,* performed by one of Suzuki's favorite musicians, cellist Pablo Casals.[27]

In the midst of this extraordinary outpouring of creativity and effort, addressing so many areas of social reform, early childhood music education remained the most conspicuous of Suzuki's endeavors. In fact, the popularity of talent education was making for a bit of a spectacle. In 1951, more than one hundred children from throughout Japan gathered at the foot of Mount Kirigamine outside Matsumoto to make music together at the first TERI summer school. It was the beginning of a tradition that continues today on a larger scale in the city of Matsumoto, from late July to early August every year.

With the movement spreading, the indefatigable Suzuki found himself visiting studios all over Japan to give lessons and closely monitor the progress of individual students. As he witnessed more and more young violinists emerging, he decided to establish a graduation event to celebrate their growth. True to his philosophy, he was not looking to either pass or fail students. He wished only to commend and acknowledge mastery when it was achieved. The first graduation ceremony for those who had completed an entire course of violin instructional repertoire took place in Tokyo on October 25, 1952. The system was completely meritocratic; anyone could graduate, at any age, as long as they had finished the course. One of the 196 graduates that year was a five-year-old who had completed the approximate equivalent of today's Suzuki Method Book 6.[28]

Also that year, Suzuki studios began incorporating the revolutionary technology of reel-to-reel recording. With a reel-to-reel machine on hand, students would be able to record and listen to their own playing, fostering a powerful new avenue for learning. He researched all products then available before coming upon a Philips recorder that, to his mind, delivered the highest sound quality. (Totsuko, a precursor company of Sony, produced a machine domestically, but it did not match up.) The Philips might have been the best, but it was not cheap. This imported model cost 68,000 yen, approximately eight months of starting salary for a university graduate and almost as much as a refrigerator, a coveted household luxury item for which there was a great deal more demand. Yet, insisting on the critical importance of the device, Suzuki made it TERI's institutional mission to purchase them. The first was installed at a studio in Kanagawa, and by 1955 most of the regional TERI chapters, which oversaw studios across Japan, were equipped with this state-of-the-art technology. Suzuki also pleaded with parents to invest in a machine for home use; to defray costs, he came up with a scheme whereby TERI would buy the machines and resell them to families at a subsidized rate paid in monthly installments.

With the advent of reel-to-reel came a new tradition, that of graduation recordings. Students would record their performances to commemorate their graduations, and Suzuki would listen to every one of the recordings. He then recorded comments to be sent back to the student, together with a hand-painted commemorative watercolor containing words of congratulations in his calligraphy. It made for quite a diploma. Later, when the talent education project expanded to include cello, piano, and eventually flute instruction, Suzuki kept up the practice, listening

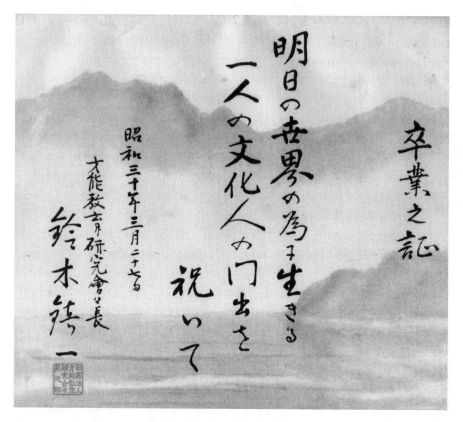

A commemorative watercolor, hand-painted and inscribed by Suzuki for one of his graduates. The text, dated March 27, 1955, reads, "Celebrating the beginning of a new life, of a person of culture, who lives for the world of tomorrow." *Talent Education Research Institute*

to every student's graduation recording and responding with his insights. Well into his nineties, he would wake up when it was still dark in order to squeeze in some listening before commencing the rest of his work. The recording technology changed—from reel-to-reel, to cassette, to CD—but Suzuki's commitment did not. Indeed, that commitment has outlived him. To this day, graduating students in Japan submit recordings of themselves to the TERI office in Matsumoto, where a group of senior instructors share the workload that Suzuki used to tackle singlehandedly.

Suzuki's feedback was always supportive. He considered graduation not a culmination but an educational tool, and like every such tool he developed, this one was designed to encourage. He used to say that, by listening to the recordings, he could clearly visualize the students; he could tell, for instance, if someone was playing with a raised shoulder or a stooped back, and in his recorded comments he would explain, in a conversational and loving tone of voice, what could be done to fix those problems. Student recordings also helped Suzuki keep tabs on his instructors, so he could guide their continuing development. And as the repertoire came to be divided into multiple levels of advancement—ten levels for violin and flute, nine for piano and cello—students and instructors could aspire to smaller graduations along the way before reaching the final level. Graduations thereby became an ongoing incentive, while Suzuki gained granular insight into the teaching and learning carried out under his aegis. Students took joy in graduation, and Suzuki found the growth reflected in a series of recordings deeply meaningful.

Around the same time that reel-to-reel recording was enabling a key institutional tradition for the talent education community, Suzuki was preparing for the first Grand Concert—the spectacular performance at Tokyo Metropolitan Gymnasium described in chapter 1. By any conceivable public relations standard, that March 1955 event was a resounding success. In particular, it was this concert that announced Suzuki's movement to the outside world. Crucial in this regard was Kenji Mochizuki, then in his final year of undergraduate studies at Oberlin College in Ohio. Though not a musician himself, Mochizuki had been introduced to talent education through his young violin-playing cousin, and he had long admired Suzuki's achievements as a teacher. Mochizuki heard about the Grand Concert and tried to get hold of the footage, hoping to show off this phenomenon in Japanese education to Oberlin's highly respected music teachers. But copying films was expensive, and TERI did not have space in its budget. So Mochizuki waited and waited. Finally in May 1958, after three years of inquiries, he was able to secure a reel and show it to a group of violin instructors who were at Oberlin for a conference. The instructors were astounded to the point of incredulity, but eventually they came around. Several of them would go on to play pioneering roles in propagating Suzuki's musical pedagogy in the United States and beyond. One of the instructors, John Kendall, was so impressed that he traveled to Matsumoto in 1959 to glimpse

Suzuki in action. He could not rest until he saw for himself how those young violinists had been trained.[29]

So much was unleashed in 1959, as it was also the year in which Suzuki finally completed the ten violin instruction books he had been publishing in installments since 1948. He felt that those ten books together eliminated the need for etude compilations. His repertoire pieces, he believed, integrated all of the important technical points for foundational studies and were presented in an effective, incremental sequence that emulated the gradual process of mother-tongue acquisition. Well-known etude books like those of Heinrich Ernst Kayser and Rodolphe Kreutzer were, in Suzuki's words, "fine materials" from which he himself benefitted. But they were unnecessary for early learners and packed in excessive technical demands. The problem was not that the material was too difficult but that there was too much of it all at once, so that students became overwhelmed. Suzuki was no less committed to technique than were earlier pedagogues; he just had a more thoughtful, stepwise approach to instruction. Thus he also provided supplementary study materials to accompany the main instructional books, covering, for example, "tonalization" exercises, score-reading skills, and music theory. But rather than subject students to multiple potentially unrelated challenges in a single lesson as etude books did, Suzuki focused on discrete problems, one at a time. It was an approach redolent of Klingler's lessons years earlier in Berlin.[30]

One might expect that Suzuki was delighted by the rising profile of talent education at home and abroad in the second half of the 1950s. But publicity was also a source of frustration, for alongside greater recognition came further misunderstanding. In Japan, those movie-goers who viewed the black-and-white newsreel footage of the Grand Concert likely saw the event as a curious spectacle, not as a proud demonstration of an educational movement relevant to society as a whole. The word "talent" was right there in the name of the organization that sponsored the performance; the automatic reaction of the audience would have been that the young violinists partaking in this unusual event were especially talented—that is, gifted. The news report offered compelling entertainment but did little to promote Suzuki's philosophy, or even the sense that he had a philosophy. Quite the opposite, the report upheld the notion of talent that Suzuki aimed to overwrite.

The sense that viewers were witnessing something extraordinary and irreplicable must have been compounded by the sight of the many luminaries in attendance, including Yoshichika Tokugawa, who, forever supportive of Suzuki, sat on TERI's board. Though he was stripped of his aristocratic title after the war and his fortune was greatly diminished, he was still a revered figure whose family name struck every Japanese with awe. Also in attendance was the young Crown Prince Akihito, an amateur cellist. Thus was a mission to achieve universal opportunity made into an artifact of tremendous privilege.

And when the concert footage found its way overseas, Americans embraced Suzuki's methods only as an approach to string instrument instruction, not to general education. The Americans who saw the Grand Concert on film were not policymakers or education-reform activists. Their goal was not to change the world, or even a particular school system, but to learn effective methods for teaching young children to play classical music on violins.

I suspect that Suzuki was ambivalent about these outcomes. He appreciated the opportunity to reach people, but he could not have seen a great wave building behind the broader aims of his movement. Japan loved his concert yet also seemed satisfied with an education system that he relentlessly criticized. In a research paper published in 1958 but written a couple of years earlier, Suzuki notes that, in 1955, 159 students had died by suicide after failing university entrance examinations. To him, this number was proof that something was terribly wrong with Japanese education. It was a system that reserved the most sought-after jobs for the very few who were able to pass the right exams, while those who failed were made to feel that life was not worth living. Incredibly, this was happening in the name of democracy and equal opportunity, even as the postwar system merely recreated, at a larger scale, the same hyper-pressurized exam culture that Suzuki had been condemning since the 1930s. It was infuriating to Suzuki that teachers and parents continued to accept such an arrangement, acting as if nothing could be done to change it. "They have no self-awareness," he writes in the 1958 paper, "that they themselves make up the society they live in."[31]

Meanwhile, Suzuki could at this point have been forgiven for losing faith in adults. With TERI's success in promoting violin instruction, Suzuki had opportunities to observe many more adults—parents and teachers—behaving badly. Even parents who were devoted to his philosophy lost sight of its purpose, focusing excessively on musical skills and insufficiently on holistic education and character. In a 1956 article, Suzuki cites an exchange with a "Mr. K" to demonstrate this point. Mr. K was the kind of person who should have understood Suzuki's goals. He was a schoolteacher with two daughters learning to play the violin, and he clearly thought highly of Suzuki. Mr. K's letter to Suzuki sounds like a confessor addressing his priest. The letter describes a practice session with his younger daughter during which he became so frustrated by her slow progress that he lost his temper. When his wife intervened, he hit her with their daughter's violin, shattering it into blood-soaked pieces. The abused Mrs. K wrote to Suzuki, separately—a further demonstration that these parents were committed to the method—worried not so much for herself as her daughters, on whom she and her husband had, she said, inflicted such trauma. Suzuki's response is remarkably hopeful, given all that transpired. He tries to encourage not only Mrs. K but also her husband, in spite of his grave mistake. Suzuki tells Mrs. K that her experience moved him and his sister to tears, he praises her awareness of the suffering her daughters are experiencing, and he assures her that she and Mr. K both have the ability to reflect and learn. Chillingly, he also tells Mrs. K that her family's struggles are not unique.[32]

Mr. K.'s confessional letter mentions Koji Toyoda as a model for his daughters, describing him as the embodiment of all that a Suzuki upbringing could achieve, both musically and personally. By the late 1950s, Toyoda had become an inspirational presence in the talent education movement, even though he was no longer physically present in Suzuki's everyday life in Matsumoto. In 1952, at the age of nineteen, he had left for Paris on a French government scholarship. There he studied with René Benedetti at the Conservatoire de Paris, from which he graduated in one record-breaking year. He was eager to obtain his degree so that he could start his studies with the great but ailing Romanian violinist Georges Enescu. Enescu would die in 1955, but he took Toyoda under his wing in the final two years of his life.

To onlookers in Japan, it seemed like Toyoda was sailing smoothly into the world of Europe's top classical musicians, but actually the young man faced considerable challenges. Musically, Toyoda felt ill-equipped to attend even the conservatory's first-year course in solfège, since he had previously had little exposure to systemized ear-training. "I was so clueless, I could only laugh," he later recalled with self-deprecating humor. Dispirited by such a basic failure, he began to question the fundamentals of his technique.

Yet, whatever criticism he received, Toyoda was inspired to keep going. Yehudi Menuhin, a protégé of Enescu's, gave Toyoda lessons and encouragement. Toyoda felt that Menuhin understood the challenge of unlearning ingrained habits, as he too had struggled in the transition to musical adulthood. And Enescu praised Toyoda from the start—particularly his bowing. "You have an exceptional talent," Enescu noted, something Toyoda relates to Suzuki in a letter. More than anyone, Toyoda knew the depth of his old teacher's obsession with talent. "Please forgive them," he writes. By "them," Toyoda was referring to both Enescu and Pablo Casals, for whom Toyoda had played during a summer festival, earning a "t-word" review. Writing to Suzuki, Toyoda apologetically explains that the maestros used the word owing to "force of habit" and that what they really had in mind was a kind of "musical sense" that differentiated musicians from mere players of music. But, of course, this would not have captured Suzuki's vision of talent, either.[33]

But then there were people who really did understand what Suzuki meant by talent, even if they weren't sure they agreed. One of these was Bernard Leach, who is widely referred to as the "father of British studio pottery." Leach spent the first four years of his life in Japan and from 1952 through 1954 traveled there with friends including fellow potter Shoji Hamada and philosopher Soetsu Yanagi—both critical figures of *Mingei Undo*, Japan's arts and crafts movement. In September 1954, Leach met Suzuki in Matsumoto. They were brought together by Kaneko Yanagi, Soetsu's wife and an alto singer who had taught with Suzuki at Teion. Kaneko insisted on the meeting, Leach writes in his diary, telling him to look up this "leading teacher of the violin in Japan," who was "a remarkable man." And so Leach and his companions observed Suzuki's class at the ongakuin one afternoon. Leach's notes provide an account reminiscent of Robert Owen's stories from New Lanark; it is a vivid rendering of Suzuki's group-teaching from this period.[34]

There were about fifteen boys and girls between the ages of five and thirteen in the large room and a number of parents sitting against the walls on chairs. [Suzuki] called the youngest, a boy of five, who came out into the middle of the room, quite unabashed, with a tiny fiddle under his arm. Without any fuss, fully concentrated, he put his bow to the strings in no uncertain manner, and played a short and simple piece by Bach which made me sit up in astonishment. It was so pure. Then one of the older girls played a Bach Chaconne. I was going to say like a concert artiste only it was better than many, there was no seeking for effects it was just Bach. I had never heard a child play like that. Mr. Suzuki then took the whole group in unison. Standing before them he started a few notes on his own violin on fragments of one piece after another—Chopin—Mozart, without explanation or warning, and in a second they were all with him as one, true and free. Tears came to my eyes and I saw that the rest of our party were also deeply touched. After that this strange Japanese teacher divided the group, waving to one half to stop, and then to the other, at any moment, leaving the rest to continue without pause or break. Next he asked them all sorts of questions while they continued to play. "How many electric bulbs are there in this room?," "Tell me what is written on that scroll," "If you cannot see, go and look, but don't stop playing," "Now, stand on one leg and play, now the other, now squat." Then he asked half the group to go downstairs to the floor below, walk along the corridor and come up the other stairway and see if they could return to the room having kept perfect time with those who had remained. They did so. These children obviously loved their teacher, but directly they began bowing they were completely engrossed in the music.

Intrigued and delighted by what they had witnessed, Leach and his friends invited Suzuki and his whole class to their hotel, where they continued with "good music and food and fun."

Leach came to understand the basic claims of Suzuki's philosophy in the limited time they shared. "Mr. Suzuki concludes that latency"— meaning ability—"is due entirely to post-natal conditions." But Leach found this "difficult to accept." True, Leach, as a Japanese speaker, was

Suzuki, in the center of the circle, leads a group lesson as spectators look on.
Talent Education Research Institute

a living testament to Suzuki's mother-tongue approach and to the overwhelming importance of the early childhood environment. (Although Leach was modest about his Japanese language skills and did not read or write the language, his spoken Japanese was excellent.) But it was the seemingly exaggerated emphasis Suzuki was willing to put on nurture over nature that gave Leach pause. At one point, in a public lecture, Suzuki even suggested that left-handedness was caused by mothers holding their babies in a certain way, squishing their right arms in their first days on earth. Leach, being an artist himself and surrounded by artists of the highest caliber, believed there were certain qualities that one simply could not learn no matter how hard one tried. These were the qualities that distinguished an artist from an artisan, and art from craftsmanship.[35]

Whatever his intellectual reservations, Leach was moved to tears by what he saw and heard in Suzuki's class. He could not deny the essential importance and remarkable achievement of Suzuki's endeavor. "Whether ante- or post-natal, a more or less infinite potential seems to be revealed," he writes, concluding that "this man holds the magic of release." Indeed, Suzuki seemed to transport his students to some other plane through music-making. But his magic was "not in music alone." Leach felt that Suzuki "saw the infinite potential in the human soul, he knew his gift and was alight. So were his children." Leach and his artist friends began "to relate [Suzuki's] conclusions with our own."[36]

8

THE WORLD IS HIS STAGE

WHEN BERNARD LEACH visited Matsumoto in 1954, he was under the impression that Suzuki's marriage to Waltraud, which had produced no children, had long since ended. That was also the common perception among Suzuki's students and their parents. In fact the marriage had not broken down, although the couple had largely separate lives, their contact limited to Waltraud's occasional weekend visits from Tokyo. Then, in 1956, Waltraud quit her job at the bank and "came home." She and Suzuki moved into a traditional Japanese wooden house in Matsumoto, to which they added a Western-style salon where the acoustics were more conducive to Suzuki's private lessons. According to Waltraud, she financed the renovation.[1]

For Waltraud, life in Matsumoto after a decade of independence must have been a challenge. Colleagues considered her a difficult, even terrifying, person to deal with; she was known to make young female TERI staff cry. But Waltraud also had great sense of purpose in her new incarnation as Mrs. Shinichi Suzuki of the talent education movement. She assigned herself the role of chief liaison officer to the outside world, and she did the job well. True, before her homecoming, foreign musicians—including David Oistrakh, the conductor Malcolm Sargent, and the pianists Alfred Cortot and Walter Gieseking—had all witnessed Suzuki's undertaking firsthand. But it is no coincidence that Waltraud's move to Matsumoto marks the beginning of intense contact with overseas music educators. Waltraud facilitated what would prove critical visits, like that of John Kendall, whose interest in Suzuki was piqued by the Grand Concert footage he saw at Oberlin. Kendall wrote repeatedly,

Suzuki turns a dial on a reel-to-reel recorder, circa 1954. The technology became a critical tool of talent education, used to encourage children's aural development. *Talent Education Research Institute*

but Suzuki kept putting off his letters until Waltraud coaxed him to reply and finally arrange their 1959 meeting.

Musicians on concert tours made a point of stopping in Matsumoto. Real eminences showed up, like the Belgian violinist Arthur Grumiaux, who had become Koji Toyoda's mentor after Enescu's death, came in 1961. The Academy Choir from Vienna visited Suzuki in 1960. When such guests appeared, Suzuki would call on some students to play for them. One of those students was Ryugo Hayano, who started private lessons in Suzuki's house when he was four years old. Hayano recalls Suzuki's special way of communicating with children, and lessons that involved equal measures of repetition and playfulness. (Suzuki also left an impression with his frailty; to Hayano's childhood eyes, he looked like an old man, his fingers yellowed from chain-smoking.) Tomiko Shida, Hayano's neighbor, would also play for visitors. She fondly remembers dropping everything she was doing when a call from Suzuki came. She and Hayano would dash over to Suzuki's house with their violins.[2]

Another prominent musician who witnessed Suzuki's students in 1961 was Pablo Casals. The eighty-four-year-old maestro came to Japan to lend

World-renowned cellist Pablo Casals congratulates Suzuki after a 1961
student concert. *Talent Education Research Institute*

moral support to his pupil Takeichiro Hirai and conduct Hirai's professional debut concert. As Casals could not visit Matsumoto, Matsumoto
came to Casals. On April 16, at Bunkyo Kokaido Hall in Tokyo, Suzuki
led 400 children in a special concert. The black-and-white footage of the
event shows a stage filled with young violinists playing the first movement of a Vivaldi concerto. In the audience Casals is all smiles. Sitting
beside him is his wife Marta, looking at once incredulous and delighted.
At the end, Casals climbs up on stage and affectionately congratulates
the young performers. Tearful, overcome with emotion, he speaks of the
importance of what he has just witnessed and wonders aloud if music
might save the world after all.[3]

As ever, the increasing fame generated by such episodes proved a
double-edged sword. Suzuki continued to promote talent education—a

movement for broad social change through the reinvention of general education. He consistently argued that music learning was just one manifestation—albeit a powerful manifestation—of every child's ability to turn their potential into talent as he understood it. But the more his violin pedagogy in particular was embraced at home and adapted in foreign countries, the harder it became for him to convey the enormous social goal of which music instruction was only a part.

Of particular importance, Suzuki's social mission largely disappeared from American applications of his ideas. Social reform also has little presence in Suzuki Method instruction in Europe and elsewhere, but the Suzuki Method is especially popular in North America, making US approaches influential. To be clear, it is not that Americans refused to think about Suzuki's core philosophy and its all-encompassing scope. Kendall, in a 1959 report for the American organizations that funded his research trip to Matsumoto, extensively describes the social and historical contexts surrounding the emergence of the talent education movement. He also cites Suzuki to the effect that "investigat[ing] methods through which all children can develop their various talents" was perhaps "more important than the investigation of atomic power"—a bold statement at the height of the Cold War. But, despite Kendall's awareness of the movement's grand vision, his primary interest was always violin pedagogy. To that end, he would fret over pedagogical questions, like whether Suzuki's teaching approach could be used outside Japan, given that "the American way of life" was "so essentially different from the Japanese." Suzuki himself disabused Kendall of that concern, affirming that it made no difference if children were "Japanese, American, African, or any other national or ethnic group." Any could learn to play the Vivaldi A Minor concerto at a high level, he suggested.[4]

In 1966, Kendall published a booklet, "Talent, Education and Suzuki: What the American Music Educator Should Know about Shinichi Suzuki." As his title hints, Kendall attempts to communicate Suzuki's philosophy both as a social movement and as a method for violin instruction. By the time the booklet was revised in 1973, however, it was retitled "The Suzuki Violin Method in American Music Education." In other words, it did not take long before Americans whittled Suzuki's ambitious social movement down to a pedagogical method. This position became institutionalized in the Suzuki Association of the Americas, which was committed, since its 1972 founding, to establishing "Suzuki" as a brand-name in music education.

In Japan as well, there was a great deal more interest in teaching the violin than in revamping education wholesale. By the 1960s, the postwar emergency had ended and Japan was beginning to become an affluent society. The popularity of violin practice as an after-school activity grew, so much so that, in 1962, NHK launched the instructional television program *Violin Lessons (Baiorin no Okeiko)*. On the show, groups of Japanese, ranging from primary schoolers to adult learners, were invited to receive lessons from the country's top violinists and conservatory instructors. The program was broadcast regularly—sometimes twice a week—all over Japan for twenty-two seasons, ending its run in 1984. Throughout, Toshiya Eto, Suzuki's first child student, was a frequent host.

Eto was a returning hero of sorts. He had come back to Japan after making his name in the United States. His mesmerizing success story included some serious philosophical conflicts with Suzuki, who had guided him from the age of four. At twelve, Eto left Suzuki's studio on an acrimonious note. As Koji Toyoda remembers, disagreements emerged between Suzuki and Eto's father over the boy's career path. Suzuki felt that the time was not yet right for Eto to perform professionally. Suzuki was particularly alarmed by the media hype that surrounded Eto after he won the Eighth Annual Music Competition and got his own genius label. His father did not want to hold back and allowed Eto to record Mendelssohn's violin concerto against Suzuki's wishes, leading to a severing of ties. After a period of self-study, Eto became a student of Alexander Mogilevsky and earned his degree at Ueno, where he signed on as a faculty member immediately upon graduation. In 1948, sponsored by a music-loving Pennsylvania lawyer attached to the US occupation forces, Eto became one of the first Japanese in the postwar era to study abroad. His destination was the Curtis Institute of Music and his new teacher was Efrem Zimbalist. Eto's professional debut came at Carnegie Hall in 1951. Within a few years, he was made professor at Curtis, was signed by Decca Records, and married a fellow violinist. Eto opted to return to Japan in 1961, bringing his young family with him. He came back because he wanted to teach others and thereby raise the overall level of performance by Japanese players of Western classical music. He proved an exceptional instructor, most notably as a professor at Toho Gakuen School of Music, a private college of which he became president in 1997.[5]

Eto's goal was to prepare violinists fit to compete on the international stage, and as such his interests and philosophy stood in stark contrast to Suzuki's. Eto, who was often referred to as "the Suzuki Method's first student," had complicated feelings about the method's premises. Writing for a major music journal in 1979, he comments unhappily on the "recent popularity" of violin lessons for young children. He expresses disappointment in the many parents who treat lessons like just another extracurricular activity, meant primarily to keep restless youngsters occupied. Too often he would see students refusing to give their best in lessons. Worse, they would excuse their lukewarm efforts by announcing that they had no professional aspirations. Eto's views certainly sound like thinly veiled criticism of Suzuki's, which prioritized well-rounded human beings over professional violinists. In the article, Eto also implicitly faults Suzuki's instruction books for failing to equip students with the rigorous technical and musical background that would lead them to conservatories.[6]

Although they diverged on the goals of violin studies, Suzuki and Eto agreed about the rewarding byproducts of music-making. "It is all right if one gives his all to music, and then decides to go a different way," Eto writes, because the effort is worth it even if one doesn't become exceptionally skilled. He believed that the experience of devoting oneself to music-making, even for a limited period of time, confers a high degree of focus, which is useful in any walk of life. Moreover, the child who studies the violin with commitment—if not necessarily outstanding results—ever after enjoys "wholly different levels of communing with music, so different from people who simply and passively enjoy listening to records." This view, endorsing various positive spillover effects of musical education in nurturing what we now call emotional intelligence, seems to reinforce rather than reject the essential claims of talent education. Where Suzuki differed from Eto was in the comprehensive nature of his goals. For Suzuki, it was not enough to agree that learning music—and other subjects—came with practical benefits. He was also adamant that such benefits should be enjoyed by any and all children, leaving absolutely no one behind.

At about the same time Eto returned to Japan, Suzuki decided to do something about the yawning gap between the goals of talent education—maximum personal development for all human beings through effective learning—and the role of talent education in practice, which tended toward effective musical training for children whose parents were willing and able to spend significant resources supporting their studies. He was not ready to give up on realizing the greatest good for the greatest number and so decided to take his business to the boss—the prime minister of Japan, Hayato Ikeda.

The exact date of their meeting is unknown, but it must have been sometime between 1960 to 1964, the years when Ikeda was in office. Suzuki's proposal to Japan's top-ranking politician reiterated much of what had been laid out two decades earlier in *Powerful Education*. Suzuki argued that the Japanese state—actually, all the world's states—should take charge of early childhood education. Public school reform for older students would be important too, but what mattered most, he insisted, was that the state get involved in schooling at a much earlier stage. This could be done, he said, by stationing counselors all over the country to advise new parents. Pediatricians and social workers gave out basic operating instructions, but they were too busy to really nurture young parents. This was a key part of the message: not only children but also parents need caring guidance to grow as reflective and thoughtful human beings capable of raising a well-loved and well-taught generation.

One can imagine how such talk would go down with men in high office. In a 1980 lecture, Suzuki, with his typical self-deprecating humor, said that he had repeated this same appeal to other prime ministers, always to no avail. There was a template to the responses: "That's a fine idea. Yes, yes, very good. Good-bye."[7] And it was not just the ears of prime ministers that were deaf to Suzuki's pleas. According to his secretaries, he wrote to every education minister whenever there was turnover in the cabinet, which was not infrequent in those days. Alas, he never received any answers. To professional policymakers, Suzuki's proposals must have seemed meddlesome, quixotic, and far-fetched. However well-connected Suzuki might have been, politicians and elite bureaucrats preferred to see him only as a famous eccentric from the Nagano mountains. Why should they listen to him, when everything was going fine?[8]

During the period of high economic growth from the early 1960s to the mid-1980s, pretty much the whole of Japan was under the spell of progress. And since life would only continue to get better, then it must be that the government and the bureaucrats who devised policy were doing something right. It was Prime Minister Ikeda, the first leader to whom Suzuki made a direct appeal, who unleashed this postwar resurgence of confidence. His pet project, rooted in his background as a Finance Ministry official, was the Income-Doubling Plan, whereby he promised that Japan's gross national product would double within a decade. This goal was achieved. Alongside income growth, Japanese took advantage of huge investments in infrastructure, welfare, and healthcare. Living standards kept improving, explaining why most Japanese of this period identified as members of the middle class. The stable upward trajectory, coming as it did after the annihilation of Japan's national life, was intoxicating.[9]

Beneath the surface, though, there was much for a man of egalitarian vision like Suzuki to object to. For example, the same Japan where everything was hunky-dory was routinely sterilizing people with disabilities and hereditary disorders. The Eugenic Protection Law (*Yusei Hogoho*), promulgated in 1948, was touted as a progressive piece of feminist legislation, which legalized sterilization and abortion for the sake of preserving women's health. But as its name suggests, the legislation was sinister. With the official aim of preventing the births of "inferior" offspring, the state sterilized approximately 25,000 people with disabilities—about 16,500 of them without their consent. Appreciating that many would not give in without a fight, the Ministry of Health and Welfare condoned the use of physical restraints, anesthesia, and even outright deception for purposes of coercion. The law remained in place until 1996.[10]

Eugenics was utterly incompatible with Suzuki's thinking. Eugenics holds that societies improve with the absence of certain inborn traits, so bearers of these traits must be prevented from entering the gene pool. Suzuki, in marked contrast, thought society would be improved if all individuals, regardless of their inborn qualities, could live their lives to the fullest. A good society was a society in which all people could lead lives of purpose and accomplishment, not one in which accidents of birth decided everything. Suzuki therefore encouraged his instructors to accept students with obvious challenges. There are various accounts of him advocating, for instance, for a girl with an arm and hand malformed by thalidomide, a girl with only three fingers on her left hand, an autistic boy who suffered panic attacks, a boy with a brain injury and resulting intellectual disability, and a blind boy, all of whom eventually learned to play the violin using Suzuki's approach.[11]

In this determinedly nondiscriminatory endeavor, Suzuki had a brother-in-arms. Masaaki Honda, a longtime TERI board member and a medical doctor, was inspired by Suzuki as well as by Glenn Doman, an American physical therapist who worked with brain-injured children. Starting in the early 1970s, Honda incorporated incremental physical and memorization exercises in his clinical work, alongside music lessons for children, which seemed to help with a variety of impairments. Honda's success in turn strengthened Suzuki's belief that all children could benefit from his approach.[12]

But for every Masaaki Honda, there were plenty others who did not care about what it meant to live in a society where the eugenics law could persist and where thousands could be brutalized in the name of so-called progress. After all, Japan had so many glittering achievements. In 1964, with the strong support of the United States, Japan became a member of the Organization for Economic Cooperation and Development, signaling a triumphant return to the world stage as a commercial powerhouse. The country's first bullet train made its debut the same year, inaugurating the world-famous *shinkansen* system of superfast rail. To top it off, that autumn Japan became the first Asian country to host the Olympic Games. These were the Olympics that could have taken place in 1940, which were cancelled due to international outrage over the full-scale Japanese invasion of China that had begun a few years earlier. The most eloquent physical testament to Japan's comeback was National Stadium, constructed in the late 1950s and used as the main venue for the 1964 Olympics. Seating more than 50,000 spectators, it dwarfed the nearby Tokyo Metropolitan Gymnasium, where the 1955 Grand Concert was held.

And for those focused on the talent education movement's violin pedagogy, there was still more to celebrate. As in other quarters of Japan, so too in Suzuki's 1964 was a banner year. It was then that Suzuki and his young violinists made their first international tour, which brought them to the United States. Suzuki devotees still refer, with quasireligious reverence, to the Ten Children Tour. The tour idea was broached by Kendall after another trip to Japan in 1962. Robert Klotman and Oberlin's Clifford Cook, who had visited Matsumoto in 1963, joined forces with Kendall to help coordinate.[13]

But money, as usual, was tight in Matsumoto, and the Americans were unable to provide any of the funding themselves. At the time, TERI was without a headquarters, having grown out of its original wooden building; expensive adventures abroad were unthinkable. And expensive they were: in those days, the US dollar was pegged at 360 Japanese yen, a lopsided exchange rate that worked in favor of Japan's export industry, contributing much to its postwar "economic miracle," but which made it extremely difficult for Japanese to travel in the United States. It would have taken nearly 400,000 yen—the annual salary of a mid-level white-collar worker—to cover the cost of just one adult's airfare. Kendall suggested to Kenji Mochizuki—the student who introduced the Grand Concert footage to the American violin world and who now worked at the Japanese Consulate in New York—that Suzuki make the trip by himself. But Mochizuki strongly opposed the proposal for the same reason he had insisted that Americans see the footage. Moving images of young violinists had accomplished a good deal already—what might live performances achieve?[14]

At the urging of board member Dr. Honda, who had lived in the United States as a child and who believed that the trip would benefit the talent education movement in the long run, it was finally decided that some of the money reserved for the completion of the new headquarters would instead be used to cover the cost of Waltraud's and Suzuki's travels. Ten children, ranging from ages five to twelve, were chosen from among the families who could afford travel expenses themselves. Ryugo Hayano—by then a bright, gregarious twelve-year-old—was one of the ten. To this day, he has the travel receipts as a memento.

Money was not the only problem, however. Just getting out of the country proved a formidable task. Two weeks before departure, the Ministry of Education quibbled with the children's passport applications on the ground that it was not advisable for them to miss school. Honda

Suzuki, back row at right, with members of the first Ten Children Tour, March 1964. *Talent Education Research Institute*

pleaded with his contacts in the Foreign and Education Ministries, and at the eleventh hour, the passports were granted. Together with the ten children, Suzuki, Waltraud, Suzuki's sister-in-law Shizuko (who would provide piano accompaniment for the young violinists), Hachiro Hirose (an instructor), Honda, and four chaperoning mothers left Tokyo's Haneda International Airport on March 5, 1964. Their first port of call was Seattle. The group was driven straight from the airport to the University of Washington, where the children performed for a packed auditorium. As they played piece after piece, the stunned silence that pervaded the hall gradually turned into excitement, and at the end of the program the audience stood and broke into rapturous applause. For the next three weeks, the group traveled across the United States, making stops in Chicago, Boston, New York, Philadelphia, Oberlin, Detroit, Wichita, Tucson, Los Angeles, San Mateo, and finally Honolulu.[15]

When the Ten Children Tour stopped at Juilliard in New York, the violinist Louise Behrend was in the audience. For the ten violinists, it was merely a short matinée performance before the evening's main event with a youth symphony in Westchester. But the Julliard concert was life-altering for Behrend. Suzuki's students "blew us all away," she recalled more than forty years later. She was impressed by the young violinists' superb technique, including their intonation. Their musical flair was even more astonishing. Since she taught young children herself, and thought she was doing the job "pretty well," this was a humbling moment. She was so affected that she decided shortly afterward to visit Suzuki, as Kendall had done before her. In order to finance the trip, she asked her management company to organize a Far Eastern recital tour, during which she took a break to spend two weeks in Matsumoto absorbing as much as she could. Based on this experience, in 1970 she founded the School for Strings, New York's first Suzuki program. Behrend became an influential voice in the international Suzuki community. She even persuaded her friend David Nadien, a legendary violinist and concert-master of the New York Philharmonic under Leonard Bernstein between 1966 and 1970, to record the repertoire that accompanied the interna-tional edition of the Suzuki Method books.[16]

Back in 1964, the Philadelphia performance was one of the most anticipated events of the tour, as the children would play for partici-pants at the Music Educators National Conference. Hirose, the in-structor, recalled that soon after the children began to play, many in the audience started to cry. When the performance was over, some of the audience members rushed over to Suzuki and hugged him. One listener that day, William Starr, a professor at the University of Tennessee and concertmaster of the Knoxville Symphony, would join the ranks of the Suzuki Method's most committed promoters. Starr went on to cofound the Suzuki Association of the Americas in 1972 and served as its first president. In 1968, four years after the Philadelphia conference, Starr and his wife Connie, a pianist and violist, took a radical step. With two huge crates, twenty suitcases, a slew of books, and a typewriter, they and their eight children relocated to Matsumoto for fourteen months. In Matsumoto, the husband and wife observed Suzuki's lessons and re-corded them with their Sony video camera, one of the first such devices on the market. The Starrs came to Matsumoto not only to research the Suzuki methodology but also to practice it as parents of Suzuki violin-ists. After their experience, they returned to the United States as effective evangelists of the Suzuki way, at least as it applied to teaching classical violin.[17]

The second Ten Children Tour came in 1966, and thereafter the tour became an annual event for the next twenty-eight years. Suzuki violinists visited twenty countries and 384 cities all around the world and gave 483 concerts. The first tour to Europe was in 1970, to Southeast Asia in 1994. Unlike the original tour, the trips that followed were paid for at least in part by a special TERI fund. Professional music managers, initially Sheldon Soffer Inc. and later Ibbs and Tillet, also helped with children's travel costs. The children were chosen by Suzuki from among the participants at the Matsumoto summer school.[18]

Experiences like the Starrs' and Behrends' were repeated by others. Young Suzuki violinists would impress music instructors abroad, who then felt compelled to travel to Matsumoto and learn the master's secrets firsthand. Not everyone took their visit all that seriously; some, to prove that they had "studied" with Suzuki, would demand a certificate with his signature after just a week and then would disappear. Others stayed for several years to finish the teacher-training course properly.[19]

Masami Kojima, a young correspondent for the major national daily *Mainichi*, was based in and around Matsumoto in the late 1970s and early 1980s. When he first arrived, he was struck by the sight of numerous foreigners in what he had always thought of as a provincial city. Once he found out that they were almost invariably followers of Suzuki's, his journalistic curiosity was piqued. In 1980, he started researching the talent education movement extensively, speaking with Suzuki and sitting in on many of the lessons he gave in a classroom filled with smoke from his cigarettes. (Suzuki was by then teaching in the TERI headquarters, completed at last in 1967.) Dozens of serialized newspaper articles later, in 1985, Kojima published a book examining Suzuki's singular philosophy. When Kojima expanded and updated the book in 2016, he asked himself again what the movement was really about, this time proposing that the answer could be found in Suzuki's own words, as recorded in an exchange with Bernard Leach, the British potter.

In 1964, Leach returned to Matsumoto, where he took part in a round-table conversation with Suzuki and Sanshiro Ikeda, a master woodworker and Leach's travel companion. Ikeda posited that Suzuki's work, despite focusing on a Western instrument, reminded him of the essence of Buddhism. What Ikeda meant was that Suzuki tried to show his students ways to achieve inner peace while accommodating the world. Leach heartily agreed and added that the talent education movement had become almost like a religion. "That's what everyone says," Suzuki responded, smiling. "What you see here is a religion of bringing up children. That's how precious children are," he explained. Suzuki did not want to be thought of as a cult leader, but children were indeed precious beings. Ikeda and Leach meant no offense. They likened Suzuki's movement to a religion because they saw him as a fellow seeker of truth and beauty and as someone who taught others how to find and create truth and beauty, so that life was worth living.[20]

This was becoming something of a constant for Suzuki—the guru treatment. He would always stress that children were the heart of his movement, not he. Nevertheless, for many aspiring instructors, the journey to Matsumoto was like a pilgrimage. In observing and interacting with Suzuki in person, and above all being guided by his way of doing things, one could touch the hem of his proverbial gown. Perhaps Suzuki's adolescent devouring of the teachings of Dogen, the thirteenth-century Zen Buddhist monk, had left a deep impression. In their discussion, Leach and Ikeda reference another influential Suzuki of the twentieth century, D. T. Suzuki, whose writings did much to introduce Zen Buddhism to the West. It was not lost on either Leach or Ikeda that their own Suzuki had about him an otherworldliness that was at once appealing and enigmatic. This aura probably had to do with Suzuki's remarkable level of self-control and the depth of belief in his own philosophy. Some people even thought he possessed healing energy—*ki* or *chi*. The Soviet violinist Leonid Kogan, while on tour in Matsumoto, developed a harsh allergic reaction to a cold medicine and later claimed that Suzuki had healed him by channeling energy to the affected area of Kogan's hand, just in time for his concert engagement. There are numerous other stories like this one.[21]

Suzuki traveled far and wide in his sixties, seventies, and even eighties. He went anywhere he was requested, be it a major city or small town. This way those who could not come to Matsumoto could meet him elsewhere. He toured in Europe, North America, South America, East Asia,

Suzuki did not limit his travels to major cities. Here he is welcomed by a crowd in Pendleton, Oregon, in 1969. *Talent Education Research Institute*

Southeast Asia, and Australia, all the while collecting honorary degrees. The first, in 1966, came from the New England Conservatory of Music in Boston. The long list of US institutions that recognized Suzuki includes the Eastman School of Music, Oberlin College, and the Cleveland Institute of Music. "Dr. Suzuki" became the customary way of addressing him among his foreign followers, even though he did not insist on it himself. The title was certainly never used for him in Japan, as the respectful "sensei" had always sufficed. Sensei, widely used in reference to teachers, literally means "born before" and was the title preferred by Suzuki, who said that he only happened to be born before his students, and that order of birth—not any superiority—qualified him to guide others. As for all the institutional accolades and honors, he seems to have adopted the old Japanese dictum of "Don't refuse what comes your way, and don't chase what leaves you" (*kuru mono wa kobamazu, saru mono wa owazu*), in the belief that whatever recognition he received would lead to a broader understanding of his movement.[22]

To move and travel the way he did, Suzuki must have been blessed with unusual strength and energy despite the serious afflictions he had suffered as a young man and immediately after the war. In April 1976, there was a gala in Tokyo to celebrate his seventy-seventh birthday the previous autumn. (The seventy-seventh birthday is considered particularly auspicious in Japanese culture.) This special gathering included a touching reunion of his students from the prewar years. Among those present were Koji Toyoda, who had become concertmaster of the Berlin Radio Symphony and then a professor at the Berlin University of the Arts; Takeshi Kobayashi, a former concertmaster of the Brno Philharmonic; Kenji Kobayashi, a soloist and concertmaster of the Tokyo Metropolitan Symphony Orchestra; and Takaya Urakawa, a former concertmaster of the Bamberg Symphony. But the most noteworthy guest may have been Toshiya Eto. Despite their fraught parting and nearly four decades of estrangement, Eto agreed to perform for his old teacher. After listening to the superb performances of his former students, Suzuki lauded them by reminding the audience that if the students do not surpass their teacher, then the teacher has not done a very good job. Suzuki liked to jest, but these words were true to his convictions. Addressing budding instructors during the embryonic stages of the talent education movement in 1949, he was already insisting that they must constantly strive to improve their teaching, so as to help their students achieve things that they themselves had been unable to.[23]

At this point, a dozen years after the first Ten Children Tour, there was huge demand for Suzuki's presence, especially in the United States. In the course of forty summer days in 1976, he taught in California, Wisconsin, New York, and Washington. For American Suzuki practitioners, summer institutes provided invaluable opportunities to see the man in action. Andrew Bird, the Chicago-based multi-instrumentalist, was only three years old at the time, but he took part in the Suzuki Summer Institute held at the University of Wisconsin at Stevens Point. "Dr. Suzuki would come and we'd all play in this gymnasium, all the different levels playing at once," he recalls. This was the group-playing format Suzuki devised for the grand concerts and other talent education festivals, dating back to the 1950s. Participants would "play down," starting with the most advanced pieces in the repertoire and finishing with the "Twinkle" variations, enabling a large group of mixed-level

Suzuki sits for a photograph at his seventy-seventh birthday gala, April 1976. In the first row, left to right: Kenji Kobayashi, Waltraud Suzuki, Shinichi Suzuki, Toshiya Eto. Second row, left to right: Takaya Urakawa, ongakuin instructor Yasuo Mito, Takeshi Kobayashi, Koji Toyoda. *Talent Education Research Institute*

players to come together for the conclusion of the performance. That year in Wisconsin, about 3,000 people participated in the institute.[24]

After that heady summer, Suzuki returned to Japan to face an acute reminder of the impermanence of life: in September, his long-time supporter Yoshichika Tokugawa died just short of his ninetieth birthday. Despite his advanced age, Tokugawa had been well enough to attend

Suzuki's gala earlier in the spring, making his passing a sudden one. For Suzuki, it was a moment of real anguish. Yet the pressing awareness that we all have limited time on earth seemed to leave him that much more determined. He had no intention of taking it easy, perhaps partly because he always felt that he started his life's quest a bit late, having picked up the violin at seventeen. "Late starters like me have to live longer to make up for the lost time," he would say. With so much more to be done, he often joked that he would not retire until he was 110.[25]

Tokugawa was gone, but by then Suzuki's cause had acquired other high-profile cheerleaders. One was Masaru Ibuka, a cofounder of Sony. As well as running a hugely successful global corporation that embodied Japan's postwar recovery, Ibuka was a committed philanthropist with a profound personal interest in early childhood education. His second daughter had been born with an intellectual disability, and he desperately sought ways to help her become as independent and active in society as possible. In 1969 Ibuka founded a think tank to research accessible educational approaches for children starting from infancy. He also opened a TERI affiliate dedicated to research in early childhood education. Ibuka partnered with Suzuki and Seiji Kaya, a physicist, moral reformer, and former provost of the University of Tokyo, to write a book on early childhood development, and in 1971 Ibuka published *Kindergarten Is Too Late*, a best seller that linked early education to social improvement. Like Suzuki, Ibuka felt that too many Japanese unthinkingly left major questions to elite bureaucrats and politicians in exchange for the implicit promise of stability, security, and affluence, thereby forgoing true self-governance. Ibuka wondered how people so oblivious to the national future could conscientiously raise the children who would participate in it.[26]

Another powerful ally who shared Suzuki's philosophy was Toru Kumon. Kumon, who went on to start the globally popular Kumon method of learning, was originally a high school math teacher. He admired Suzuki from a frontline educator's point of view. Alongside everything else, Suzuki had developed an innovative approach to mathematics education—formulated while he lay still on his futon at Asama Onsen, recovering from his severe postwar ailment—and Kumon borrowed from it. Suzuki's method combined memorization, recitation, physical exercise, and game-playing, such as counting up and down different sets of numbers, as if to play the ascending and descending scales on the violin. This approach was used at Hongo Elementary School's experimental program and at the Yoji Gakuen, the TERI-run preschool in Matsumoto. In the late 1950s Kumon developed his own learning program that integrated worksheet-guided self-study with aspects of Suzuki's methods, such as emphasis on repetition and incremental learning at an individually determined pace. Underpinning the Kumon method was a faith, identical to Suzuki's, in "the potential of each individual student" and in the possibility of developing each student's "ability to the maximum." Today, these are the maxims of Kumon's world-spanning project. Kumon and Suzuki agreed that their respective enterprises were basically one and the same, in terms of both methodology and philosophy.[27]

If their methods were similar, however, their lives were quite different. Kumon, though highly respected, was never the quasireligious leader that Suzuki became in the eyes of his followers. And Kumon steered clear of the loaded term "talent," preferring to stick to "potential." Kumon also had the practical sense to secure the survival of his business. Only very late in life did Suzuki begin to think about what would come after him.

Perhaps the leader of a movement that draws its strength from its principal's charisma is just not allowed to die, or even to slow down. A 1977 New York Times profile was headlined, "At 79, Suzuki's Tempo Is Still Agitato." According to the report, Suzuki would wake up at three o'clock in the morning to listen to graduation recordings and record his own comments. This and other desk work would continue for six hours, after which Suzuki would appear at TERI headquarters. He would work there until seven at night, teaching students and instructors-to-be. The article, reported from Matsumoto, points out that Suzuki considered retirement unthinkable because too many people were relying on him—people like Linda and Roger Stieg, American violin teachers who had made tremendous financial sacrifices so that they could travel to Japan for instruction by Suzuki himself.[28]

Suzuki in his seventies behaved like a man in his prime. But a part of him knew that he could not go on forever. On top of his strenuous schedule of teaching, lecturing, writing, and running TERI, he devoted considerable time and energy to training the future instructors who would inherit leadership of the talent education movement. Helen Higa, an instructor who came to Matsumoto from Hawaiʻi in the early 1970s, recalled a loose institutional structure for her course of studies. There was no set schedule for graduation, although the course usually lasted about three years. On any given day, she might get a five-minute lesson, a twenty-minute lesson, or an hour-long lesson from Suzuki, depending on what he decided to teach. Trainees also observed each other's lessons, studied the repertoire pieces together, and performed in front of each other in preparation for leading group lessons. From Suzuki's free-flowing teaching, Higa learned the importance of observation and reflection. Suzuki was always alert to students' needs, always taking note and re-thinking his plans when the situation demanded. In particular, Suzuki was hyperaware of whether students were mastering material and would stop a lesson in its tracks until the student worked out one or another challenge and was ready to proceed. He would even allow lessons to end with material uncovered if students needed extra time. Suzuki felt strongly that overloading students frustrated them, defeating the purpose of learning. A good teacher, then, was attentive to students' stepwise progress. Higa well knew that Suzuki's was more a philosophy, not an inflexible method; there were no hard-and-fast rules. Teaching the Suzuki way meant "watching and observing and then trying something out, and it would work or it wouldn't."[29]

Megumi Taoka, another instructor trainee from this period, reminisced about how Suzuki kept researching and developing better ways to teach. It was another manifestation of his boundless energy and his endless pursuit. If he thought of some new approach, he would stop by the trainees' lounge and summon them to the classroom so that he could test his new ideas on them. There were no holidays, and taking a break was never an option for him. If he felt tired of one task, he would choose another to focus on. With a mixture of concern, annoyance, and pride, Waltraud told the *New York Times* reporter that her husband "never relaxes . . . That's the trouble with him. He's always trying to find a new way to teach a point to a particular student."[30]

Waltraud also told the reporter about an old problem—her husband's carelessness with money. How could the talent education movement, now a mature and still-growing global operation, possibly have been struggling financially in 1977? TERI's instructional materials were selling all over the world; that alone should have been enough to cover costs.

But somehow Suzuki always managed to be in debt. "Sensei liked to give, and gave more than he had," his secretary Mitsuko Kawakami remembered, "so much so that when it was time to file taxes, we had nothing left to pay them!" As unbelievable as it sounds, there was no institutional oversight over Suzuki's access to a large amount of money. All he had to do was ask someone in the TERI office, and it was turned over to him so that he could give it away. That such a thing was possible was a sign of amateurish accounting but all the more so the absolute power Suzuki had over his staff.[31]

Suzuki's gift-giving was at once nonchalant and insistent, as Mineo Hayashi discovered. In the 1950s and 1960s, Hayashi was one of the first talent education cello students, and he went on to a performance career. As a young man, Hayashi was a recipient of Suzuki's excessive generosity on more than one occasion. Once, when he heard that Hayashi had a minor automobile accident, Suzuki gave him "a considerable amount of money" as a consolation. In another instance, Hayashi found himself hanging around at TERI headquarters with some time to kill before a concert. On a whim, he decided to give a couple of free lessons. Afterward, he was taken aback when Suzuki compensated him with 100,000 yen—at the time, almost as much as the starting monthly salary of a university graduate. If money was not to hand, Suzuki gave away expensive violin bows and works of art without a second thought. The recipients of his largesse were often young people.[32]

What Suzuki gave away typically belonged to TERI, since he did not have a great deal of his own. As such, he is one of many Japanese who did not reap major financial rewards for inventions and ideas that became global phenomena, whether the Suzuki Method, karaoke, or sudoku. Perhaps this was the self-conscious discipline of the post-Meiji business ethos at play, curbing greed in the name of the greater good. It is worth pondering. To this day, Japan, for all its business successes, avoids the excesses of greed that drive capitalism elsewhere. To illustrate, in March 2021, Toyota Motor Corporation CEO Akio Toyoda received a pay package equal 1/2,700 of what Tesla CEO Elon Musk received in the same period.[33]

Yet Suzuki was unusual in his disregard for money. Other Japanese organizational leaders may have taken relatively low pay, but they knew the importance of finance in the context of businesses and nonprofits alike. Suzuki, by comparison, was indifferent, even averse, to the subject of money. His neglect of the issue jeopardized TERI's survival and worried and puzzled close observers, including Ibuka and Kumon, who knew very well the challenges of running a major enterprise. Both of them repeatedly urged Suzuki to put accounting and legal specialists in charge of administration at TERI. But Suzuki seemed to abhor their suggestions, as he did any mention of money that did not involve him giving it away.[34]

Meanwhile, especially in the United States, the increasing popularity and fame of what was being called the Suzuki Method made it an enticing target for the commercially minded. At the fortieth anniversary of the Suzuki Association of the Americas, in 2012, William Starr described how David Sengstack—president of Summy-Birchard, the publisher of John Kendall's Suzuki-related literature in the 1960s—offered to protect Suzuki's name by claiming the trademark himself. Sengstack was an old hand at this game. Earlier, his company had acquired publishing rights for Suzuki's materials for the entire world outside Japan from the Japanese publisher Zen-On. This seems to have resulted from an utter lack of business sense on the Japanese side: Suzuki granted all his publishing rights to TERI, which then licensed those rights to Zen-On, which clearly had no idea what to do. In any case, over the course of the 1970s and 1980s, Sengstack registered copyrights and trademarks using the Suzuki name. Sengstack claimed his motivation was to prevent the movement from splitting apart "as potential teachers rushed to Japan, found favor with Suzuki, then returned to present his latest ideas." But Sengstack certainly wanted to profit from the Suzuki brand name as well. Ostensibly in order to ensure "the growth of a pure Suzuki movement in America," Sengstack put tremendous pressure on the Suzuki Association of the Americas to persuade Suzuki to grant him control of the Suzuki brand name. Waltraud made sure Suzuki rejected such a proposition.[35]

Starr also mentioned Suzuki's close encounter with one David Smith, putatively a multimillionaire Atlanta businessman. In Starr's retelling, Smith declared in the *Wall Street Journal* that he would like to give millions to his chosen cause—the Suzuki Method. He did indeed give generously. In an early 1977 newsletter, Suzuki announced a plan to construct a much-needed annex to the TERI headquarters, which would be paid for, unexpectedly, by "an American named Smith-san." Remarkably, Smith did not want anything in return for this gift.[36]

The truth, according to Starr, was messier. In April 1978, Suzuki and his violinists made another tour of the United States, first giving a joint concert of a hundred Japanese and a hundred American violinists at the Kennedy Center in Washington, DC. The concert was attended by President Jimmy Carter, who said he wanted to take his daughter Amy on his impending visit to Japan so that she could be taught by the master. This highly publicized event was followed by concerts at Carnegie Hall in New York and then in Atlanta, where Suzuki was made an honorary citizen. During Suzuki's stay in Atlanta, he and his retinue were taken to Smith's various offices—he seemed to have his fingers in many pots. At one point, Waltraud was peeled away from Suzuki's side. Her absence lasted about five minutes, during which Smith presented Suzuki with a legal document that granted him all the rights to the Suzuki name, which, Smith explained, he would then license. The idea was preposterous, but, amazingly, Suzuki signed. He was convinced that by donating a whole building without asking for anything in return, Smith had demonstrated integrity and selflessness and therefore could be trusted.

When Waltraud found out what had happened in her brief absence, she was horrified and seized the document. To her great relief, she discovered that her husband had signed in the wrong place, nullifying the agreement. For the rest of the Atlanta visit, Waltraud, Starr, and Sandy Reuning, another pioneering member of the American Suzuki movement, took turns clinging to Suzuki. In the end, Smith realized no tangible returns on his "investment" of an annex building, though he did leave his name to posterity as a cofounder of the Suzuki School in Atlanta, a Montessori school that was, according to its website, opened "with Shinichi Suzuki's endorsement." In his fortieth-anniversary speech, Starr added that Smith was shot dead in a New York alley a few years after the Atlanta meeting. There were no leads as to the killer. For his part, Suzuki recorded, regretfully, that Smith was killed in an accident while traveling in Italy.[37]

For some years, the annex in Matsumoto—commonly known as Sumisu Kaikan (Smith Hall)—was only partially used, becoming another symbol of all that was on Suzuki's heaping plate. Allen Lieb, an instructor at the School for Strings in New York who studied with Suzuki in the late 1970s and became CEO of the International Suzuki Association, remembers stacks and stacks of English-language textbooks collecting dust in the once eagerly anticipated space. These might have been materials from the English-learning program Disney World of English, which is popular in Japan to this day. Created in 1978 with the help of Anne Dow, a Harvard academic and Suzuki believer, the materials feature Micky Mouse and friends and dovetail with Suzuki's mother-tongue approach. It is probable that he considered incorporating the textbooks in the preschool curriculum at the Yoji Gakuen but never saw to it. There was simply too much to do.[38]

In the early 1980s, the octogenarian Suzuki finally took up fundraising. Looking to the future, he realized that the talent education movement would need direction in his absence. Since the movement was now a global one, that direction would have to come from an international organization—and someone would have to fund the new body. In addition, just as Sengstack had warned, there were too many "Suzuki" associations around the world; a global organization could bring them under a single roof. These assorted associations were usually founded with Suzuki's endorsement—which he was prone to giving freely— though they operated independently. Some were run by teachers taught by him personally, others by teachers who merely said they were. Anyone might lay claim to Suzuki's philosophical, methodological, and even spiritual legacy. Emphasizing the importance of establishing formal leadership that could oversee the preservation of his work, Suzuki pleaded with Japanese instructors and student families to pay an annual membership fee to get the global organization up and running. They obliged, and gradually their fellows in other countries followed suit. This led to the founding of the International Suzuki Association (ISA) in 1983.

Around the same time, Suzuki also relented on the "Suzuki Method." With Waltraud's help, he came to realize that he would have to trademark the term and embrace it, lest others took advantage. A New York attorney, Pasquale Razzano, worked closely with the Suzukis to make the legal arrangements. After so many years of giving out his name and work to nearly all takers, there was much to do. First Razzano had to register the trademark in the United States and other countries in which there were Suzuki associations. Then the various organizations

Suzuki leads an international group of youngsters at the sixth World Suzuki Convention, Matsumoto, July 1983. *Talent Education Research Institute*

under the auspices of the newly established ISA became licensees of that trademark. There was also a long and difficult conversation to be had with Birch Tree, Summy-Birchard's corporate successor. Ultimately an agreement was reached whereby the old Summy-Birchard copyrights and trademarks were reassigned to Suzuki, who in turn assigned them to ISA.[39]

Suzuki, one imagines, was not closely concerned with these legal processes. Far more worrying was that talent education and the mother-tongue approach were being eclipsed by the narrower concept of the Suzuki Method. What had been a movement for social reform was becoming more of a personal legacy, tied to the violin and a few other instruments. Suzuki's teaching style would outlive him, as would his name. But he could not be sure about the future of his revolution.

9

"SUZUKI MESSODO"–IN MY TIME

In my memory, it is the late 1970s, and I am six or seven years old. I'm in the southern Tokyo neighborhood of Meguro, on my way to catch the school bus, when I see a rather small, discreet sign hanging from a tall camellia hedge. A metal sheet, slightly weathered and rusty but pleasing in its graphical simplicity, the sign is painted dark green so that it almost blends in with the plump leaves. On it are the words "Suzuki Method violin lessons available." The words "Suzuki Method" are printed in white katakana letters, the characters used to indicate words borrowed from other languages. There are Japanese words that translate as "method," and of course Suzuki is a common name, usually written as 鈴木. But the sign, implying the Suzuki Method's foreignness, reads, スズキメソッド, which sounds like "Suzuki Messodo"—"messodo" being a translation of "method." I saw that green-and-white sign every day while heading to school. It is etched in me.

Without really knowing anything about Shinichi Suzuki's educational philosophy, I had developed the notion that the Suzuki Method was meant for a "special" kind of child—the smart and well-spoken type whom parents, teachers, and other adults all adore, kids too good for the ubiquitous Yamaha music schools. There must have been some people at my school who were receiving Suzuki musical training, but it never came up in conversation. Suzuki instruction was something they did after school, something that did not have much to do with our shared student life.

Another memory from the same period. I am sitting in my family's living room, furtively channel-surfing; my mother disapproved of children watching a lot of television. I come across the NHK show *Violin Lessons*, and the host that evening is Toshiya Eto. I can still see Eto instructing a girl around my age. Despite his avuncular appearance, he exudes a steely air behind his silver-rimmed glasses. The girl solemnly places her violin on her shoulder. Everything seems so formal, effortful, and contrived. I quickly switch the channel before she even makes a sound.

For a long time, I did not take much notice of the violin, until I started to hear about the adventures of the Osaka-born teenager Midori Goto. Midori—who became internationally famous under her first name—was instructed by her mother, who had aspired to be a professional violinist. Midori became a household name in Japan in the mid-1980s, after her star turn performing Leonard Bernstein's *Serenade,* with the composer conducting, at the Tanglewood Music Festival. During the performance, she broke the E-string—the highest-pitched and the thinnest of the four strings—first on her own violin, then on one she borrowed from the concertmaster. She finished the piece on yet another instrument. The following day, the footage proving her virtuosity and uncommonly graceful calm was repeatedly broadcast on Japanese news programs, as commentators voiced words of amazement and praise, blended with a hint of nationalistic pride. The subtext, as I understand now, was, "Look at this violinist, so young, and so Japanese, and moreover blowing the minds of the Western audience!" Midori was a latter-day Nejiko Suwa, who fulfilled the promise on which Suwa was unable to deliver all those years ago.

The Midori phenomenon fascinated me, not because I was suddenly fond of violin music but because this modern Cinderella—like Suwa, she came from a broken family—was just a few weeks older than myself. I was impressed by the large and glamorous life she seemed to be leading in a faraway country, and on the sheer strength of her art. I thought of my unexciting life in Tokyo and pitied myself. While Midori was an overnight global sensation, I was stuck in the routine of mind-numbing work at school and uninspiring piano practice at home.

But in 1989, something changed: I fell deeply in love with the sound of the violin. I was seventeen, finishing high school, and unable to cope very well with the intense stresses of late adolescence. In many ways, I was experiencing the banal anxieties of teenagers, but mine came with an extra layer of confusion and alienation. My father's work had temporarily taken our family to New York, and I was feeling sad and friendless in a foreign country, struggling for belonging. I was tongue-tied in a language that felt so unnatural. Midori had ended up in New York, but unlike her, I felt I had no business being there, with no special talents to offer to anyone. All of this added up to a minor existential crisis. And for the first time in my life, I actively sought solace in the company of music.

Playing the piano in our living room was not an enticing option. I did not want to give my mother false hope about the possibility of my restarting serious piano practice any time soon; I had only just wriggled out of it on account of being too overwhelmed in a new environment. For me, listening to music became a substitute for playing. I listened to everything, from cheesy pop to heavy metal, musical theater, classical, and jazz. Then, a moment of revelation came when I watched a PBS broadcast, "Mozart by the Masters," featuring Itzhak Perlman, Pinchas Zukerman, and Victor Borge in performance with the Chicago Symphony Orchestra. My eyes and ears were opened, not least because it was the first time I saw Borge's inimitable comic sketches, executed with great timing and innate musicianship, even though his playing always stopped frustratingly short after only a few inviting measures. Borge, the Clown Prince of Denmark, was irreverently poking fun at, and having fun with, classical music. Watching Borge, I unhappily recalled how my mother would stop me whenever I improvised silly tunes on the piano, robbing me of the little fun I was trying to draw from the instrument.

Alongside Borge, what struck me that evening was the voice of Perlman's violin. He played Fritz Kreisler's transcription of the rondo from Mozart's *Haffner Serenade* to Borge's uncharacteristically complete piano accompaniment, as well as the *Sinfonia Concertante* with Zukerman on viola. I knew right then that if I had heard the sound of Perlman's violin as a child, I would have given everything to learn how to play the instrument. I would have willed myself to put up with all the screechy sounds of my own violin in the faint hope of being able to create something resembling this sound.

Not long after that broadcast, I went home to Tokyo during a break. One day, while browsing in a bookstore, I noticed by chance a slim volume on a shelf of reprinted classics. I slipped the book out, instinctively reacting to its title *Ai ni Ikiru*—to live for love, or *Nurtured by*

Love in the published English translation. I saw that the book was originally released in 1966 by an author named Shinichi Suzuki. On the back cover was a headshot of a smiling old man in a suit, with a pleasant face and combed-over gray hair. The earnestness of the title touched something in my extremely introverted mind. I was very much in my own head at the time, owing to my feeling of belonging nowhere: isolated in the United States but no longer completely at home in my native country either. Japan was at the height of its bubble economy, a nation obsessed with luxury brands and anything else that cost a lot of money. It made me uncomfortable, despite my genuine homesickness and tendency to idealize my country when I was away from it.

Gripped by the idea of a love-preaching old man in the midst of a decadent society, I skimmed the first few pages of the book and soon learned that Suzuki was the founder of the "Suzuki Messodo" I remembered from the green metal sign of my childhood. I also noted that Suzuki fell in love with the violin at the age of seventeen—around my age—when he heard Elman's recording of Schubert's *Ave Maria*. I purchased the book, hurried home, and finished it in one sitting. By the end of the book, I was determined that, should I ever have a child, I would start him or her on the Suzuki Method. This was, of course, also the summer when I tried and failed to learn the violin with Koko Kato.

Not long after my unrequited love affair with the violin began, I also started college, where I majored in history. Unexpectedly, Suzuki popped up in one of my course books on US-Japan relations. The book noted that it was the Suzuki Method that drew eleven-year-old Amy Carter to Japan on a state visit with her parents, President Jimmy Carter and First Lady Rosalynn Carter. I later learned that Amy had been taking Suzuki violin lessons for a couple of years and often played at events and concerts. She had also had a lesson with Suzuki himself at the White House the previous year. This time, in Japan, Suzuki declined to see her on account of having a previous engagement; in his niece Hiroko Suzuki's opinion, the snub showed his characteristic aversion to being seen as a sycophant of power. On June 26, 1979, Hiroko was sent in his stead to the US embassy in Tokyo, along with a group of children to play together with Amy. In spite of his tightly packed schedule, the president made sure to drop in and listen for fifteen minutes, in between his visit to the Akasaka Palace and a meeting with a former prime minister. At a time of growing trade friction between the two countries—the United States worried that Japan was becoming too powerful—this musical interlude signified a diplomatic victory for both countries. Amy, for her part, progressed steadily, and her violin-playing continued to prove an asset for the White House. For instance, when King Baudouin and Queen Fabiola of Belgium visited in April 1980, Amy and five other young violinists provided a post-luncheon entertainment including Karl Böhm's "Perpetual Motion," a staple Suzuki repertoire piece.[1]

Carter's presidency was marked by his commitment to civil rights and international cooperation. This particular American First Family's involvement with the Suzuki Method, in my mind, makes so much sense because it speaks to the Suzuki philosophy's humanism. Around the time Amy began her violin studies, more than 300,000 students were following the Suzuki Method—two-thirds of them in the United States, while Japan claimed only 20,000. Forty years on, the United States remains home to about 300,000 Suzuki Method students, about three-quarters of the global total. As "Suzuki Messodo" suggested, Suzuki's pedagogy had been dissociated from its original aspirations. Not only had talent education largely disappeared, but the project that bore Suzuki's name was no longer primarily a Japanese one.[2]

Meanwhile in Japan, an increasing sense of incongruity plagued the talent education movement. The Suzuki Method was a reasonable success in numerical terms, yet no progress was being made with respect to educational and social reform. Suzuki's revolution never found purchase in the official spheres of Japanese society, whether public schools or music conservatories. Public schools remained under the control of an unrepentant Ministry of Education, while conservatories focused on training professional musicians, a status that was rarely the goal for Suzuki's students.

Even in Matsumoto, talent education's birthplace, few people seemed to know anything about it. Overseas visitors would get lost in the mile between the train station and TERI's headquarters because no one could direct them. The office is located in the heart of Matsumoto, on its main boulevard—and yet. Suzuki's former secretary Mitsuko Kawakami, cited the old proverb "It's darkest under the lamp post" while describing talent education's place in the city. She remembered one instructor from Australia who had trouble finding his way to Matsumoto because

Suzuki leads a group class at Seattle's Holy Names Academy in 1964. The school was one of the first institutions outside Japan to establish a Suzuki instructional program. *Talent Education Research Institute*

people in Tokyo had no idea how to get there. When he did manage to reach Matsumoto, no one at the train station had heard of talent education. Repeating the name Suzuki was no help either, with so many Suzukis in town.[3]

On a visit to Matsumoto in the summer of 2019, I could see what Kawakami meant. After spending some hours talking with Koji Toyoda at TERI headquarters, I hailed a taxi to my next destination, the Shinichi Suzuki Memorial Museum. It was only a mile away, but it was in a residential area I did not know well. I told the middle-aged driver where I wanted to go to. "The what?" he responded. I explained that it was the house where Shinichi and Waltraud Suzuki had lived for forty years. It had been left to the city of Matsumoto, which turned it into a museum. Even after I told him the exact address, he seemed unsure, so I added, "You know, the Suzuki Messodo, for violins?" Finally, with a sigh of genuine relief, the driver said, "Ah! The violinist. Oh yes, I think I know, though I've never been."

As it turned out, the driver did not really know where the museum was. It took us a long time to get there; he did not believe in using GPS, so I resigned myself to getting lost with him. He told me about his life as he drove. He was born and raised in Matsumoto, albeit in a less posh neighborhood than the one we were now navigating. I asked him whether there was anyone he knew who took lessons with Shinichi Suzuki. "Violin? No way! That's something rich people did, and our school wasn't in that kind of neighborhood." But then, upon some reflection, he said maybe one or two of his classmates played the violin after all. Another student played the "big violin," by which he meant the cello. But no, no one he knew well was part of this Suzuki Messodo scene.

The more we talked, the more I sensed something in the tone of the driver's voice that I rarely confront in Japan—something resembling class resentment, which is not supposed to exist in the country's officially classless postwar society. I tried to shift the focus of the conversation slightly. As another Suzuki summer school was about to start in one week, I remarked on how busy Matsumoto would be. He had no idea what I was talking about. He said summer months, especially August, are busy anyway, but yes, come to think of it, there is one week when he sees a lot of children carrying violin cases. When we finally reached our destination, he said cheerfully, "Nice talking! There's so much you don't know about your own town, things that are right under your nose, right?"

The Shinichi Suzuki Memorial Museum was open for just another hour. Deputy Director Yukiko Todoriki greeted me with a warm smile. I was shown into the salon, in the Western-style annex that Waltraud had built so that Suzuki could give private lessons at home. Sitting on a sofa was a small man in glasses, probably in his sixties. He introduced himself as Toshimitsu Osawa, an accountant who happened to live across the street from the museum. He was not there merely to have a neighborly chat. Though he had had no personal connection with the talent education movement during Suzuki's lifetime—if he had, its financial state might have been different—in recent years he had gotten interested in its philosophy. He thought it a shame that so few people visited the museum, so in his spare time he did what he could by connecting with potentially interested people and proposing events in the hope of placing the museum on Matsumoto's overcrowded cultural map. The city is now home to formidably high-profile attractions, like Yayoi Kusama's permanent collection at the Matsumoto Museum of Art and the summer concert series during the Seiji Ozawa Matsumoto Festival.

Over tea, we talked about my book project, and after a while I told them about the difficulty I had in traveling the short distance from the TERI office to the museum. This more than proved Osawa's point. The museum should be a "mecca," he said, for Suzuki followers the world over, yet it was almost forgotten. I also related my exchange with the taxi driver, who identified violin lessons with elitism. "It's true," Osawa interjected. "I had lots of classmates who played the violin, but that's because I went to a school that's affiliated with Shinshu University." It was a publicly funded school, but one attended by students whose parents tended to be well-to-do professional types, like lawyers, doctors, and academics. I was troubled by his comment, especially considering our location. We were sitting in Shinichi Suzuki's living room. It could have been the epicenter of a revolution for all children. To think of Suzuki's tireless work as a pipedream—or worse, an unwitting handmaiden of elitism—was dispiriting.

My troubled thoughts began to drift in search of something more affirming. What about Venezuela's El Sistema movement and its successful youth symphony, Orquesta Sinfónica Simón Bolívar? Isn't that a testament to the power of Suzuki's philosophy as a vehicle for social change? The orchestra consists of underprivileged children who learned music through a state-funded foundation, commonly known as El Sistema. Led by a highly effective publicist and alumnus, conductor Gustavo Dudamel, El Sistema came to international attention in 2007, when the youth symphony made sensational debuts at the Royal Albert Hall in London and Carnegie Hall in New York. Media outlets embraced the inspiring backstory of social advancement and personal transformation through music. El Sistema seemed like an answer to Suzuki's plea for improving lives by making valuable, early opportunities available to all children regardless of their backgrounds.

That El Sistema seems to provide at least some of what Suzuki hoped to achieve is no coincidence. In 1970 William Starr, whose passion for promoting the Suzuki Method did not stop at the US border, traveled to Venezuela, taking footage of Suzuki's lessons. In 1971 and again in 1973, he returned with student groups on goodwill tours and introduced the

Suzuki Method to local violin teachers. Starr did not meet José Antonio Abreu, the mastermind behind El Sistema, so a direct link between Starr's activities in Venezuela and the 1975 founding of El Sistema is uncertain. What cannot be disputed, however, is that in June 1979, Takeshi Kobayashi, the older of the Kobayashi brothers who began studying with Suzuki before the war, arrived in Venezuela on a three-month cultural mission that turned into a Suzuki Method roadshow of sorts. Abreu, aware of the method's popularity in the United States, jumped at the chance to meet someone who had been Suzuki's student. And that was not all. A shrewd operator, Abreu arranged for a group of thirty-four indigenous Pemon children to be flown into Caracas so that Kobayashi could teach them how to play the violin the Suzuki way.[4]

By this point, Kobayashi was one of Japan's preeminent violinists. He had never taught young children, nor did he consider himself a true product of the Suzuki Method, as Suzuki was still developing the approach when Kobayashi was his student. Kobayashi had expected to give recitals and concerts in Venezuela, as he had done on previous cultural missions to South and Southeast Asia. He was nonetheless happy to act as an ambassador for his old teacher, whom he adored, and even to give lessons to aspiring instructors.

With that in mind, before his departure, Kobayashi went to Matsumoto to sit in on Suzuki's classes, in the hope of picking up some of the basics of Suzuki's teaching approach. But when Kobayashi arrived in Caracas and found out that he was expected to teach a large group of complete beginners, he felt poorly qualified—after all, certified Suzuki instructors usually spent years in training. Not only that, but Abreu had promised the Venezuelan culture minister that the children would be able to play symphonies during Kobayashi's stay. Kobayashi ended up teaching the children day in and day out. Indeed, by the end of his three months, they were able to play Suzuki's "Twinkle" variations and even some passages of Beethoven's Ninth Symphony with both professional and youth orchestras. Not surprisingly, it was the politically astute Abreu, not Kobayashi, who stood proudly at the conductor's podium. Kobayashi's frustrations aside, the children's performance was a singular achievement. When he left, with a tremendous sense of relief, he donated all the Suzuki instruction books he had brought with him to El Sistema.

Buoyed by the success, Abreu toyed with the idea of establishing a national Suzuki academy in Venezuela, headed by Kobayashi. Despite his somewhat bitter experience, Kobayashi, who was a born adventurer, was tempted. He returned to Caracas with a letter from Suzuki endorsing the founding of a talent education school there. On this occasion too, Kobayashi was asked to give Suzuki-style lessons. But the slowness of negotiations and a number of miscommunications—sometimes, the lack of communication—exasperated him. "The Venezuelan way of doing things exhausted me excessively," he later said. Venezuela's Suzuki academy never came to fruition. Even so, the Suzuki methodology, the know-how, and the philosophy of "anyone can" persisted and was absorbed into El Sistema.[5]

To be sure, El Sistema, despite its success and despite its role as a public institution, has not been a perfect realization of Suzuki's goals. For example, the Pemon children Kobayashi taught in 1979 were not given the opportunity to continue their studies; they were flown back to their homes in the jungle, never, one suspects, to play the violin again. And these days, fifteen years after El Sistema's global ascent, the seemingly triumphant narrative is no longer so straightforward. Criticism has mounted within Venezuela, as the people of a country mired in poverty wonder whether it makes sense to maintain the expensive program, which, though inspiring, is not quite of top caliber. Still, it is notable that the Venezuelan government, propelled by Abreu's adroit maneuvering under shifting political regimes, has been consistently willing to take a chance on the kind of social reform Suzuki could only dream of in Japan. State support for El Sistema stands in stark contrast to the Japanese government's habitual indifference to Suzuki's endeavor, despite the great services that Suzuki and his students performed for the Japanese state.

It was not just Amy Carter and US-Japan diplomacy. Japan had a highly unpredictable neighbor in the Soviet Union, and throughout the Cold War, Soviet-Japan relations were strained over both ideological differences and disputes concerning the postwar Soviet occupation of Japan's northern territories, namely the Kuril Islands of Suzuki's youthful travels. When David Oistrakh—one of the Soviet Union's most celebrated artists—first toured Japan in February 1955, he made a splash not only because of his artistry but also because his visit offered

Soviet violinist David Oistrakh, on tour in Japan in 1955, sits in the front row listening intently to a young performer. *Talent Education Research Institute*

hope for promoting mutual understanding through music. During the tour, Suzuki's violinists delighted Oistrakh, affirming what Japan and the Soviet Union shared: a musical language. Here again, Suzuki played the diplomatic role, fostering on both sides a foundation on which to build. This encounter also paved the way for Oistrakh's attendance at a Grand Concert a dozen years later. On that occasion, he took part by conducting the mass performance of Suzuki's book 1 composition, "Allegro."

Given Oistrakh's meeting with Suzuki and his students in 1955, it is safe to assume that Soviets were aware of the talent education movement years before the American "discovery" of the Suzuki Method. But the Soviet response to this phenomenon differed greatly from that of its Cold War rival. Rather than import and promote Suzuki's teaching style, the Soviets cherry-picked his prized students. In 1958, the year in which the Bach Double footage was shown at Oberlin, Leonid Kogan—the Soviet violinist who was convinced that Suzuki miraculously healed his dermatological allergy—was touring in Japan. While in the country, he heard one of Suzuki's precociously advanced students, Yoko Sato. The following year, Kogan brought Sato, who was barely ten years old, to the Moscow Conservatory as a Soviet state-funded scholar. She would graduate the top of her class in 1971, having won numerous international prizes.

During the time of détente—the easing of Cold War tension between the East and West—and of commercial liberalization in the People's Republic of China, Suzuki's violin diplomacy had a further part to play. On October 23, 1978, thirty Suzuki violinists were called to the Japanese prime minister's residence to welcome the Chinese leader Deng Xiaoping, heralding both the deepening of Sino-Japanese economic ties and China's emergence as a state backer of education in Western classical music. (This performance preceded two historic 1979 visits to China by Western classical musicians: the Boston Symphony Orchestra under the baton of Seiji Ozawa in March and violinist Isaac Stern in October.) Deng was intrigued enough by the young Japanese violinists to want to know more. In March 1983, twenty-two Suzuki violinists from Japan and the United States were invited to China. The Chinese government made sure that they were enthusiastically received as they played in Shanghai, Xian, and Beijing. In September of that same year, eighty-one Suzuki string players traveled to East Germany at the invitation of its cultural ministry and gave concerts during a twelve-day stay.

The Japanese government did nothing to foster the growth of talent education, yet Suzuki did quite a bit for the Japanese government as an unofficial ambassador. In the annals of soft power—appealing to others through cultural outreach, rather than coercing them through force, economic warfare, and other means—few educators have been more active than Suzuki was.

By the time my thoughts had returned from Venezuela—and elsewhere—to Japan, it was well past the museum's closing time and Todoriki kindly called a taxi for me. I hoped it would arrive without getting lost. While waiting, I looked at the glass display cases full of photographs, letters, and other Suzuki memorabilia. I also glanced at a copy of Albert Einstein's self-portrait, hung prominently on the wall. It was signed, in German, "To Shinichi Suzuki in friendly memory" and dated November 1926, around the time Suzuki and his brother Umeo had Einstein test their father's master violins. I took in a striking wedding photo of young Waltraud and Suzuki, a framed cover jacket of the remastered Suzuki Quartet album, a huge board with a timeline of the talent education movement, medals and other commendations that various governments and institutions bestowed on Suzuki during his lifetime. There were no real surprises. I had seen most of these items on my previous visits, in published materials, or on the museum website. At Todoriki's invitation, I proceeded to the opposite wing of the house to look at Suzuki's study.

It was a modest room of about a hundred square feet. There were no chairs, just a low desk and a floor cushion. The room was arrayed with an assortment of simple furniture set against the farthest wall. There were a few chests of drawers, a slim bookcase with a random selection of books, and a side desk with a palette of dried-up watercolor paints. In this study, while the world was still asleep, Suzuki spent countless hours listening to student recordings, recording his comments, and painting commemorative watercolors with personal messages for graduating students. Todoriki walked over to the desk to produce a number of Suzuki's passport books, mostly from when he was in his eighties and nineties. The passports, lovingly kept in one of the small drawers, were full of the stamps Suzuki earned as he traversed the globe to promote his movement.

All this was too much for me to take in. The old wooden house suddenly felt musty, like a thrift shop overloaded with secondhand clothes. There was a whiff of decay, intensified by the midsummer humidity of the Matsumoto Basin at dusk. I could not breathe. Mercifully, the taxi arrived just in time.

CONCLUSION

EARLY ONE SUMMER NIGHT IN 1994, less than half a mile from Suzuki's home, something strange was floating in the air. Yoshiyuki Kono, a forty-four-year-old office worker and father of two, heard something rattling in his backyard. He went outside to check and saw one of his dogs shaking violently and foaming at the mouth. Another dog of his lay motionless. "I think we ought to phone the police," he called to his wife. There was no reply. When he reentered the house, he saw his wife convulsing just like the first dog, moaning in agony. He called an ambulance. Soon enough, he started feeling queasy. He heard a roaring sound inside his head. Unable to see clearly or to stand, he felt death approaching. He collapsed and was transported to the hospital with his wife.

Kono, his wife, and his dogs were victims of sarin poisoning. This much was clear early on, but it would take months for the police to determine who was responsible: a fanatical cult called Aum Shinrikyo. Little-known at the time, the group was led by Shoko Asahara, a poorly educated, half-blind yogic guru who resembled Grigori Rasputin in his ill-kept appearance. Asahara preached that the world was coming to an end, and only his followers would survive to inherit what remained. Asahara, though, was willing to orchestrate this outcome himself. After a Matsumoto real-estate deal fell through, preventing his cult building a huge complex there, he decided that the whole city deserved to be punished. On the fateful evening, Asahara's followers released their poison gas in several residential areas of Matsumoto, harming approximately six hundred people and claiming eight lives. The casualties included Kono's wife, who died after fourteen years in a vegetative coma.[1]

The day after the attack, as Kono lay suffering, Nagano Prefectural Police pointed to him as the prime suspect. Officials noted that he had been the first to report anything unusual, he possessed a stock of pesticide, and he had an engineering degree and a record of employment at a pharmaceutical company. Kono's personal profile, the police insisted, suggested that he could have produced the deadly gas from the pesticide. (As would later become clear, Kono could not have synthesized sarin using any chemicals he had on hand.) The police put tremendous pressure on him to confess to the crime, while the uncritical media pilloried him as the "poison gas man." Kono's horrific experience was one of the most shameful episodes of false accusation in Japan's postwar history.

Eventually, Kono's innocence was proven by the process of elimination. On March 20, 1995, nine months after the Matsumoto attack, sarin gas poured into Tokyo's central subway network. The attack occurred during the morning rush hour, when the volume of commuters was highest. Five locations on three different lines were struck, killing thirteen people and injuring more than 5,800. But the perpetrators left traces of their involvement, and a senior cult member's confession led to a series of arrests and ultimately Asahara's capture. In addition to the sarin attacks, the cult is thought to have been involved in at least forty-five criminal incidents from the late 1980s to the mid-1990s, a dozen of which resulted in fatalities.[2]

At the time of the Matsumoto attack, Suzuki was almost ninety-six. He and his circle were fortunate to have escaped what he called a "harrowing" crime.[3] Yet no one in Japan was unaffected. As the source of the attacks came into focus, there was much soul-searching in the press and the public at large. The members of Aum Shinrikyo were, to all appearances, model Japanese. If the leader was a half-crazed demagogue, his followers were the very picture of success within the rigid systems of education and career that Suzuki had tried so long and so desperately to change. The cult's senior members were conquerors of exam hell who had made it to top universities including the University of Tokyo, the University of Kyoto, Keio, Waseda, and the Tokyo Institute of Technology. They were lawyers and physicists and cardiac surgeons. And, somewhere along the way, they discovered that their souls were empty. The Japanese dream they had been living left them bereft of purpose or efficacy or community, so they instead found what they needed in a millenarian cult.[4]

The celebrated writer Haruki Murakami called 1995 "Japan's Year Zero"—the moment the country was forced to wake from decades of complacency. Already the economic miracle had begun collapsing on itself, as runaway real estate speculation drove a bubble that burst in the early 1990s with predictable results. And, in January 1995, only a month before the subway murders, the Great Hanshin-Awaji Earthquake hit the port city of Kobe, killing more than 6,000 people and leaving hundreds of thousands without homes. Tall buildings and express highways, supposedly state-of-the-art products of earthquake-proof Japanese engineering, crumbled while the government in Tokyo dithered, delaying rescue efforts and exacerbating the tragedy. "We believed in our system," Murakami said in a 2003 interview. "We had been getting richer and richer and we thought our system would be stable forever. . . . But after 1995 . . . we have come to think that there is something wrong with our system." Japan was no longer so rich, and after a series of calamities, it did not seem very safe either.[5]

In the anxious days between Aum Shinrikyo's Matsumoto and Tokyo attacks, Suzuki's age finally caught up to him. Kenjiro Yuki, Suzuki's aide, recalls the frosty early morning of November 28, 1994, when he was woken by a panicked telephone call from Waltraud. When Yuki reached their house, he found Waltraud sitting on the floor outside the bathroom, holding Suzuki in her arms like she was Michelangelo's Madonna della Pietà. Suzuki was still in pajamas. There was no color in his face, and he was not breathing. Yuki carried him to the bedroom and set him down on the bed, whereupon he started breathing again. He was diagnosed with cerebral thrombosis and remained in the hospital for the next nine months.[6]

During Suzuki's hospital stay, the couple did what came naturally to them: they made plans for his return to work. They decided to move out of their home of forty years and into a new house that was simpler to access and was much closer to TERI headquarters, so that Suzuki could more easily resume life at home and at the office. (The Suzuki Museum occupies the couple's old house, which was donated to the city of Matsumoto in April 1996.) Others around Suzuki were also eager to see him back in the swing of things. There are those who recognized such wishful

Waltraud and Suzuki at his ninety-fifth birthday concert, in 1994, held at Tokyo's Suntory Hall. *Talent Education Research Institute*

thinking for what it was: "People used to tell me how energetic and extraordinarily young my uncle was," his niece Hiroko recollected in our 2014 interview, "but in those final years, in his private moments, he looked and behaved just like a man of his age, like any ordinary grandpa." Yet Suzuki's colleagues could be forgiven for thinking him rather invincible. His routine had barely eased in the years leading up to his episode. Only in 1992 did he finally delegate the graduation recordings to younger instructors, on account of his deteriorating hearing. It took thirty of them to pick up the slack. In his nineties, he visited the United Kingdom, the United States, and Australia, and in 1993 he attended the Eleventh Suzuki Method World Convention in South Korea.[7]

Joining Waltraud and Suzuki in Seoul was Koji Toyoda. The couple had been strengthening their old ties, particularly since 1987, when the Suzukis visited Berlin, where Toyoda was based. "Ko-chan," after so many years, remained Suzuki's golden boy, the son he never had and his only conceivable successor. "I am counting on you after I am gone," he told Toyoda at one point. At the same time, Suzuki was still insisting that he was not planning to retire any time soon. He even extended his declared retirement age to 120. In any case, Toyoda was not prepared to drop everything and move to Matsumoto. A professor at Berlin University of the Arts since 1969, he was grounded in Europe, where he and his pianist wife Motoko raised their two sons. He also knew that succeeding Suzuki would not be easy. Therefore, like everyone else, he wished that his old teacher would live on.[8]

Yet Suzuki and Toyoda did speak often about how best to ensure the future of talent education after its creator was gone. Suzuki's wish was to establish a teaching college that would train future educators according to his philosophy, but the project stumbled, ostensibly due to lack of financing. Some TERI insiders, however, believe that the real obstacle was opposition in the United States, where Suzuki Method practitioners did not think they should have to cross the ocean and earn a formal degree to become bona fide instructors. Whatever the truth, the failure was a huge blow to Suzuki, who reportedly shed tears in front of close associates when they finally convinced him it would never happen. As a consolation prize, in 1997 Suzuki got the International Academy of the Suzuki Method, a specialty school offering a teacher-training course. In reality, it was a glorified new name for the training program that had been operating at the Matsumoto Ongakuin for decades. Suzuki became the head of the international academy, but this too was a nominal gesture. In October of the same year, his health declined precipitously, preventing him carrying out any duties.[9]

Suzuki died on January 26, 1998, with Waltraud by his side. He was ninety-nine years old. Waltraud would follow him almost three years later, dying on Christmas Eve of 2000. Theirs was not the easiest or most constant marriage, yet one wonders if either could have lived such long and meaningful lives without the other.

After Suzuki's death, Toyoda finally agreed to take the helm at TERI. He became its president in September 1999 and moved to Matsumoto in the spring of 2000. The decision was made reluctantly, as Toyoda understood the enormity of the task that lay ahead. But once he took up his new job, he pursued it with great energy. Toyoda believed in implementing a thoroughgoing reform plan, including reassessing the qualifications of instructors, revising the method books, and generally raising the level of expectation for student performance. In all this, he believed he was pursuing a mandate from Suzuki himself.

Toyoda was especially troubled by what he regarded as instructors' slavish dependence on Suzuki's teachings, which the instructors treated as an inviolable sutra. Yet Suzuki, of all people, would have insisted that they exercise independence and initiative. That, after all, was Suzuki's modus operandi. He was constantly researching, innovating, and pursuing self-improvement, but many instructors practicing under his name appeared to have lost sight of their master's own practice. Toyoda was certain that if he did not act soon, the talent education movement would be lost forever.

Toyoda's reforms faced considerable hostility. To be sure, his passion and uncompromising attitude won him respect in certain quarters, but his leadership also caused discomfort, even anger. Some of his TERI colleagues believed that Toyoda—whose teaching career had mostly been at the conservatory level—had no business running an organization devoted to early childhood education. And, in general, there was much resistance to Toyoda's go-it-alone approach, which contravened the International Suzuki Association's policies. When Toyoda tried to force through revisions to the violin method books, an ISA committee stopped him, pointing out that he was not authorized to change the core Suzuki materials without the ISA's agreement. Although Toyoda felt that Suzuki had personally supported his revision effort, he failed to convince the ISA committee, which decided to produce its own new edition. The committee's edition ultimately became the global standard.

One drastic change Toyoda did institute was in the area of graduations. Suzuki had approved the graduation of any students who sent him a formal recording, on the theory that, even if a performance left something to be desired, it was the student's teacher, not the student, who was responsible for any deficiencies. Toyoda thought otherwise. Under his leadership, a group of judges would assess the recordings for all students in Japan seeking graduation, and, especially at advanced levels, those who did not meet certain standards would be denied graduation. Not everyone agreed with this reform, either, but sometimes Toyoda got his way. His unstinting efforts drove home the message that the talent education movement—or the Suzuki Method—could not maintain momentum by sitting still.

After Toyoda's tumultuous presidency came Mineo Nakajima, who took the top job at TERI in 2008. Nakajima had been one of the first children to enroll in the ongakuin after the war, the pharmacist's son who reminisced fondly of having been taught by a teenaged Toyoda. Nakajima had become one of Japan's foremost international relations scholars, with expertise in modern Chinese politics, and was known as an early critic of Maoism. (His short international relations textbook was treasured reading for me when I was in graduate school. I was oblivious to his Suzuki connection then.) Throughout his busy adult life, Nakajima played the violin for pleasure. At the onset of China's Cultural Revolution, in 1966, he even played with a Red Guard, who accompanied him on piano. But a love of the violin was not the only imprint on Nakajima from his Matsumoto childhood. He was instrumental in founding Akita International University, which sought to provide Japan with the kind of truly humanistic liberal arts education that he believed it lacked in the postwar era. He became Akita International's first president in 2004 and quickly turned it into one of the most popular and competitive universities in Japan. Nakajima continued in that post even after becoming president of TERI. His goal for both institutions was the same: to teach future generations to embrace life and become sensitive, well-rounded individuals who could think for themselves. As TERI president, he revisited Suzuki's fervent wish to institutionalize talent education philosophy within a college curriculum. But Nakajima, too, was unable to get the project off the ground. What could have been a great chance to resuscitate the talent education movement was cut short in early 2013, when Nakajima was struck by illness and met an untimely death in the middle of his presidency.[10]

In many ways, Hiroko Suzuki's tenure as TERI president, which followed Nakajima's, was a balm. Much loved and admired as a veteran violin and viola teacher, she demonstrated through actions more than words how a Suzuki instructor could guide children and their adult guardians. Her uncle's direct influence on her was obvious and inevitable, for she had received her first violin lessons from him during the war years, which they spent together in the Kiso Valley. She was known to joke that she was raised in a "pure laboratory culture" of Suzuki's approach. The first time I saw her in action was in 2012, when my five-year-old daughter and I attended a Suzuki summer institute in Sapporo. I noticed immediately her close resemblance to Suzuki. Her speech was clear, spirited, and disarming, as was her smile. Watching her, it was easy to imagine what her uncle might have been like with small children.[11]

But nostalgia could not be the only engine to sustain Suzuki's legacy, and that was precisely the problem that fell to Ryugo Hayano, who in 2016 became TERI's fifth and current president. One of the ten Suzuki violinists on that first tour of the United States in 1964, Hayano had become a leading particle physicist. When he assumed his role at TERI, he was one year short of retirement from the University of Tokyo but still had a full complement of compelling projects in the pipeline. Hayano was by then an intellectual celebrity of sorts and was greatly in demand. Through social media and volunteer projects, he tried to promote a reasoned, scientific debate on the impact of the nuclear meltdowns that followed the earthquake and tsunami that hit Japan's northeastern region on March 11, 2011. That, in turn, led to a web of other obligations, such as devising proposals on how to dispose spent nuclear fuels from the Fukushima Daiichi nuclear energy complex. To assume the presidency of TERI on top of it all was a monumental task. But—like Toyoda, who could have retired comfortably in Berlin—Hayano could not escape his loyalty to Suzuki.

Hayano was just the leader TERI needed. His charisma and high profile insulated him from TERI's internal politics, leaving him well placed to make major changes to the organization. To him, the need for paring down was obvious. The boldest step he took came in 2018, when he discontinued the International Academy of the Suzuki Method. When Suzuki was in his prime, would-be instructors from all over the world flocked to Matsumoto in order to be taught by him directly. But in Suzuki's absence, that was no longer the case. With dwindling enrollment, maintaining the teacher-training course and retaining instructors made little sense. In place of the academy, Hayano proposed a system of teacher certification that could be carried out across Japan. Now that it was no longer necessary for trainees to relocate to Matsumoto, the course of training became less of a total, communal experience, for good and ill. In general, Hayano has brought TERI out of the provincial shadows. He opted not to relocate to Matsumoto himself and shifted many administrative duties to an office in Tokyo. In doing so, Hayano signaled that dedication to the cause of talent education is compatible with a full life in the place of one's choosing.

Featuring prominently in Hayano's practical and unsentimental leadership is the question of how to make talent education more relevant in today's world. Indeed, Hayano believes that Suzuki's cherished notion of talent education strikes the wrong chord. "Our officially registered name might remain the Talent Education Research Institute, but that's not a good enough reason not to make better use of the global brand power of the 'Suzuki Method,'" he told me in 2018, while attending an International Suzuki Association meeting in New York. He drew a comparison to the Panasonic brand name, which also was reverse-imported to Japan. For many years, Panasonic was a brand name for products exported by the company Matsushita. But the Panasonic name became so recognizable abroad that, in 2008, the company adopted it as its new name. Fully aware that talent education is a loaded, potentially confusing, and often-misleading term, Hayano has ventured to replace it with the Suzuki Method wherever possible, including on TERI's official website.

This name change, Hayano believes, must be matched by substantial changes in the way Suzuki lessons are being given. After inspecting numerous Suzuki studios all around Japan, his impression was that they had been frozen in time. Too many studios operated on the assumption that parents and other guiding adults could be counted on as volunteers. These adults were often put in charge of organizing special events, booking recital venues, collecting fees, and preparing snacks for students. Such reliance on parents' time and goodwill is outdated in Hayano's view. Today's Suzuki Method studios need to be more "user-friendly," he told me, especially in urban parts of Japan where education-minded but busy families with disposable income tend to concentrate. Hayano argues that, if set up properly, Suzuki studios could flourish in such environments, despite, or even because of, Japan's declining birth rate.[12]

But Hayano is not simply charging ahead without reflecting on the past. Some of his initiatives aim to affirm Suzuki's mother-tongue approach and no-children-left-behind philosophy. TERI has partnered with University of Tokyo neurobiologist Kuniyoshi Sakai, who uses MRI studies to investigate the role of early music education in brain development. Sakai's team has so far demonstrated, among other things, unique brain activity patterns related to emotion and melody in those with early exposure to the Suzuki Method. Another TERI project provides instruments and instruction for after-school orchestra programs in areas ravaged by the 2011 earthquake, tsunami, and nuclear disaster.[13]

All these developments suggest that talent education, the all-inclusive ideology of social reform, has run its course, leaving Suzuki's revolutionary aspirations unrealized. But the Suzuki Method, with all its possibilities for personal enrichment through the practice, enjoyment, and appreciation of music, has persevered. The spruced-up TERI homepage under Hayano's presidency is revealing. Writ large is the slogan, "Rich sensitivity and the power to live life to the fullest" (*Yutakana Kansei, Ikinuku Chikara wo*), presenting the Suzuki Method as a kind of self-help tool that enables children everywhere to navigate whatever obstacles they might encounter later in life. The focus here is decidedly on individuals rather than communities.[14]

And why not? Deep down, Suzuki's talent education philosophy was always about individual fulfillment. It was never a blindly egalitarian doctrine claiming that everyone was created equal. Rather, talent education was an argument to the effect that the inequalities we are born with should not dictate what kinds of people we will become. Great potential can be wasted, and lesser potential can lead nonetheless to meaningful accomplishment. Suzuki believed that every child should live in a world that respected and nurtured their potential, whatever it amounted to. The world where people were trying to be the best they could be, by extension, would be better than the one he lived in. So there was much for society to gain, but as a byproduct of individual pursuits.

The world Suzuki lived in shaped his ideas and his passion. The twentieth century, with all its promise and difficulty, made him the thinker and teacher he was. It was a dramatic hundred years that brought unprecedented material wealth as well as great poverty, narrow-minded nationalisms and universalist ideologies, devastating violence, and the profound tension of the nuclear age. In such uncertain, threatening, and disorienting times, Suzuki saw within individuals the greatest source of strength. "In a person's lonely, ephemeral life," he wrote in 1956, "the only solace" can be found in the "efforts each one of us makes to nurture love, and live for love, so that we create an oasis within ourselves."[15] Today's challenges include those of yesteryear, alongside new ones, from climate change and global terrorism to cyberwar. We face a world no less daunting that Suzuki's. And so we, too, need to create our own oases, where we may try to live life to the fullest.

Holding tight to their violins, children stride up the foothills of a Nagano mountain, together with their favorite teacher. *Talent Education Research Institute*

Notes

Suzuki's writings and lecture notes are compiled in the eight-volume collection *Suzuki Shinichi Zenshu*, published by Kenshu Shuppan, 1989, and abbreviated *SSZ1* to *SSZ8* below. All translations of Japanese sources are the author's unless otherwise specified.

Introduction

1. Andrew H. Malcolm, "At 79, Suzuki Tempo Is Still Agitato," *New York Times*, November 13, 1977.
2. Eric Hobsbawm, *The Age of Extremes: The Short Twentieth Century, 1914–1991* (London: Michael Joseph, 1994).
3. Shinichi Suzuki quoted in Masaaki Honda, "Saino Kyoiku to Watashi," in *Nijuisseiki no Kansei Kyoiku*, ed. Saino Kyoiku Kenkyukai (Kobe: Rokko Shuppan, 1999), 21.
4. Suzuki's notion of "natural ability" and its relationship with his definition of talent is elaborated in Shinichi Suzuki, "Noryoku wa Hiyakusuru" (1948), reprinted in Shinichi Suzuki, *Suzuki Shinichi Zenshu*, 8 vols. (Tokyo: Kenshu Shuppan, 1989), 1: 185–189 (hereafter *SSZ*).
5. Shinichi Suzuki, "'Ochikobore'ka 'Ochikoboshi'ka" (1977), reprinted in *SSZ*, 3: 272.
6. As featured in *The Art of Violin: The Devil's Instrument*, documentary, dir. Bruno Monsaingeon (2000).
7. Yehudi Menuhin, *Unfinished Journey* (New York: Knopf, 1977), 154.
8. Penelope Trunk, "Why I Love Suzuki Method for Music Education," February 4, 2014, ... PT ... *, http://education.penelopetrunk.com/2014/02 /04/why-i-love-suzuki-method-for-music-education.
9. Shinichi Suzuki, "Futatsu no Ofuku Shokan" (1956), reprinted in *SSZ*, 2: 173–174.

10. Mari Yoshihara, *Musicians from a Different Shore: Asians and Asian Americans in Classical Music* (Philadelphia: Temple University Press, 2007), among others, provides a valuable take on the spread of classical music and music lessons in Japanese society.

11. Andrew Bird with Sarah Bylander Montzka, "Unfretted/Unfettered: The Evolution of Andrew Bird," *American Suzuki Journal* 40, no. 2 (March 21, 2012), https://suzukiassociation.org/news/unfretted-unfettered-evolution-andrew-bird.

12. "Portrait Arabella Steinbacher (Interview)," Pentatone, February 4, 2014, https://www.youtube.com/watch?v=8SB6MfjpY5c; Kyoko Takezawa interview, *Suzuki Method* 152 (May 2005), http://www.suzukimethod-obog.com/takezawa.html.

13. Stravinsky quoted in Robert Craft, *Stravinsky: Chronicle of a Friendship* (New York: Alfred A. Knopf, 1972), 6. This statement is frequently misattributed to W. H. Auden.

14. *The Piano: A Love Affair,* documentary, hosted by Alexander Waugh, aired April 15, 2007, on BBC Four.

1. No Ordinary Childhood, No Ordinary Environment

1. Sauveur Antoine Candau quoted in Shinichi Suzuki, "Zuno no Seino Iden ni tsuite" (1956), reprinted in Shinichi Suzuki, *Suzuki Shinichi Zenshu,* 8 vols. (Tokyo: Kenshu Shuppan, 1989), 1: 259 (hereafter *SSZ*).

2. Oistrakh quoted in *Mainichi Shimbun,* January 27, 1956, and reprinted in the program pamphlet for the 1956 Grand Concert.

3. See, for example, a segment of the concert footage: "Dai Ikkai Suzuki Messodo Zenkoku Taikai," Monthly Suzuki, August 29, 2016, https://www.youtube.com/watch?v=Cc2nCWp5I7I.

4. Dorothy L. Sayers, *Gaudy Night* (1935; New York: Bourbon Street Books, 2012), 526.

5. Keizaikikakucho (Economic Planning Agency), "Keizai Hakusho" (white paper), 1956, 42.

6. Suzuki, "Zuno no Seino Iden ni tsuite," 251.

7. John Kendall interviewed in *Nurtured by Love: The Life and Work of Shinichi Suzuki* (2006), documentary, dir. Laura J. Wong, Brian Neff, and Thomas Ball.

8. Satsuki Inoue, *Nihon no Vaiorin-o—Suzuki Masakichi no Shogai to Maboroshi no Meiki* (Tokyo: Chuo Koron, 2014), 23–28.

9. Margaret Mehl, *Not by Love Alone: The Violin in Japan, 1850–2010* (Copenhagen: Sound Book Press, 2014), 30.

10. Inoue, *Nihon no Vaiorin-o,* 36–41.

11. Inoue, *Nihon no Vaiorin-o,* 46; on the cost of Western imports, see Yoko Shiotsu, "Meijiki Kansai Vaiorin Jijo," *Osaka Ongaku Daigaku Ongaku Hakubutsukan Nenpo* 20 (2004), 33.

12. Suzuki, *Aruitekita Michi* (1960), reprinted in *SSZ*, 6: 29; Inoue, *Nihon no Vaiorin-o,* 60.

13. Inoue, *Nihon no Vaiorin-o*, 46.

14. Robin Kay Deverich, "Violin Pedagogy: How Did They Learn? Classes for the Masses in England," Violin Online, n.d., http://www.violinonline.com /classesforthemassesinengland.htm.

15. Laurie Niles, "Interview with David Schoenbaum: A Social History of the Violin," Violinist.com, March 13, 2013, http://www.violinist.com/blog/laurie /20133/14476.

16. Inoue, *Nihon no Vaiorin-o*, 182.

17. Suzuki, *Aruitekita Michi*, 26–27.

18. Soseki Natsume, *I Am a Cat* (1905–1906), trans. Aiko Ito and Graeme Wilson (Tokyo: Tuttle, 2002), 408, 419.

19. Terada's love affair with violin is recounted in Yoshiharu Suenobu, *Terada Torahiko—Baiorin wo Hiku Butusrigakusha* (Tokyo: Heibonsha, 2009).

20. Jawaharlal Nehru, *An Autobiography: With Musings on Recent Events in India* (London: John Lane, 1939), 16.

21. Suzuki, *Aruitekita Michi*, 36–37.

2. Formative Encounters

1. Shinichi Suzuki, "Zuno no Seino Iden ni tsuite" (1956), reprinted in Shinichi Suzuki, *Suzuki Shinichi Zenshu*, 8 vols. (Tokyo: Kenshu Shuppan, 1989), 1: 259 (hereafter *SSZ*).

2. James L. McClain, *Japan: A Modern History* (New York: W. W. Norton, 2002), 230.

3. Shinichi Suzuki, *Aruitekita Michi*, reprinted in *SSZ*, 6: 12–14; Shinichi Suzuki, "Wagako wo Ifu suru Kokorokoso—Koen Kiroku" (1980), reprinted in *SSZ*, 3: 245.

4. Suzuki, *Aruitekita Michi*, 15–16.

5. Katei Takahashi, "Diado Shoken (5)—Chikuonki," *Fuzoku Gaho* magazine (1901).

6. Suzuki, *Aruitekita Michi*, 17.

7. Suzuki, *Aruitekita Michi*, 18. For information on Burmester's recording, see the Discography of American Historical Recordings (DAHR), a University of California, Santa Barbara, project to create a comprehensive list of master recordings made by US companies.

8. Fritz Kreisler, interview by Abraham Chasens, on Kreisler's 80th birthday, February 2, 1955, https://www.youtube.com/watch?v=ydJC8IhFAAo&t=1s; "Gossec's Gavotte," *Suzuki Skeptic* website, November 16, 2011, https:// suzukiskeptic.wordpress.com/2011/11/16/gossecs-gavotte.

9. Suzuki's account is related in *Aruitekita Michi*, 18–25, which disagrees with the contemporaneous local newspaper report on some points of fact, such as the date of the incident. I have opted to follow the newspaper account, while preserving personal details in Suzuki's recounting.

10. "Meisho Seito no Gyakushu," *Shin Aichi*, December 16, 1915.

11. Satsuki Inoue, *Nihon no Vaiorin-o—Suzuki Masakichi no Shogai to Maboroshi no Meiki* (Tokyo: Chuo Koron, 2014), 151; figures given in "Suzuki Masakichi Monogatari," a life story of Masakichi Suzuki recounted on the official company website of Suzuki Violin, https://www.suzukiviolin.co.jp /about/history, and in Inoue, *Nihon no Vaiorin-o,* 152.

12. Toru Mori, "Nihon no Kekkakuryuko to Taisaku no Hyakunen," *Nihon Naikagaku Zasshi* 91, no. 1 (January 2002), 129.

3. Enchanted Circles

1. William Starr, "Visiting the Past, Vitalizing the Future," keynote address from the 2012 Suzuki Association of the Americas Conference, December 14, 2012, https://suzukiassociation.org/news/saa-is-40-visiting-past-vitalizing-future. The student recollection is from Hiroko Masaoka, "Omoide no Kazukazu," in *Utsukushiki Oto Utukushiki Kokoro wo* (Kanazawa: Saino Kyoiku Kenkyukai Episodo Henshu Sewaninkai, 1997), 53–54.

2. Shinichi Suzuki, *Aruitekita Michi,* reprinted in Shinichi Suzuki, *Suzuki Shinichi Zenshu,* 8 vols. (Tokyo: Kenshu Shuppan, 1989), 6: 37–40.

3. Yoshichika Tokugawa, "Kitachishima Kiko," in Tokugawa, *Kumagari no Tabi* (Tokyo: Seika Shoin, 1921), 69–70.

4. Suzuki, *Aruitekita Michi,* 27–28, 45–46.

5. Fumimaro Konoe, "Eibei Hon'i no Heiwa Shugi wo Haisu," reprinted in *Sengo Nihon Gaikoronshu,* ed. Shinichi Kitaoka (Tokyo: Chuo Koronsha, 1995), 52.

6. Junzo Ara, "Tokugawa-san no Kurisumasu," in Ara, *Azabu Honmuracho* (Tokyo: Ra Teru Shuppankyoku, 1995), 51–54.

4. Berlin, the Golden City

1. Shinichi Suzuki, *Aruitekita Michi,* reprinted in Shinichi Suzuki, *Suzuki Shinichi Zenshu,* 8 vols. (Tokyo: Kenshu Shuppan, 1989), 6: 55 (hereafter *SSZ*).

2. William Grange, *Cultural Chronicle of the Weimar Republic* (Lanham, MD: Rowman and Littlefield, 2008), 3.

3. Richard J. Evans, *The Coming of the Third Reich* (New York: Penguin, 2004), 105.

4. Statistics for state-supported travel in Tetsuro Kato, *Waimaruki Berurin no Nihonjin: Yokochishikijin no Hantei Nettowaku* (Tokyo: Iwanami Shoten, 2008), 27, 38; Suzuki, *Aruitekita Michi,* 54.

5. Satsuki Inoue, *Nihon no Vaiorin-o—Suzuki Masakichi no Shogai to Maboroshi no Meiki* (Tokyo: Chuo Koron, 2014), 187.

6. Suzuki, *Aruitekita Michi,* 57.

7. Suzuki, *Aruitekita Michi,* 61–62, 90.

8. Inoue, *Nihon no Vaiorin-o,* 188, 191; Suzuki, *Aruitekita Michi,* 59.

9. Photos of Klingler's handwritten communications (in German) can be viewed at "Founder Shinichi Suzuki," Talent Education Research Institute, https://www .suzukimethod.or.jp/suzukimethod/career.

10. Suzuki, *Aruitekita Michi*, 72–73.

11. Suzuki, *Aruitekita Michi*, 82–83, 89–92.

12. Waltraud Suzuki, *My Life with Suzuki* (Evanston, IL: Summy-Birchard, 1987), 1, 3 6, 8–9.

13. Suzuki, *Aruitekita Michi*, 67–71.

14. Suzuki, *Aruitekita Michi* 65–69; Inoue, *Nihon no Vaiorin-o*, 193–194.

15. Suzuki, *Aruitekita Michi*, 62–63.

16. Inoue, *Nihon no Vaiorin-o*, 199.

17. Tsutomu Kaneko, *Ainshutain Shokku: Taisho Nihon wo Yurugaseta Yonjyu-sannichikan* (Tokyo: Kawade Shobo, 1991), 1: 209–210; Inoue, *Nihon no Vaiorin-o*, 203.

18. Suzuki, *Aruitekita Michi*, 75; Margaret Mehl, "Cultural Translation in Two Directions: The Suzuki Method in Japan and Germany," *Research & Issues in Music Education* 7, no. 1 (2009), 9–10.

19. Einstein's inscribed portrait and letter to Masakichi Suzuki, dated November 2, 1926, can be viewed at "Ainshutain Hakase kara no Oreijo to Jigazo," https:// kinenkan.suzukimethod.or.jp/exhibition.html; Michaelis' letter to Einstein mentioning Suzuki is dated January 25, 1927, as given in Margaret Mehl, *Not by Love Alone: The Violin in Japan, 1850–2010* (Copenhagen: Sound Book Press, 2014), 182. The letter, in German, can be viewed at https://kinenkan .suzukimethod.or.jp/images/exhibition_phto1.jpg.

20. Michael Cooper, "Violin World Yowls at Challenge to Fabled Teacher," *New York Times*, December 8, 2014.

21. Suzuki, *Aruitekita Michi*, 73–78; Tomio Sonehara, interview with author, December 28, 2014, and July 22, 2015, Yokohama.

22. Shinichi Suzuki, *Nurtured by Love*, rev. ed., trans. Kyoko Iriye Selden and Lili Selden (Van Nuys, CA: Alfred Publishing, 2013), is a superior translation.

23. Suzuki mentions having received Klingler's private recording of Bach's unaccompanied sonata as a Christmas present one year. Suzuki, *Aruitekita Michi*, 60.

24. This episode and the subsequent two are from Suzuki, *Aruitekita Michi*, 73–78. Einstein's and Suzuki's conversation with Kessler is from Shinichi Suzuki, "Saino wa Umaretsuki dewa Nai" (1951), reprinted in *SSZ*, 2: 54–55.

25. Reiko Takei, "Suzuki-sensei no Te," in *Utsukushiki Oto Utukushiki Kokoro wo* (Kanazawa: Saino Kyoiku Kenkyukai Episodo Henshu Sewaninkai, 1997), 65.

26. Suzuki, *Aruitekita Michi*, 76–78; Albert Einstein to Walter Kaufmann, January 19, 1927, call number 57–3, Albert Einstein Archives at the Hebrew University of Jerusalem; Walter Kaufmann quoted in Shalva Weil, "The Walter Kaufmann Story: The Exile Who Invented All-India Radio's Signature

Tune," *Asian Jewish Life* 17 (February 2018), https://asianjewishlife.org /asia/india/ajl-issue17-the-walter-kaufmann-story; Abaigh McKee, "Walter Kaufmann (1907–1984)," Music and the Holocaust, ORT, n.d., http:// holocaustmusic.ort.org/resistance-and-exile/kaufmann-walter.

27. Waltraud Suzuki, *My Life with Suzuki*, 9–10.

28. Masami Kojima, *Sekai ni Yoji Kakumei wo: Suzuki Shinichi no Ai to Kyoiku* (Tokyo: Sofusha, 2016), 111–112.

29. Shinichi Suzuki, violinist, "Violin Sonata in A Major, 3. Recitativo-Fantasia: Ben moderato," by César Franck, recorded n.d., 1928, with Manfred Gurlitt, track 6 on disc 67 of *DG120: 120 Years of Deutsche Grammophon,* Deutsche Grammophon DG 4836149, 2018. Audio available at https://www .youtube.com/watch?v=7YP9QgJR14w.

5. For the Sake of Beautiful Tone

1. Waltraud Suzuki, *My Life with Suzuki* (Evanston, IL: Summy-Birchard, 1987), 13, 17–20.

2. Shinichi Suzuki, *Aruitekita Michi,* reprinted in Shinichi Suzuki, *Suzuki Shinichi Zenshu,* 8 vols. (Tokyo: Kenshu Shuppan, 1989), 6: 98 (hereafter *SSZ*); Satsuki Inoue, *Nihon no Vaiorin-o—Suzuki Masakichi no Shogai to Maboroshi no Meiki* (Tokyo: Chuo Koron, 2014), 245.

3. Suzuki, *Aruitekita Michi,* 100.

4. Margaret Mehl, "The Suzuki String Quartet and Kate I. Hansen's 'Slesvig,'" Margaret Mehl website, May 28, 2018, https://margaretmehl.com/the-suzuki -string-quartet-and-kate-i-hansens-slesvig.

5. Suzuki, *Aruitekita Michi,* 100–101; Koji Toyoda, liner notes to CD *Suzuki Kuwarutetto no Isan* (Quartet House Japan, 2008).

6. Inoue, *Nihon no Vaiorin-o,* 277.

7. Waltraud Suzuki, *My Life with Suzuki,* 20, 22.

8. Eria Kubo, "Setagayaku Daida no Ongakugakko—'Teion' no Rekishi to Igi," *Setagaya Daida Chiiki Keikyu,* March 2018, 15.

9. Suzuki, *Aruitekita Michi,* 106.

10. Kubo, "Setagayaku Daida no Ongakugakko," 17–18.

11. Teikoku Ongaku Gakko, "Nyugaku Annai" (prospectus), n.d.

12. Suzuki, *Aruitekita Michi,* 86.

13. Yukiko Hagiya, *Suwa Nejiko: Bibo no Vaiorinisuto Sono Gekiteki Shogai 1920–2012* (Tokyo: Arufabeta, 2013), 36.

14. Suzuki's comment in the *Nagoya Shimbun,* February 4, 1933, quoted in Inoue, *Nihon no Vaiorin-o,* 273–274.

15. Inoue, *Nihon no Vaiorin-o,* 275.

16. Hagiya, *Suwa Nejiko,* 41–42, 205–206.

17. Suzuki, *Aruitekita Michi,* 103.

18. Shinichi Suzuki, *Chikarazuyoki Kyoiku* (1941), reprinted in *SSZ,* 1: 24.

19. Toshiaki Eto, "Toshiya wo Sodatete," in *Eto Toshiya Vaiorin to Tomo ni* (Tokyo: Ongaku no Tomosha, 1999), 26.

20. Shinjiro Baba's testimony appears in Masami Kojima, *Sekai ni Yoji Kakumei wo: Suzuki Shinichi no Ai to Kyoiku* (Tokyo: Sofusha, 2016), 115–116; Shinichi Suzuki, *Dare ni demo Naoseru Vaiorin no Oto no Kyoseiho* (Tokyo: Kyoeki Shoasha Shoten, 1937).
21. Hagiya, *Suwa Nejiko*, 66–67.
22. Samuel Chotzinoff, *A Little Nightmusic: Intimate Conversations with Jascha Heifetz, Vladimir Horowitz, Gian-Carlo Menotti, Leontyne Price, Richard Rogers, Artur Rubinstein, Andrés Segovia* (New York: Harper and Row, 1964), 12.
23. "Tsukareta Kokoro ni Hibiku Yorokobi," *Asahi Shimbun*, May 4, 1934.
24. Shinichi Suzuki, "Ongaku no Noryoku Kyoiku" (1954–1955), reprinted in *SSZ*, 2: 245–247.
25. Hagiya, *Suwa Nejiko*, 61–62, 71.
26. Hagiya, *Suwa Nejiko*, 77.

6. "No Such Thing as a Born Genius"

1. Shinichi Suzuki, *Aruitekita Michi*, reprinted in Shinichi Suzuki, *Suzuki Shinichi Zenshu*, 8 vols. (Tokyo: Kenshu Shuppan, 1989), 6: 111 (hereafter *SSZ*).
2. Agata Schindler, "Walter Kaufmann," in Claudia Maurer Zenck, Peter Petersen eds., *Lexikon verfolgter Musiker und Musikerinnen der NS-Zeit* (Hamburg: Universität Hamburg, 2006), https://www.lexm.uni-hamburg.de/object/lexm_lexmperson_00001488; Simon Wynberg, liner notes to CD "Walter Kaufmann: Chamber Works," ARC Ensemble, *Chamber Works by Walter Kaufmann* (Chandos, 2020), 7.
3. Shinichi Suzuki, *Ningen to Saino* (Tokyo: Daitokyosha, 1985), reprinted in *SSZ*, 2: 189–194.
4. Shinichi Suzuki, "Echudo wa Mo Iranai," *Saino Kyoiku*, July 1957, reprinted in *SSZ*, 2: 277–288.
5. Takeshi Kobayashi, interview with author, July 22, 2015, Yokohama.
6. Masami Kojima, *Sekai ni Yoji Kakumei wo: Suzuki Shinichi no Ai to Kyoiku* (Tokyo: Sofusha, 2016); Koji Toyoda, liner notes to CD *Suzuki Kuwarutetto no Isan* (Quartet House Japan, 2008).
7. Laura Volpi, "Once upon a Tempo: A Dip into the History of Classical Music Competitions," *Bachtrack*, November 8, 2018, https://bachtrack.com/feature-history-music-competitions-naumburg-queen-elisabeth-geneva-long-thibaud-crespin.
8. Yukiko Hagiya, *Suwa Nejiko: Bibo no Vaiorinisuto Sono Gekiteki Shogai 1920–2012* (Tokyo: Arufabeta, 2013), 63–64, 94–95.
9. Suzuki, *Aruitekita Michi*, 111, 113.
10. According to the pianist Christopher Oldfather, these tests were still being administered into the late 1960s and 1970s, and to much older students. Oldfather was a sophomore at Macalester College when he was made to sit for Seashore's tests. In Oldfather's experience, the playback equipment used

was of poor quality, making it impossible to distinguish microtones. Christopher Oldfather, email exchange with author, December 14, 2021.

11. *Ai no Ikka,* dir. Masahisa Sunohara, Nikkatsu Studio (1941).

12. Kojima, *Sekai ni Yoji Kakumei wo,* 131.

13. Takeshi Kobayashi, interview with author, July 22, 2015; Koji Toyoda, interview with the author, July 1, 2015, Matsumoto, Japan.

14. Anonymous, "Tokumei Kibo," *SSZ,* 8: 177.

15. Shinichi Suzuki, *Chikarazuyoki Kyoiku* (1941), reprinted in *SSZ,* 1: 38.

16. Yasumitsu Nawata, "Rekishiteki ni Mita Nihon no Jinko to Kazoku," *House of Councillors Rippo to Chosa* 260 (October 2006), 95–96; "Birth rate, crude (per 1,000 people)," the World Bank, https://data.worldbank.org /indicator/SP.DYN.CBRT.IN, accessed March 17, 2022.

17. Katsumasa Harada et al. eds., *Showa Nimannichi no Zenkiroku,* 19 vols. (Tokyo: Kodansha, 1989), 1: 212.

18. Shozo Aso, *Katei Kyoiku no Genri to Jissai* (Tokyo: Hokubunkan, 1915); Kichisaburo Sasaki, *Katei Kairyo to Katei Kyoiku* (Tokyo: Meguro Shoten, 1917); Genzo Ichikawa, *Katei Kyoiku* (Tokyo: Jido Hogo Kenkyukai, 1924); Kuniyoshi Obara, *Haha no tame no Kyoikugaku,* 2 vols. (Tokyo: Idea Shoin, 1925 and 1926).

19. Haruko Hatoyama, *Wagako no Kyoiku* (Tokyo: Fujo Kaisha, 1923), 5–6, 179, 181.

20. Kobayashi, interview with author, July 22, 2015; and Takeshi Kobayashi, *Vaiorin Iccho, Sekai Hitoriaruki* (Tokyo: Geijyutsu Gendaisha, 1981), 18.

21. Shinichi Suzuki, *Yoji no Saino Kyoiu to sono Hoho* (Tokyo: Zenkoku Yoji-kyoiku Doshikai, 1946), reprinted in *SSZ,* 1: 84; Toyoda interview, July 1, 2015; Kobayashi interview, December 28, 2014.

22. Ministry of Education, "From Elementary Schools to National Schools," March 1, 1941, (translation), http://www.mext.go.jp/b_menu/hakusho/html /others/detail/1317388.htm.

23. Suzuki, *Chikarazuyoki Kyoiku,* 11–22.

24. Suzuki, *Chikarazuyoki Kyoiku,* 49.

25. Suzuki, *Chikarazuyoki Kyoiku,* 61, 63.

26. Ian Donnachie, "Education in Robert Owen's New Society: The New Lanark Institute and Schools," *Encyclopedia of Pedagogy and Informal Education* (online), 2000, 2003; updated March 16, 2020, https://infed.org /mobi/education-in-robert-owens-new-society-the-new-lanark-institute-and -schools.

27. Suzuki, *Chikarazuyoki Kyoiku,* 43.

28. Currer Bell (Charlotte Brontë), *Jane Eyre: An Autobiography* (London: W. Nicholson and Sons, 1900), 92.

29. Suzuki, *Yoji no Saino Kyoiku to sono Hoho,* 186.

30. Suzuki, *Chikarazuyoki Kyoiku,* 24, 28.

31. Nobuko Imai interview, in "Akogare wo Oimotome, Jonetsu no mama ni Viora no Sekai wo Kiri Hiraku," *Nippon Steel Monthly* (March 2009), 7.

32. Kojima, *Sekai ni Yoji Kakumei wo,* 119, 124, 134.
33. Suzuki, *Yoji no Saino Kyoiku to sono Hoho,* 90; Waltraud Suzuki, *My Life with Suzuki* (Evanston, IL: Summy-Birchard, 1987), 28.

7. Picking Up the Pieces

1. "Chero no Meishu Senso no Giseini," *Chunichi Shimbun,* August 12, 2012.
2. Waltraud Suzuki, *My Life with Suzuki* (Evanston, IL: Summy-Birchard, 1987), 28.
3. Shinichi Suzuki, *Yoji no Saino Kyoiu to sono Hoho* (Tokyo: Zenkoku Yoji-kyoiku Doshikai, 1946), reprinted in Shinichi Suzuki, *Suzuki Shinichi Zenshu,* 8 vols. (Tokyo: Kenshu Shuppan, 1989), 1: 102–103 (hereafter *SSZ*).
4. This account of the origins of Suzuki's Matsumoto venture is based on Masami Kojima, *Sekai ni Yoji Kakumei wo: Suzuki Shinichi no Ai to Kyoiku* (Tokyo: Sofusha, 2016), 173–185.
5. Heishiro Kanda, *Saino Kyoiku wa Kosumoporitanizumu,* undated manuscript, in Takeshi Kobayashi's private archive, 7.
6. Mineo Nakajima with Fumiko Sato, "Watashi no Hansei," *Shinanomainichi Matsumoto Senbaijo WEB* 1 (2006), http://www.matsusen.jp/myway/nakajima/nkj03.html.
7. Heishiro Kanda, *Saino Kyoiku wa Kosumoporitanizumu,* undated self-published manuscript in Takeshi Kobayashi's private archive, 13–14.
8. Shinichi Suzuki, *Aruitekita Michi,* reprinted in *SSZ,* 6: 129.
9. Koji Toyoda, interview with author, July 24, 2019, Matsumoto, Japan. There appear to be a number of subtle discrepancies in Suzuki's and others' writings, especially concerning the chronology of his illness, convalescence at Asama Onsen and Kirigamine, and final move to Matsumoto. I rely more on Masami Kojima's account, checked against Koji Toyoda's memory of events.
10. Kojima, *Sekai ni Yoji Kakumei wo,* 185.
11. Suzuki, *Yoji no Saino Kyoiku to sono Hoho,* 190–191.
12. Kazue Fukui, "Kokoro no Ressun e Fukai Kansha," in *Utsukushiki Oto Utukushiki Kokoro wo* (Kanazawa: Saino Kyoiku Kenkyukai Episodo Henshu Sewaninkai, 1997), 101.
13. Junko Yasuda, "Takai Hado wo Ukete," in *Utsukushiki Oto Utukushiki Kokoro wo,* 73; Hiroko Masaoka, "Omoide no Kazukazu," in *Utsukushiki Oto Utukushiki Kokoro wo,* 52–54.
14. Kojima, *Sekai ni Yoji Kakumei wo,* 221–225.
15. Kinuko Sasaki, "Omoide," in *Utsukushiki Oto Utukushiki Kokoro wo,* 34.
16. Shinichi Suzuki, "Naze Chugaku dake de Yamesaseta ka," *Saino Kyoiku,* Winter 1971, reprinted in *SSZ,* 3: 266–268.
17. Suzuki, *Yoji no Saino Kyoiku to sono Hoho,* 166; Kojima, *Sekai ni Yoji Kakumei wo,* 185.
18. Suzuki, *Yoji no Saino Kyoiku to sono Hoho,* 67–68.

19. Miyoko Goldberg Yamane, *Nijyusseiki no Kyojin Szymon Goldberg* (Tokyo: Genki Shobo, 2009), 56–58.

20. Shinichi Suzuki, *Sino Kyoiku* (Matsumoto: Saino Kyoiku Kenkyukai, 1948), reprinted in *SSZ*, 1: 218; Koji Toyoda, interview with author, October 18, 2018, New York.

21. Kojima, *Sekai ni Yoji Kakumei wo*, 140; Koji Toyoda interviewed by Fumiko Sato, "Watashi no Hansei," *Taun Joho*, November 27, 2002.

22. Koji Toyoda, interview with author, July 1, 2015, Matsumoto, Japan.

23. Shinichi Suzuki, *Yoji no Noryoku Kaihatsu* (Tokyo: Sanseido, 1970), reprinted in *SSZ*, 3: 77–93.

24. Kojima, *Sekai ni Yoji Kakumei wo*, 315.

25. Kojima, *Sekai ni Yoji Kakumei wo*, 320; Katsumasa Harada et al., eds., *Showa Nimannichi no Zenkiroku*, 19 vols. (Tokyo: Kodansha, 1989), 8: 217.

26. Kojima, *Sekai ni Yoji Kakumei wo*, 144.

27. Shinichi Suzuki, "Kokoro wo Sokonerareta Kora," *Saino Kyoiku*, March 1951, reprinted in *SSZ*, 2: 342–344.

28. Shinichi Suzuki, "Vaiorinka no Sotsugyo ni tsuite," *Saino Kyoiku*, July 1952, 72.

29. Kenji Mochizuki, "Amerika wo Yuriugokashita Suzuki Mesodo," *Saino Kyoiku*, March 1968, reprinted in *SSZ*, 7: 340.

30. The first volume of the ten instructional books was Shinichi Suzuki, *Vaiorin Shidokyokushu—Dai Isshuu* (Tokyo: Kawada Shobo, 1948). On existing practice books, see Shinichi Suzuki, "Echudo wa Mo Iranai," *Saino Kyoiku*, July 1957, reprinted in *SSZ*, 2: 280.

31. Shinichi Suzuki, "Rakugosasenai Kyoiku ni tsuite," *Fujinae*, April 1958, reprinted in *SSZ*, 2: 134.

32. Shinichi Suzuki, "Aruhi no Dekigoto," in *Ikuji no Sensu* (Tokyo: Risosha, 1956), reprinted in *SSZ*, 2: 163–164, 166, 174.

33. Shinichi Suzuki, *Suzuki Mesodo ni yoru Yoji no Noryoku Kaihatsu*, reprinted in *SSZ*, 6: 185; Koji Toyoda, interview with author, July 1, 2015, Matsumoto, Japan.

34. See Robert Owen, *The Life of Robert Owen by Himself* (New York: Alfred Knopf, 1920), 198.

35. Leach's Japanese language skills are evident in an audio recording of a conversation with Hamada and Yanagi, in which Leach, utilizing highly polished and sometimes-technical vocabulary, discusses Japanese and other ceramic traditions. The recording is available on YouTube; its source is uncertain, but it was most likely part of an exhibit at the Japanese Folk Crafts Museum in Tokyo. See "Banado Richi, Yanagi Soetsu, Hamada Shoji tono Kicho na Taidan," July 22, 2017, https://www.youtube.com /watch?v=Vzs3R762vu8. On left-handedness, see Shinichi Suzuki, "Wagako wo Ikei suru Kokoro koso—Koen Kiroku" (November 1981), reprinted in *SSZ*, 3: 244.

36. Bernard Leach, *A Potter in Japan* (London: Unicorn, 2015), 209–211.

8. The World Is His Stage

1. Bernard Leach, *A Potter in Japan* (London: Unicorn, 2015), 211; Waltraud Suzuki, *My Life with Suzuki* (Evanston, IL: Summy-Birchard, 1987), 65.

2. Tomiko Shida, interview with author, April 24, 2019, Brussels, Belgium.

3. "Kazarusu Rainichi," video clip of April 14, 1961, recital attended by Pablo Casals, posted by Monthly Suzuki, August 29, 2016, https://www.youtube .com/watch?v=C5RojfCTWAI.

4. John D. Kendall, "Talent Education: The Violin Teaching Methods of Mr. Shinichi Suzuki," unpublished report, 1969, 4, 6–7.

5. Koji Toyoda, interview with author, July 24, 2019, Matsumoto, Japan.

6. Toshiya Eto, "Vaiorin Kyoiku no Tenbo," *Ongaku Geijyutsu,* May 1971, reprinted in *Eto Toshiya Vaiorin to Tomo ni* (Tokyo: Ongaku no Tomosha, 1999), 211–212.

7. Shinichi Suzuki, "Katei ni okeru Ressun nit suite," lecture published in *Saino Kyoiku,* autumn 1980, reprinted in Shinichi Suzuki, *Suzuki Shinichi Zenshu,* 8 vols. (Tokyo: Kenshu Shuppan, 1989), 3: 248 (hereafter *SSZ*). There was one occasion on which Suzuki felt buoyed by a prime minister's active interest in his proposal. In March of 1970, Prime Minister Eisaku Sato invited Suzuki and Masaru Ibuka, a cofounder of Sony, to hear their views on state support for early childhood education. However, nothing materialized from this meeting either. Shinichi Suzuki, *Yoji no Noryoku Kaihatsu* (Tokyo: Sanseido, 1970), reprinted in *SSZ,* 3: 69.

8. Mitsuko Kawakami and Michiru Hodaka, jointly interviewed by author, July 25, 2019, Matsumoto.

9. Surveys of middle-class self-identification available via Naikakufu (Cabinet Office), "Kokumin Seikatu ni kansuru Yoronchosa," https://survey.gov-online .go.jp/s39/S40-01-39-16.html.

10. "Joint Bill Finalized to Compensate Those Forcibly Sterilized under Japan's Defunct Eugenics Law," *Kyodo News,* March 1, 2019.

11. Masaaki Honda, "Saino Kyoiku to Watashi," in Saino Kyoiku Kenkyukai ed., *Nijuisseiki no Kansei Kyoiku* (Kobe: Rokko Shuppan, 1999), 22–25; Kenko Aoki et al., "Chichioya no Kyoryoku ga Ookina Sasae," roundtable discussion, *Saino Kyoiku,* October 1971, reprinted in *SSZ,* 7: 209–210; Shinichi Suzuki, *Nurtured by Love,* rev. ed., trans. Kyoko Iriye Selden and Lili Selden (Van Nuys, CA: Alfred Music, 2013); *Nurtured by Love: The Life and Work of Shinichi Suzuki* (Cleveland, OH: Cleveland Institute of Music, 2006).

12. Honda, "Saino Kyoiku to Watashi," 22–23.

13. Masami Kojima, *Sekai ni Yoji Kakumei wo: Suzuki Shinichi no Ai to Kyoiku* (Tokyo: Sofusha, 2016), 35.

14. Ryugo Hayano with Haruo Yamada, "'Dono ko mo Sodatsu' Suzuki Shinichi no Ongakukyoiku wo Taiken shite," *Ontomo,* March 30, 2018, https:// ontomo-mag.com/article/interview/ryugohayano01.

15. Kojima, *Sekai ni Yoji Kakumei wo,* 38.

16. Louise Behrend, interview, part 3 of 8, posted by School4Strings, January 6, 2012, https://www.youtube.com/watch?v=aIYEd8aVCm0.

17. Hirose's observations are recorded in Kojima, *Sekai ni Yoji Kakumei wo,* 43; William Starr, "Visiting the Past, Vitalizing the Future," keynote address from the 2012 Suzuki Association of the Americas Conference, December 14, 2012, https://suzukiassociation.org/news/saa-is-40-visiting-past-vitalizing-future.

18. Masaaki Honda, *The Vehicle of Music: Reflections on a Life with Shinichi Suzuki and the Talent Education Movement* (Van Nuys, CA: Alfred Music, 2002), 252.

19. Hodaka, interview with author, July 25, 2019.

20. Leach, *A Potter in Japan,* 211; Shinichi Suzuki, Sanshiro Ikeda, and Bernard Leach, "Mukei no Sekai ni Manabu," transcript of *Saino Kyoiku* round-table discussion, April 1969, reprinted in *SSZ,* 7: 81.

21. Kogan's story was recounted to Yoko Sato, a child violinist Kogan brought to Moscow as his protégé, who had originally been taught by Suzuki. Yoko Sato, "Watashi ni totte no Suzuki-sensei," *Chiiki to Sozo,* February 1980, reprinted in *SSZ,* 7: 181.

22. Megumi Taoka, "Seikatsu no Subete ga Ressun," in *Utsukushiki Oto Utuku-shiki Kokoro wo* (Kanazawa: Saino Kyoiku Kenkyukai Episodo Henshu Se-waninkai, 1997), 89; Andrew H. Malcolm, "At 79, Suzuki Tempo Is Still Agitato," *New York Times,* November 13, 1977.

23. Shinichi Suzuki, *Saino Kyoiku* (Matsumoto: Saino Kyoiku Kenkhukai, 1948), reprinted in *SSZ,* 1: 220.

24. Andrew Bird with Sarah Bylander Montzka, "Unfretted/Unfettered: The Evolution of Andrew Bird," *American Suzuki Journal* 40, no. 2 (March 21, 2012), available at https://suzukiassociation.org/news/unfretted-unfettered-evolution-andrew-bird.

25. Suzuki, *Yoji no Noryoku Kaihatsu,* 58.

26. Suzuki, *Yoji no Noryoku Kaihatsu,* 60; Masaru Ibuka, Shinichi Suzuki, and Seiji Kaya, *Watakushi no Yoji Kaihatsuron* (Tokyo: Kodansha, 1970); Masaru Ibuka, *Yochien dewa Ososugiru: Shin no Yojikyoiku towa nanika* (Tokyo: Sesami Books, 1971).

27. On Suzuki's mathematics education system, see Suzuki, *Saino Kyoiku,* 206–210; "The Kumon Method and Its Strengths," https://www.kumon.com/about-kumon/kumon-method; Toru Kumon, celebratory note appearing in concert program, 31st Grand Concert, Nippon Budokan, Tokyo, 1985, and Shinichi Suzuki, "Noryou wo Sodateru Undo no Tenkai," in *Kumonshiki no Nijyugonen* (Osaka: Kumon Kyoiku Kenkyukai, 1983), both reprinted in Press Release, TERI, November 1, 2012, 8, https://16thwc.suzukimethod.or.jp/_src/61343/release121101.pdf?v=157637746063.

28. Kawakami and Hodaka, interview with author, July 25, 2019.

29. Helen Higa, interview by Margaret Watts Romney, "Matsumoto Memoir," Building Noble Hearts podcast, Suzuki Association of the Americas, June 23, 2017, transcript, https://suzukiassociation.org/building-noble-hearts/episodes/s1-matsumoto-memoir-helen-higa.

30. Taoka, "Seikatsu no Subete ga Ressun," 88–89; Malcolm, "At 79, Suzuki Tempo Is Still Agitato."

31. Kawakami quoted in Higa, "Matsumoto Memoir."

32. Mineo Hayashi interviewed in "Yokoso Senpai Supesharu: Suzuki Messodo Konjyaku," *Suzuki Method* no. 154 (2005), 19–20.

33. Jiro Yoshino, "Toyota Shacho no Hoshu wa Masukushi no Nisennanahya-kubun no Ichi," *Nikkei Business,* September 10, 2021, https://business.nikkei.com/atcl/NBD/19/00117/00170/.

34. Kawakami and Hodaka interview, July 25, 2019.

35. Starr, "Visiting the Past, Vitalizing the Future."

36. Shinichi Suzuki, announcement in newsletter "Matsumoto Shibu Dayori," no. 71 (January/February, 1977), 1.

37. The Suzuki School, https://www.suzukischool.com/about-suzuki-school; Shinichi Suzuki, "Debiddo Sumisu-shi no Totsuzen no Fuho wo Kanashiite," *Saino Kyoiku* (summer 1982), reprinted in *SSZ,* 6: 353–356.

38. Allen Lieb, interview with author, June 17, 2019, New York.

39. Pasquale A. Razzano, email to author, August 27, 2019.

9. "Suzuki Messodo"—In My Time

1. Hiroko Suzuki, interview with author, July 10, 2014, Matsumoto, Japan.

2. Andrew H. Malcolm, "At 79, Suzuki Tempo Is Still Agitato," *New York Times,* November 13, 1977; "'Talent Education' Expands through the World," Suzuki Method, Talent Education Research Institute website, n.d., https://www.suzukimethod.or.jp/english/E_mthd121.html; Ryugo Hayano, interview by Matsuka Madoka, Mainichi Media Café (online), n.d., http://mainichimediacafe.jp/interview/109.

3. Mitsuko Kawakami, interview with author, July 24, 2019, Matsumoto, Japan.

4. Kathleen Starr, William Starr's daughter, confirmed her father's travels to Venezuela in an email to the author, July 9, 2019. On Starr's visits, see also Masami Kojima, *Sekai ni Yoji Kakumei wo: Suzuki Shinichi no Ai to Kyoiku* (Tokyo: Sofusha, 2016), 68. For discussion of the Suzuki Method as an inspiration for El Sistema, see Shinichi Yamada, *Eru Shisutema: Ongaku de Hinkon wo Sukuu* (Tokyo: Kyoiku Hyoronsha, 2008).

5. Takeshi Kobayashi quoted in Yamada, *Eru Shisutema,* 153.

Conclusion

1. Yoshiyuki Kono, "Inochci no Honoo wo Moyashite Ikiru," *Chichi,* March 2007, excerpted at https://www.chichi.co.jp/web/20180711kouno-1; Yutaka Shiokura, "Hito wa Machigau, Dakara Yurusu," *Asahi Shinbun* digital, August 3, 2019, https://www.asahi.com/articles/ASM702SKXM70ULZU001.html; casualty numbers from Matsumoto City Comprehensive Medical Association, *Matsumoto Sarin Jiken Higaisha no Kenko Chosa ni Kansuru Hokokusho,* October 2015.

2. Koancho, "Kohyo Shiryo," official data released by Japan's Public Security Intelligence Agency, http://101.110.15.201/psia/aum-24nen.html.
3. Kenjiro Yuki, interview with author, July 11, 2014, Matsumoto, Japan.
4. Ikuo Hayashi, *Omu to Watashi* (Tokyo: Bushun Bunko, 2001), 31.
5. David Pilling, *Bending Adversity: Japan and the Art of Survival* (London: Allen Lane, 2014), 110.
6. Kenjiro Yuki, email correspondence with author, September 5 and September 11, 2019.
7. Hiroko Suzuki, interview with author, July 10, 2014; Hiromu Yasuda, email to author, October 18, 2020.
8. Koji Toyoda with Fumiko Sato, "Watashi no Hansei," *Taun Joho*, December 27, 2002.
9. Tomio Sonehara, interview with author, December 28, 2014, and July 22, 2015, Yokohama.
10. Mineo Nakajima, "Watashi to Vaiorin," *Bungei Shunju*, March 1974, 87–89.
11. Hiroko Suzuki, interview with author, July 10, 2014.
12. Ryugo Hayano, interview with author, October 14, 2018, New York.
13. Kuniyoshi L. Sakai et al., "Music-Experience-Related and Musical-Error-Dependent Activations in the Brain," *Cerebral Cortex* (2021), https://doi.org/10.1093/cercor/bhab478.
14. See Saino Kyoiku Kenkyukai homepage, https://www.suzukimethod.or.jp.
15. Shinichi Suzuki, "Aruhi no Dekigoto," *Ikuji no Sensu* (Tokyo: Risosha, 1956), reprinted in Shinichi Suzuki, *Suzuki Shinichi Zenshu*, 8 vols. (Tokyo: Kenshu Shuppan, 1989), 2: 166–167.

Acknowledgments

It should come as no surprise that a book covering the nearly hundred-year-life of a peripatetic man could be written only with the help of others. Still, I feel humbled by just how much has been provided to me by so many.

First and foremost, I would like to thank my uncle Naotaka Fukui, whose own lifelong contributions to Japan's music and higher education merit a whole separate book. He was instrumental in connecting me with the Talent Education Research Institute when I began my research in 2014.

I was fortunate to speak with Koji Toyoda at length on several occasions. The depth of his reflection and the strength of his memory astounded me, and I could not help but feel that he was the most powerful real-life connection that I had to Shinichi Suzuki. I am forever grateful for the time he shared with me. I am also thankful to the late Hiroko Suzuki, whose recollections of her uncle helped me grasp his personality. Ryugo Hayano lent my project full and unconditional support in his capacity as the TERI president.

The veteran instructor Hiromu Yasuda and former TERI employees Mitsuko Kawakami and Michiru Hodaka were full of valuable insights and anecdotes. Kenjiro Yuki and Yukiko Todoriki welcomed me at the Shinichi Suzuki Memorial Museum and were always ready to answer my questions. I cannot express enough gratitude to Mikiko Shin, who helped track down most of photographs used in this book. He also helped verify important historical facts and always responded to my queries in an impressively timely fashion.

Others in Japan who helped me construct the portrait of Suzuki were Kimiko Nakazawa, Tomio Sonehara, Masami Kojima, and above all Takeshi Kobayashi. I treasure Kobayashi's memories of his teacher dating back to the prewar years and of his experience unwittingly launching the El Sistema movement.

In Europe, I was assisted by Gustaaf Borchardt, who introduced me to the two primary figures in the Suzuki movement in Belgium, Tomiko Shida and Anne Marie Oberreit. Shida's account of growing up in Matsumoto and leaning to play the violin under Suzuki's direct guidance were particularly helpful in explicating the early years of the talent education movement.

The American end of my research was immensely facilitated by Allen Lieb. He was generous not only in offering me his insights but also in allowing me access to his remarkable network of Suzuki-related contacts. They include, among others, Mark Bjork, Sandy Reuning, Jackie Corina, Larry Corina, Tanya Carey, Helen Higa, the late William Starr, and Kathleen Starr, all of whom provided helpful input. Special thanks are due to Beatriz Aguerrevere, who illuminated aspects of the Suzuki movement in Venezuela, and to Pasquale Razzano, who patiently walked me through the intellectual property issues surrounding the Suzuki Method brand.

Alexander Goehr, Christopher Oldfather, Simon Wynberg, Christopher Szpilman, Margaret Mehl, Kristen Krauss, Patinka Kopec, Agata Schindler, Ikumi Okamoto, Andreas Janousch, Juan José Herrera de la Muela, Li Lin, and Shalva Weil provided scholarly, musical, pedagogical, and personal insights. I thank them for their willingness to talk with me and share their invaluable knowledge.

I am heavily indebted to George Andreou for believing in this book. His team at Harvard University Press has given me much-needed support throughout the publication process. Robin Bellinger brought new perspectives to my attention. Emily Marie Silk became my ideal reader, who truly grasped what I was trying to achieve. Simon Waxman helped enormously with finalizing the manuscript, improving the style and giving it more clarity. On the practical side, Olivia Woods offered tireless assistance with the art and manuscript production, Anne McGuire thoroughly checked the notes, and Stephanie Vyce provided expert advice. I am grateful to all of them.

I must thank profusely three dear friends who read all or parts of the manuscript in progress. Carol Archer, Fred Sherry, and Jim Conte all gave me unique and valuable insights. Without their support and enthusiasm, I would have found it difficult to see the book to its completion. Equally appreciated are the comments provided by two anonymous peer reviewers. I would like to express my gratitude for the thankless tasks they performed.

Jin Auh of Wylie Agency was the biggest cheerleader for this book, and without her unwavering faith, I can say with certainty that this project would not have even gotten off the ground.

Lastly, I would like to give thanks to my family. My parents, Kensuke Hotta and Kimiko Hotta, were ever supportive and helped with many aspects of my research while I was in Japan. My husband, Ian Buruma, was a huge source of encouragement, believing in the project even when I was tempted to give up. With all my heart I thank him and our daughter, Josephine, whose musical, intellectual, and personal development has given me constant, joyous inspiration.

Index

Page numbers in *italics* refer to figures.

ability, 7, 141, 145, 146, 180, 201. *See also* aptitude; inborn qualities; talent; talent education

Abreu, José Antonio, 216–217

Ádám, Jenő, 144

adults, 109; children's classical music education and, 9–11; children's environment and, 124–125; early childhood education and, 134; genius and, 116; misuse of Suzuki Method by, 9–10; Suzuki studios' reliance on, 229; talent education and, 178. *See also* environment; parents

age, exposure to music and, 95, 108, 109, 111, 124. *See also* environment

Age of Civil Wars (fifteenth- and sixteenth-century Japan), 24

Ainus, 66

Akihito (crown prince, later emperor), 17, 177

Akita International University, 227

All India Radio, 95

Amati, Nicola, 28

Ando, Ko, 73–74, 79, 80, 100

Annual Music Competition (Music Competition of Japan), 127, 154–155, 187

anti-Westernism, 147. *See also* ultranationalism

Aoki, Kenko, 170

aptitude, 7, 128–129, 146. *See also* ability; inborn qualities; talent; talent education

art: artistry vs. fluency, 112; meaning of, 52; moral/intellectual improvement and, 83, 107

Art of Violin, The (documentary), 53

arts and crafts movement (Japan), 179

Asahara, Shoko, 221, 222

Asama Onsen, 157, 166, 200

Asia: freedom from Western influence, 147; Japanese expansion in, 104–105. *See also individual countries*

Association for Love and Friendship (Yuaikai), 69

auditions, blind, 161

Auer, Leopold, 80, 109, 113, 119, 165

Aum Shinrikyo, 221–222, 223

Ave Maria (Schubert), 52, 53

Baba, Shinjiro, 116

Bach, J. S., 10, 17, 55, 94, 124; Double Concerto for Two Violins, 18–19, 22, 23; Violin Concerto in A Minor, 128

Bacon, Francis, 49, 50

Bamberg Symphony, 198

Bassompierre, Albert de, 119

Baum, Vicki, 75

Beethoven, Ludwig van, 8, 10, 55, 78, 79, 94, 101, 216

Behrend, Louise, 193–194, 195

Belgium, 77, 119, 212

Bell, Joshua, 1

Benedetti, René, 178

Berlin, 2; Ando in, 73; arts in, 6, 83; Berlin Philharmonic, 80, 83, 163, 165; Berlin Radio Symphony, 198; Berlin University of the Arts, 85, 198, 225; concerts in, 79, 83–84, 85; Hotel Excelsior, 75; Suzuki in, 75–98; Toyoda in, 198, 225. *See also* Germany

Index

Issa Karuta (card game), 171
Italy: fascism in, 121, 136; view of League of Nations, 71; violin makers in, 28, 30, 87
Iwamoto, Mary Esther, 127

Jackiw, Stefan, 1
Jane Eyre (Brontë), 145–146
Japan, 14; change in, 10, 19–20, 39–40, 41, 45, 57, 64, 101 (*see also* government, Japanese; Western influences); class and, 214, 215; competitiveness in, 131; defeat in World War II, 20, 150–151, 155; discontent in, 70; end of progressive social reform in, 103; equal rights and, 58; failure of education and, 163; family structure in, 132–133; forced opening of, 24–25, 33; foreigners in, 24–25; Germans in, 98 (*see also* Suzuki, Waltraud Prange); isolation of, 24, 28, 29; merchants in, 46–47; militarization of, 135; modernization and, 41, 45; national growth, 59; patriarchy in, 163; popular entertainment in, 69–70; postwar constitution, 153; postwar recovery, 190–192, 200; sovereignty of, 22; spread of urban culture in, 51; Suzuki's return to, 98, 99; as trading nation, 59; Western culture and, 25, 39–40 (*see also* Western influences)
jazz, 135
Jews, 7, 111
Jiyu Gakuen, 133
Joachim, Joseph, 73, 80, 94, 165; Joachim Quartet, 80
John G. Murdoch & Co., 35, 59
Josefowicz, Leila, 1
joy, of making music, 5, 82, 160

kabuki theater, 27, 69
Kai, Miwako, 112
Kamensky, Boris, 165
Kamijo, Shigeru, 166–167
Kamiya, Shotaro, 45
Kanda, Heishiro, 152, 154, 163
Kato, Kiyoshi, 164
Kato, Koko, 164, 165, 211
Kaufmann, Moritz, 124
Kaufmann, Walter, 94–96, 124
Kawakami, Mitsuko, 203, 212
Kawamura, Matasuke, 89
Kaya, Seiji, 200
Kayser, Heinrich Ernst, 126, 176
Kendall, John, 23, 175–176, 183, 186, 192, 194, 204
Kessler, Ernst, 94
ki (healing energy), 196

Kindergarten Is Too Late (Ibuka), 200
Kiso Fukushima, 149, 156
Kiso Suzuki factory, 154
Kiso Valley, 149, 152, 157
Klengel, Julius, 100
Klingler, Karl, 78–83, 86, 88, 93, 176; Klingler Quartet, 78, 80, 119
Klingler, Marianne, 93
Klotman, Robert, 192
Kobayashi, Kenji, 130, 135, 163, 164, 198
Kobayashi, Takeshi, 126, 130, 135, 163, 164, 198, 199, 216, 217
Kobayashi, Yonesaku, 130, 163
Kobe, 223
Koda, Nobu, 27, 66–67, 68, 73
Kodály, Zoltán, 144
Kogan, Leonid, 196, 218–219
Kojima, Masami, 195
Kono, Yoshiyuki, 221–222
Konoe, Fumimaro, 71
Konoe, Hidemaro, 71
Korea, Japanese annexation of, 42
Kreisler, Fritz, 53, 54, 68, 83, 87, 103, 114, 210
Kreutzer, Rodolphe, 176
Kumon, Toru, 200–201, 204
Kuril Islands, 64, 66–68, 217
Kurosaki, Yoshisuke, 171
Kyoto, 21, 24

Labor organizing, Japanese, 69
language acquisition, 4–5, 95, 123, 124–125, 152. *See also* mother-tongue approach
Leach, Bernard, 179–182, 183, 195–196
League of Nations, 70–71, 105
learning: adults' responsibility for, 4–5; at-home, 133–134; incremental, 125, 140, 176, 191, 201; progressive/cumulative, 5. *See also* education; educational philosophy, Suzuki's
Leuchtenberg, Nadezhda de, 108, 117
Lieb, Allen, 205–206
Liebknecht, Karl, 76
life skills, 9
listening, 10–11, 158. *See also* ear, learning by
London Naval Treaty, 101, 103
love, 11–12, 143. *See also* environment; educational philosophy, Suzuki's
luthiery, 32. *See also* violin makers
Luxemburg, Rosa, 76

MacArthur, Douglas, 168, 169
Magic Mountain, The (Mann), 60–61
Mahler, Gustav, 71, 83, 95
Maidstone Movement, 35, 59

Index